— FOURTH EDITION —

NEW YORK CITY'S
BEST

PUBLIC Pre–K
& ELEMENTARY
SCHOOLS

A PARENTS' GUIDE

Clara Hemphill and Lydie Raschka
with Pamela Wheaton, Laura Zingmond,
and the InsideSchools staff

TEACHERS COLLEGE PRESS
TEACHERS COLLEGE | COLUMBIA UNIVERSITY
NEW YORK AND LONDON

InsideSchools

Published by Teachers College Press, 1234 Amsterdam Avenue, New York, NY 10027

Library of Congress Cataloging-in-Publication Data

Names: Hemphill, Clara, 1953– author.
Title: New York City's best public pre-K and elementary schools : a parents' guide / Clara Hemphill and Lydie Raschka, with Pamela Wheaton, Laura Zingmond, and the InsideSchools Staff
Other titles: New York City's best public elementary schools
Description: Fourth Edition. | New York : Teachers College Press, [2016]
Previous edition: 2005. | Includes index.
Identifiers: LCCN 2016032653 (print) | LCCN 2016033804 (ebook)
ISBN 9780807758045 (paperback : acid-free paper)
ISBN 9780807775127 (ebook)
Subjects: LCSH: Public schools—New York (State)—New York—Directories. Elementary schools—New York (State)—New York—Directories.
Classification: LCC L903.N75 N495 2016 (print) | LCC L903.N75 (ebook) | DDC
371.0109747/1—dc23
LC record available at https://lccn.loc.gov/2016032653

ISBN 978-0-8077-5804-5 (paper)
ISBN 978-0-8077-7512-7 (ebook)

Printed on acid-free paper
Manufactured in the United States of America

24   23   22   21   20   19   18   17   8   7   6   5   4   3   2   1

To our husbands,
Rob Snyder and Chris Raschka,
and to our children,
Max and Allison Snyder and Ingo Raschka

CONTENTS

* indicates a school with a Pre-K program

Contents

* indicates a school with a Pre-K program

* indicates a school with a Pre-K program

Contents

* indicates a school with a Pre-K program

Contents

* indicates a school with a Pre-K program

Contents

* indicates a school with a Pre-K program

PREFACE

I wrote the First Edition of this book nearly 20 years ago, when my son was entering kindergarten at Manhattan New School—still new at the time—and my daughter was a toddler. In those days, the conventional wisdom was that public schools were beyond repair, and that anyone with a choice would avoid them. But even then, there was excellence in surprising places. The formula for success was always the same: An inspired principal assembled a talented staff that shared his or her vision. Activist parents, willing to take a chance on a less-than-perfect-school, enrolled their children, then rolled up their sleeves to help out with everything from lunch duty to painting the bathrooms. Success spread from school to school: Sometimes the assistant principal of a successful school would become the principal of a new school and start the process over again. As long as there was a pent-up demand for good schools and a pool of talented principals and teachers, the virtuous cycle continued.

In the decade since the Third Edition of this book was published, both the city and the school system have changed dramatically. Real estate prices have skyrocketed, forcing out longtime residents and making it ever more difficult for newcomers to find housing. Gentrification has changed the demographics of many schools: Those that once had a mix of children of different races and income levels now are overwhelmingly white and well-off.

Meanwhile, from 2002 to 2013, during the administration of Mayor Mike Bloomberg, the number of charter schools increased from 17 to nearly 200. Charters are tuition-free schools, supported by tax levies, but run by independent organizations rather than the Department of Education. At their best, the charters offer a welcome alternative to the mostly low-performing district schools in poor and working-class neighborhoods. However, the proliferation of charters has drawn the most motivated parents, particularly in black neighborhoods, away from the traditional public schools, leaving many of those schools with declining enrollments, shrinking budgets, and an ever-higher concentration of very poor children.

Recent battles over school rezoning in downtown Brooklyn—where housing for the very rich abuts public housing—have sparked fears that the arrival of white students in formerly "minority majority" schools will be the first step in the displacement of black and Hispanic families. Equally important is the tendency for both well-off and working-class parents to see education as a zero-sum game in which my child can only get ahead at the expense of your child. My fear today is that too many parents see school as an amenity that they pay for (like off-street parking or a health club) rather than a public good that we all support; they lobby for changes (or the status quo) that serve their own child, not necessarily all children.

On the positive side, in researching this edition, we discovered promising schools in neighborhoods where (relatively) affordable housing can still be found—and parents of different races and social classes are working diligently to improve them for everyone. In a city that's increasingly segregated, we found dozens of schools that serve a mix of different income levels, races, and ethnicities. Our profiles take you inside these schools to show how skillful principals manage to make all children and parents feel welcome and to ensure that all get the education they deserve. It doesn't have to be a zero-sum game. We can increase the number of good schools in the city.

The biggest recent change to the public school system has been Mayor Bill de Blasio's ambitious, rapid expansion of prekindergarten. In just 2 years, his administration created 65,000 seats for 4-year-olds—as many seats as the entire public school system of Boston or San Francisco. While the seats are not distributed evenly throughout the city, and some parents must travel a few miles to enroll their child, the reality of universal prekindergarten is a major accomplishment of the de Blasio administration. It also opens the possibility of greater socioeconomic school integration, because middle-class parents are more willing to enroll their child in a high-poverty school for Pre-K than for older grades.

A large body of research shows that poor children do better in schools that are racially and economically integrated; indeed, integration is widely seen as the most cost-effective way to improve academic performance. More recent research shows integration can benefit *all* children. Exposing children to different points of view promotes deeper thinking, problem-solving skills, and greater understanding of others. At integrated schools, children learn about the Lunar New Year and Ramadan, Chanukah, Christmas, and Kwanzaa—not from a book but from other children's celebrations. They learn about other children's struggles and triumphs. And they learn respect and tolerance for others, which serve them well whatever they do.

Of course, parents cannot integrate the entire school system on their own. Rather, we can press city officials for changes that might make a difference: by hiring effective superintendents and principals, by creating magnet programs to attract middle-income children to high-poverty schools, by permitting low-income children to fill seats in undersubscribed schools in high-income neighborhoods, or by drawing attendance zones and assigning children in a way that avoids high concentrations of poverty in any one school. And, as this book shows, parents are not helpless. They can look beyond a school's demographics and test scores to find a school where their child will flourish and where, with their help, the school will improve.

The New York City public schools helped make my own children the adults they are today: intellectually curious, morally grounded, ever generous, and able to get along with people of all races and backgrounds. We wrote this latest edition in the hopes that it can help you have the same experience with your children.

—Clara Hemphill

ACKNOWLEDGMENTS

This book was a collaborative effort. Thanks to the staff of the New School's Center for New York City Affairs, home of the InsideSchools website, particularly Kristin Morse, Emily Springer, and Bruce Cory. Thanks to InsideSchools staffers who visited schools and compiled data: Pamela Wheaton, Laura Zingmond, Nicole Mader, Ella Colley, Aimee Sabo, Gail Robinson, Mahalia Watson, Elizabeth Daniel, and Jacquie Wayans. You take the mission to help parents navigate school choice very seriously—but keep it lighthearted in the office with humor, tea, and chocolate.

The generosity of the principals and teachers who invited us into their schools cannot be overstated. They opened their doors to us and allowed us to sit in on classes and to write candidly about everything we saw, the good and the bad.

Thanks to the Alfred P. Sloan Foundation, the Tortora-Sillcox Family Foundation, the David L. Klein Foundation, the New York Community Trust, Robert Sterling Clark Foundation, and Deutsche Bank for their support of InsideSchools, and to the Altman Foundation and the Child Care and Early Education Fund for their support of our research on prekindergarten. Thanks to Teachers College Press for backing this project for many years.

Our husbands, Chris Raschka and Robert Snyder, both authors themselves, encouraged—and sometimes edited—us. Our children, Ingo Raschka and Max and Allison Snyder, made us think deeply about what education should be. They are, as ever, our greatest love and inspiration.

—Clara Hemphill and Lydie Raschka

INTRODUCTION

If you lived anywhere else in the country, your child would probably be assigned to a school based on your home address. In New York City, it's more complicated than that. The city offers free prekindergarten classes for all 4-year-olds—but you'll have to apply to them, and there may not be room in the school nearest your house. When your children reach kindergarten, you may send them to your neighborhood school, or you may take advantage of the city's extensive system of school choice.

This book will help you navigate a complex bureaucracy to find the best schools for your child. It will help you evaluate public prekindergarten classes—which may be housed in a public school, a private school, or a community organization. It will outline your options for public kindergarten, including your neighborhood school, gifted programs, charter schools, and other schools of choice.

Profiles of our favorite schools are included here. We picked them based on hundreds of visits and interviews with parents, teachers, and administrators.

New York is a profoundly unequal city and, unfortunately, the schools reflect that reality. Schools in the richest neighborhoods tend to have more stable leadership, more experienced teachers, and parents who are able to pay for private after-school tutoring to supplement their children's education. Parent associations at some elementary schools raise more than $1 million a year to pay for everything from assistant teachers in the classroom to music and art lessons.

That said, you don't have to live on Park Avenue to get a good education for your child. For the book we particularly sought out schools in affordable neighborhoods. We include schools that we believe are poised to make gains in the coming years. These schools may not have the highest test scores—at least not yet—but they have strong leadership, lively classes, and a sense of community—necessary ingredients for success.

Getting Started: Prekindergarten

Free public education begins in prekindergarten. Most children attend prekindergarten 6 hours and 20 minutes a day, 180 days a year—the same schedule as older children. Any child who turns 4 before December 31 is entitled to attend prekindergarten

1

that year; that is, a child with a fall birthday may start school in September when he is still 3.

While some ordinary neighborhood schools have prekindergarten, the bulk of seats are in other locations. The city contracts with child-care centers, private nursery schools, religious schools, and community centers to offer free Pre-K classes. In addition, the city has established freestanding "Pre-K centers" which children attend for just one year. Your child is guaranteed a seat in one of these settings. There is no guarantee you will get your first choice, or that your assignment will be close to home. No transportation is provided (except for children with special needs and those in temporary housing).

The city offers free directories of all the prekindergarten programs, updated annually. You may also find a school near your home by searching the InsideSchools.org website.

You may apply online through the Department of Education website (schools.nyc.gov/ChoicesEnrollment/PreK/default.htm) starting in January; in person at one of 12 "family welcome centers"; or by telephone: (718) 935-2067. Application deadlines change from year to year, but generally are in early March. You'll learn where your child is accepted in May. If you miss the first deadline, you may apply in the "second round" in May. If you move to the city after the application process is complete, go directly to a "family welcome center," or telephone the number above. If you don't get your top choice, your child will automatically be placed on a wait list at your preferred programs and the school will contact you if a seat opens up. You may also call a school and ask to be placed on the wait list.

To register, go to the school in person with your child, the child's birth certificate or passport, immunization records, and proof of residence. You do not need a green card or a Social Security number, but you do need two documents with your address on it such as a lease or a recent gas or electric bill.

What to Look for in a Prekindergarten

It's a good idea to visit schools before you fill out your application. Most schools give tours. Beware of those that don't. You want a school that's welcoming to parents.

The first thing to consider is **location.** Close to home is best. Little kids tire easily, and a long commute will be difficult, particularly in the winter. Still, some parents find good programs near their work, or near a relative or babysitter who can pick the child up after school.

Look for **an exciting, orderly classroom where kids can explore.** Good Pre-Ks have fun-to-read books and objects organized in baskets on shelves to help children investigate patterns, numbers, and shapes. Look for classrooms with live animals, LEGOs, water tables, plants, and fish tanks to spark curiosity. Tables and rugs give kids choices of where to work.

In prekindergarten, children need to learn to get along with other children and to follow classroom routines. They need to build their spoken language as a foundation for learning to read. They need to get a sense of what numbers are as a foundation for arithmetic.

Children this age need opportunities to talk to one another and to grown-ups—more than they need pencil-and-paper exercises. They should create their own stories in their own words in a dress-up corner or a play kitchen. They should learn words like "bigger" and "smaller" and "above" and "below" when they build towers in the block corner.

A good Pre-K teacher should be talking to kids and listening to them, repeating back words and full sentences—upping the ante when it comes to language. The teacher should be able to maintain an orderly and predictable routine to help kids feel safe and secure.

The program leader or principal sets the tone for the school. You want someone who is approachable and easy to find, not hidden behind a door. A strong leader brings out the best in each member of the school community. The principal or director should either have experience in early childhood education or be in communication with an expert in the building.

Look for **children's work** on display, not just decorations made by the teacher. Ideally, the work should show individual creativity. You don't want to see lots of fill-in-the-blank worksheets; but kids should at least be beginning to draw, write letters, or sound out words and label their pictures. Are there science explorations—like drawings of leaves or a graph to show how many seeds are in an apple?

Often you will see a schedule of the day posted on the wall. Look for a routine with a mix of active and quiet activities. There should be a time to rest but not enforced naptime. Kids should have time to play outside every day and time to explore, often called "choice" or "center" time. All Pre-K children eat lunch in the classroom, "family style," where they can chat with friends and practice good manners. They should be allowed to go to the bathroom as soon as they need to go, and the bathroom should be close to their classroom.

Look for how teachers foster **independence**. Children are able to hang up their own coats, help prepare and serve breakfast or lunch, clean up after themselves, and put on their own coats and shoes. Good Pre-Ks often label objects so kids can begin to pair objects and words; this provides children with step-by-step pictures for procedures like hand washing. These activities instill good habits.

Options for Prekindergarten

Prekindergarten programs are housed in a variety of settings. **Child-care centers** are designed for working parents and are open year-round, usually from 8 a.m. to 6 p.m. The city pays for 6 hours and 20 minutes, 180 days a year, the same as the public school calendar. Parents must pay for the remaining hours. Also called Early Childhood Centers, these tend to have more experience caring for young children than elementary schools and may have more flexibility in routines. For example, a child who is tired may be permitted to nap rather than take part in an activity. Some child-care centers charge parents on a sliding scale depending on their income; some limit enrollment to low-income families.

Head Start Centers, part of the 50-year-old federal anti-poverty program, give priority to low-income families. The hours tend to be longer than an ordinary public school but shorter than child-care centers. The Head Start programs we have visited are high quality.

Some **private and religious schools** have contracted with the city to offer free prekindergarten classes. Some of the private preschools give preference to children who are already enrolled in their classes for 3-year-olds; if you are applying for Pre-K for the first time you may be out of luck. To meet the city requirements for separation of church and state, Roman Catholic, Greek Orthodox, Jewish, and Muslim schools do not offer religious instruction during the hours of public prekindergarten. However, they may offer religious instruction outside those hours. Apply to these schools with the regular Department of Education online application at schools.nyc.gov/prek.

Some **charter schools** also offer prekindergarten. Contact the schools directly or fill out the online application at www.nyccharterschools.org.

Some, but not all, **public elementary schools** offer prekindergarten classes. The most popular and overcrowded elementary schools simply don't have space; some may have just 18 seats in prekindergarten and hundreds of applicants.

Pre-K centers were set up by the Department of Education as a way to expand the number of seats available in school districts that had little room in the ordinary public schools. Some of these are housed in leased space; some are housed in new public school buildings that are not yet at full capacity. They have as many as 10 prekindergarten classes in one location, and children stay at these schools for just one year. The Pre-K centers we have visited are of high quality. Their teachers are certified and regular employees of the Department of Education.

We have profiles of our favorite stand-alone prekindergarten programs listed by district in the chapters that follow; descriptions of Pre-K programs housed in ordinary elementary schools are included in our profiles for those schools.

Getting Started: Kindergarten

Soon after your child is enrolled in prekindergarten, you'll have to start thinking about kindergarten—unless your child has landed a seat in a school that continues through the elementary years. Depending on the schools you want to consider, kindergarten admission may require a round of school visits, a test for a gifted and talented program, an application for district schools, and a separate application for a charter school lottery.

Any child whose 5th birthday falls before December 31 the year he or she starts school is entitled to attend kindergarten. Kindergarten typically runs from 8:30 a.m. to 2:50 p.m. Some charter schools have a longer school day; some ordinary public schools offer after-school programs, either free or for a fee.

Starting in kindergarten, your child is eligible to attend a school based on your home address. The city is divided into 32 school districts, and most districts are divided into several dozen individual school zones. (Three districts, District 1 on the Lower East Side, District 7 in the South Bronx, and District 23 in the East New York section of Brooklyn, have no school zones; children may apply to any school in these districts.)

To find the school for which your child is zoned, search the InsideSchools website or call the City of New York at 311 or (212) NEW-YORK. If your zoned neighborhood school is satisfactory, you can usually relax. Your child is guaranteed a seat except in unusual circumstances. There are a few zoned schools that are so overcrowded that they cannot admit every child who lives in the zone; in these cases, a few children may be assigned to schools nearby. (We've noted these very overcrowded schools in the text of the school profiles that follow.)

Most children attend their zoned schools. But if your neighborhood school is unsatisfactory, or if you want your child to have a crack at the dozens of alternative schools or specialized programs that accept children from outside their immediate neighborhoods, or if you're just one of those obsessive parents (like me) who needs to visit a couple dozen schools before deciding, you should start your search the fall before your child enters school. If you want your child to be considered for a gifted and talented program you must submit a Request for Testing in early November. Most schools offer tours in the fall and winter.

The Department of Education has centralized kindergarten enrollment through an online application system called Kindergarten Connect. This form, which allows you to apply to up to 12 schools, gives the impression that there is more school choice than is, in fact, available. Nothing is to stop you from putting a very popular school on your list, but don't get your hopes up. Nonetheless, there are many options beyond your zoned neighborhood school.

The deadline for applying to kindergarten is typically in January. Your child will be assigned a seat in April; if he isn't assigned to your first choice, he will automatically be placed on a wait list at all the schools you preferred. To register, bring your child, two documents with proof of residence (a lease or electric bill), your child's birth certificate, and immunization records.

If you move to the city after the application process is complete, you may register directly at your zoned neighborhood school. You may also contact other schools that interest you directly; it's hit or miss, but some very popular schools have seats open up in later summer, early fall, or even in the winter.

A word about wait lists: If you did not apply to a school you like, you may still apply after the deadline and get on a wait list. Some seats open up in September and October if, for example, a family moves. Schools receive budgets according to how many children are enrolled on October 31, so the staff is eager to fill any empty seats. Make sure your favorite school knows you still want a seat.

It's an open secret that some parents lie about their address to get into a school they like—putting their name on a friend's Con Ed bill, buying a phony lease at a stationery store, or making up a persuasive story about how their child really lives with an aunt across the street. I don't recommend it. At the very least, your child may be embarrassed when he or she has to write those inevitable essays about his or her neighborhood. And what if the school calls you at your phony address during a real emergency?

A lot of schools check addresses carefully; some even send "attendance teachers" (formerly known as truant officers) to see if you actually live where you say you do. Expect the attendance teacher to look in closets for clothes and toys and other evidence of a lived-in apartment.

Rather than lies, I recommend patience and pleasant persistence. Although the early rounds of admissions are centralized—and a computer makes the decisions based on an algorithm—principals sometimes have more leeway to admit children later in the summer. Let a school know you are eager for your child to attend and a seat just may open up.

What Are Your Options?

Besides your zoned neighborhood school, you may want to consider gifted and talented programs; unzoned schools (which typically admit children from an entire district; dual-language programs (in which children are taught in two languages); and charter schools. You may also want to consider neighborhood schools that routinely admit children from outside their attendance zone because they have room to spare. You may apply to these schools on your application. For kindergarten directories and applications see www.schools.nyc.gov/ChoicesEnrollment.

Gifted programs include five so-called citywide schools, open to children from all five boroughs who score exceptionally high on multiple-choice tests, and several dozen "district" programs, open to children who score high but not quite so high on the tests. The citywide programs are stand-alone schools; the district programs consist mostly of one class in a neighborhood school. Two other gifted programs of note: the Special Music School on the Upper West Side of Manhattan, open to children from all five boroughs who display unusual musical talent, and Hunter College Elementary School on the Upper East Side, open to Manhattan children only. These two schools have their own admissions procedures. The citywide schools are hugely popular, with far more qualified children than available seats, but a few of the district programs have room to spare.

If you want your child to be tested for one of the citywide or district gifted programs, you must submit a request to the Department of Education (DOE) in November the year before he or she starts kindergarten; the tests are given in January and February. You'll find out if your child meets the eligibility requirements in April; if he or she does, you may apply to the programs; admissions decisions are announced in May. If you move to the city after testing is complete, you may request a special test over the summer. Most children enter these programs in kindergarten. Occasionally seats are available in the upper grades.

Is a gifted class right for your child? Some of the best schools in the city refuse to group children by ability, and manage to bring all children to a high level of achievement. At a school like that, your child may do very well in a general education classroom, even if he or she is unusually capable. On the other hand, in parts of the city where the overall quality of the neighborhood schools is poor, gifted programs may offer a refuge.

Try not to feel bad if your child is refused admission to a gifted program. Most experts are dubious about whether tests given to 4-year-olds can predict future academic achievement. A shy child, or one who doesn't separate from you easily, or one who is just learning English, may do poorly on test at the age of 4—and may still be an academic star by 3rd grade.

Unzoned schools admit children from a whole district or occasionally from the whole city. Many were designed as an alternative to traditional neighborhood schools and have a progressive philosophy, with lots of projects, fieldtrips, and hands-on activities. Some are simply created to ease overcrowding at zoned schools. The city publishes lists of unzoned schools in its kindergarten directories; our favorites are profiled here.

Dual-language programs offer instruction in two languages and are designed to make children fluent speakers, readers, and writers in both. Typically, classes mix native speakers of both languages; the language of instruction alternates. Some of these programs give preference to children who live in the attendance zone, but some have room for children outside the attendance zone. Dual-language programs are offered in Spanish, French, Chinese, Arabic, Japanese, Russian, Korean, and Italian. A complete list is available in the city's elementary school directories. Apply on your Kindergarten Connect application or contact the school directly.

Other Options: Charter Schools

There has been a huge growth in **charter schools** in the past decade. First established by state law in 1998, charter schools are tuition-free schools that operate independently of the city's Department of Education and are supported by tax levies. There are more than 200 charter schools in New York City, serving 95,000 pupils, or nearly 9% of the city's school population.

A few begin with prekindergarten; most begin with kindergarten. Some serve children in grades K–8; some grades K–12. Some begin with middle school and a few begin with high school.

Admission is by lottery held in April. Most give priority to children who live in the school district in which the school is located. You may apply online, through the Common Application on the Charter School Center website, or directly to the school that interests you. If you arrive in the city after the lottery has been held, you can ask to be placed on the wait list. Some admit children in upper grades; some do not.

Just like the ordinary public schools, the quality of the charters ranges from excellent to not-ready-for-prime-time. There are super-traditional charters with discipline codes so strict that children are sent home if their shirts are untucked and super-progressive charters where kids call teachers by their first names and create their own projects.

Charters are exempt from certain rules and regulations of the DOE, and only a few have unionized teachers. Some have very high rates of teacher turnover. The school day and school year tend to be longer—a boon both to working parents and to children who need more time to learn.

Unlike other states, New York does not permit for-profit companies to run charter schools. Large nonprofit networks operate many of New York's charter schools; in some cases, a small community organization may operate just one charter—we call these "mom and pops." Our favorite "mom and pops," together with networks that have schools in just one borough, are listed along with the ordinary public schools in the geographical sections that follow.

KIPP NYC is one of the city's first charter organizations, opened in 1995 (even before the state law that codified charters). It operates five elementary schools in the Bronx, Manhattan, and Brooklyn as well as five middle schools and one high school in New York City. KIPP NYC is affiliated with the California-based KIPP (Knowledge Is Power Program) network, which now operates more than 180 charter schools across the United States, most in low-income neighborhoods.

KIPP has strict rules about discipline in its elementary schools; some parents find the approach oppressive, while others welcome it. By middle school, the atmosphere seems more relaxed. We've been impressed by the quality of instruction and the approach to reading and math on our visits to KIPP middle schools. See KIPPnyc.org for details on how to apply.

Success Academy Charter Schools, founded by former City Councilwoman Eva Moskowitz, is the largest and most controversial charter network, with more than 40 schools covering every borough except Staten Island. For Moskowitz, charter school expansion is a political cause: Both parents and children are expected to take part in rallies in Albany and New York City in support of the network's political agenda. For the network's defenders, its stratospheric test scores are a sign of high-quality teaching and hard-working students; to its detractors they are the results of incessant test-prep and a brutal culture that systematically weeds out laggards. *The New York Times* ran a series of stories excoriating the network for its harsh disciplinary practices; *PBS News Hour* criticized the network for its practice of suspending children as young as 5. A number of parents have filed federal civil rights complaints that Success Academy discriminates against children with disabilities.

Here's what our reviewer, Laura Zingmond, wrote after a visit to Upper West Success, a racially mixed school on Manhattan's Upper West Side: "Instruction is fast-paced and highly structured. . . . Many lessons and activities are timed, so teachers don't fall behind. . . .

"Every moment is packed with purpose and structure. During block time, students are given activities and goals. In art, before they paint a full picture, students practice skills such as how to use a brush, how to make different marks with the brush, and how to clean a brush before dipping it into another color. We observed one teacher playing a math game with her students while they waited on line to use the bathroom. . . .The upside to the structure is that we met students displaying impressive skills. . . . [But] for some the structure might be stifling or simply too much. A good chunk of the first few weeks of kindergarten is devoted to behavior management. Students spend a lot of time practicing how to walk silently in the hallways, sit on the rug, or ask to go to the bathroom."

See individual school profiles and parent comments on the InsideSchools website. For application information, see success academies.org.

The benefits of the charter schools are related to their drawbacks. Most are located in neighborhoods where poverty and official neglect have combined to create low-performing, even disorderly district schools. By limiting their enrollment to children whose parents know in April where they will be living in September, the charter schools avoid one of the significant difficulties facing the ordinary district schools: the constant churning of children arriving and leaving throughout the year because of unstable housing. By instituting strict discipline codes, the charters are able to exclude children who may disrupt classes in an ordinary district school. Some charters welcome children with disabilities; some are poorly equipped to teach any child who doesn't fit the mold. Depending on where you live, how your child fits in, and what charter you choose, your experience may be a nightmare—or a dream come true.

Weighing What's Important to You

If you can possibly manage it, you should visit schools before you apply. But before you do, think a bit about what's important to you. It's easier to weigh the pluses and minuses of any particular school if you've sorted out in your mind what your child needs the most.

Don't think there is some "best school" out there that your child must attend no matter what. A school that's great for one child might be awful for another. An active child might go berserk in a school without a playground or organized sports—no matter how challenging the academics. Some children are happiest in a highly structured school, where they know exactly what's expected of them; others flourish when given the freedom to follow their own interests. Some thrive on competition; others hate to be ranked and sorted.

Think about your values as well. Do you believe childhood is a time to enjoy life and to make friends? Or do you believe too much play means a child won't be prepared for the rigors of high school and college? Do you believe children need to learn to follow rules and accept authority? Or is it more important for them to challenge authority and think for themselves? There are no right or wrong answers to these questions, but you will be happiest with a school that shares most of your own values.

Consider whether you prefer a traditional or a progressive school. There are good schools in both camps. Some of the best incorporate elements of each.

Traditional schools emphasize basic skills of reading and arithmetic. Good penmanship is prized, and quick recall of facts is encouraged. Teachers may rely on textbooks to ensure that all children cover the same material. Children may be grouped by ability in honors, general, and remedial tracks. The teacher may stand at the front of the class and give lessons to all the children at once, and the children are expected to absorb the information they are given. Although very few elementary schools still have desks in rows, traditional schools are unlikely to have kids sprawled on the floor. Parents often appreciate the order and discipline of good traditional schools. Traditional schools often emphasize their pupils' scores on standardized tests, and many traditional schools listed here have high test scores.

Progressive schools encourage children to work at their own pace, to follow their own interests, and to do independent research. Progressive schools may have no assigned desks at all; children work on the floor or at small tables. Each child might be involved in a different activity: reading a book of his or her own choosing, or caring for a class pet, or figuring out a problem in multiplication using wooden blocks put together in rows. Progressive schools shy away from textbooks, encouraging children instead to read novels, science discovery books, or biographies. The content of children's written work is considered more important than the handwriting. Children of different abilities are placed in the same class, and each child may read a different book. Parents appreciate the fact that a bright child can work ahead of peers and that a child who is having trouble can get individual attention. Advocates of progressive education say it's more important to learn how to gather and interpret information than to memorize facts.

There are strengths and weaknesses to each philosophy. A bad traditional school can be oppressive; a bad progressive school, chaotic. Parents at some traditional schools say their children know the facts—dates in history or the multiplication tables—but don't know what to do with them. Parents at some progressive schools say their children understand big concepts—such as trends in history or how to go about solving a math problem—but don't know basic facts. The best schools, of course, insist children learn facts and concepts; they teach basic skills and encourage children to think for themselves. The combination is crucial, whatever the school's philosophy.

What about **gifted programs**? In some schools, a gifted program creates an unpleasant atmosphere, dividing the school into the privileged haves and the neglected have-nots. I have reservations about telling 5-year-olds they are special because they scored well on a multiple-choice exam. Children need to learn that hard work counts—not innate talent.

Will a super-intelligent child be bored in a regular class? It depends. Ellen Winner, author of *Gifted Children: Myths and Realities,* says that if a school has high standards for everyone, all but the most exceptional children are better off in regular classes. Gifted education in segregated classes, she argues, should be reserved for the true child prodigies—for the 3-year-old who's teaching himself algebra, for example. (They exist; she's interviewed them.)

Unfortunately, we live in the real world, and most of us don't have a choice between a high-performing neighborhood school with classes of mixed abilities and a gifted program 10 blocks away. Some research suggests that very bright African American and Latino children, in particular, benefit from gifted programs—perhaps because otherwise they are likely to be assigned to low-performing neighborhood schools. If your neighborhood school is uninspiring and there are no other good choices nearby, a gifted class may well be your best bet, if your child is one who scores well on tests.

Whatever you decide, an important question to ask a principal or teacher is: How do you deal with a range of abilities in a class? How do you challenge children at the top? How do you help children who are having trouble? Most schools claim to "individualize" or "differentiate" instruction, but it's worth asking for examples of how they do it. My son's kindergarten teacher, for example, had puzzles of different degrees of difficulty. When my son finished a 100-piece puzzle, she pulled down a 200-piece puzzle for him to work on.

Schools with desks in rows and the teacher standing at the front tend to focus on "whole-group instruction." In these classes, if everyone reads the same book, it's going to be too hard for some kids, and too easy for others.

But schools in which the classrooms are organized to accommodate a range of abilities are more likely to challenge the high achievers. In these schools, children work individually or in small groups, and each child reads a different book or works on a different project. One child may write an essay of a few sentences, while others write several pages.

In choosing a school, you also want to think about **what you can fix**, what you can live with, and what you cannot live without. No school is perfect—public, private, urban, or suburban. Some things are easier to fix than others. You can find after-school music lessons, or sports, or even French classes if your school doesn't have them. (See the InsideSchools list of free enrichment programs for ideas.) Not enough arithmetic drill? Flash cards at home will help. Remember: Just living in New York City is a great education. Your children will learn a lot from family trips to the American Museum of Natural History, the Metropolitan Museum of Art, the Brooklyn Botanic Garden, and the Bronx Zoo.

Consider **location**, too. In general, the closer a school is to home, the better. One thing good schools have in common is a sense of community. That's a lot easier to achieve if most children walk to school, if parents are welcome to drop in when they have a spare minute, if it's easy for children to get together and play after school. If your neighborhood school is fine, but not quite as good as one farther away, consider whether the time spent schlepping your child to another zone or district could be better used improving your neighborhood school.

Parents who are willing to roll up their sleeves and work with the principal and teachers can achieve promising results. See our profile of PS 125 in Harlem or read about the Bedford Stuyvesant Parents Committee for examples.

A wise friend told me the most important thing was to find a school that did not kill my children's natural curiosity. The tone and climate of a school may be more important than the children's scores on standardized tests. A school that's promising—and on its way up—may provide a better experience for your child than a complacent, well-established school that's resting on its laurels.

Things to Think About Before You Visit

The methods a school uses to teach reading, writing, and arithmetic may have a big impact on how well your child does. It's useful to understand the different approaches and the philosophy behind them.

The most confident schools stay away from fads or scripted textbooks, relying instead on the deep experience of their teachers to adopt different approaches for different children. They use a variety of textbooks and techniques—or no textbooks at all—to help their children learn.

For decades, textbooks companies have sought the holy grail: a magical set of books that can teach all children to read and calculate, regardless of the skill of their teachers. Unfortunately, these books don't exist—although publishers continue to print books that purport to be teacher-proof (and school systems continue to buy them).

In 2012, New York State became one of the first in the nation to adopt the new Common Core learning standards, which outlined new, tougher skills in reading and math that children were supposed to have in each grade. New York City hastily purchased new textbooks that the publishers claimed were aligned to the new standards. For reading, schools were encouraged to choose from a series called ReadyGen (which teachers instantly dubbed not-ReadyGen), one called Core Knowledge, and one called Expeditionary Learning. For math, schools were encouraged to adopt a series called GO Math!, supplemented by online exercises called Exemplars.

Each of these has its limitations, but the worst is **ReadyGen**, which, unfortunately, was adopted by hundreds of schools. Principals, teachers, and reading specialists we interviewed complain that the series lacks instruction in phonics (that is, techniques to match letters with sounds), fails to teach writing, and mostly offers only snippets of readings (rather than complete books). Moreover, the whole books it does recommend are significantly too difficult and have themes that are inappropriate for the children who are supposed to be reading them. Of all the schools we visited, only a tiny handful use this reading series successfully, mostly by picking and choosing very carefully among the components and by supplementing with other materials.

The **Core Knowledge** curriculum, based on the work of E. D. Hirsch, includes classics like *The Tale of Peter Rabbit* and *The Wizard of Oz*. Teachers read aloud books to the whole class that would be too difficult for children to read by themselves as a way to build up their background knowledge and vocabularies. The problem, principals told us, is that children don't spend enough time reading aloud to their teacher in a small group—a practice called "guided reading," which is critical to success.

Expeditionary Learning offers imaginative projects that combine lessons in reading, science, and social studies. For example, children may become "experts" on frogs by reading multiple books about different kinds of frogs; in the process, they learn about how animals adapt to their environment. While teachers we interviewed were enthusiastic, this reading program begins in 3rd grade—and offers little for teachers in grades Pre-K to 2.

The program with the deepest roots in the city's schools is the **Teachers College Reading and Writing Project (TC)**. Lucy Calkins and others at Teachers College, Columbia University, transformed the teaching of writing in the public schools with the method called the Writing Process. With it, children learn to write, even before they learn to read, by stringing together whatever letters they know to approximate words. A kindergartner might write BTN to stand for "button" or HSPTL to stand for "hospital." These early efforts at writing, sometimes called invented spelling, allow children to express complicated and interesting ideas from the very beginning, at a time when other children their age are merely tracing lines of letters. These techniques also help children learn to read as they begin to make a correspondence between a sound and a written letter. (By 2nd grade, children are expected to use "dictionary spelling," not their own approximations.)

At its best, TC produces terrific writers. Children learn sophisticated elements of a writer's craft at a young age. They develop a voice; they learn to write evocative descriptions of sights, sounds, and smells; and they learn to use dialogue effectively and to understand metaphors. Children learn, as adult writers know, that each piece of writing must be revised many times before it is "published." What the Writing Process gives children is the excitement of expressing themselves in print at a very young age—and a reason for wanting to write well.

In my experience, the TC methods are less successful for teaching reading. While children may choose their own books from rich classroom libraries, there's too much emphasis on "independent reading," that is, children reading books independently, and not enough time spent on guided reading, that is, reading in a small group with a teacher.

What's the answer? Teaching reading is a complicated skill, and experienced teachers learn to draw on elements of different approaches.

Teaching mathematics represents a different set of challenges. Before the introduction of the Common Core learning standards, children in New York State followed a shamefully slow-moving curriculum, only learning their multiplication tables in the 4th grade, for example. While the Common Core encouraged schools to have children read books that were inappropriately difficult, the standards for math stepped up the pace of instruction in a way designed to allow children to study algebra by 8th grade and calculus by the end of high school—a demanding but not impossible college prep curriculum.

Whether elementary teachers were prepared for the change is another question. Unfortunately, many elementary school teachers are frightened of math, and avoid it as much as possible. The best schools devote significant time and money to training teachers to teach mathematics; these schools understand that children need both fluency—the ability to calculate quickly—and conceptual understanding—that is, a knowledge of why numbers work the way they do.

Some of the most ambitious schools have adopted **Math in Focus,** also called **Singapore Math,** developed by that high-performing island nation. Because it requires a significant investment in teacher training, it's an expensive program. **GO Math!,** recommended by the city's Department of Education, provides a more scripted approach. Many progressive schools have adopted **Investigations**, a program developed in Cambridge, MA. In its early versions, Investigations, formerly called TERC, focused on conceptual understanding at the expense of fluency—that is, kids understood how numbers worked, but never learned to multiple and divide quickly. Later editions have a better balance. Another progressive approach, **Everyday Math**, developed by the University of Chicago, has what is called a "spiral curriculum," in which material is revisited repeatedly over months and across grades. Some of our favorite schools have an eclectic mix of math programs, drawing the best features from each set of textbooks.

Before you visit a school, you may want to consider some statistics, including its standardized **test scores.** One of the most controversial changes in education in New York State in the past decade was the introduction of new, more difficult tests supposedly aligned with the Common Core State Standards. For years, the tests were too easy—and children who graduated from high school ill prepared for college got a rude awakening. Now, the consensus seems to be that the tests, at least for reading, are too hard, or too confusing, or poorly constructed.

Whatever the flaws of the tests given to children in grades 3 to 8, they do give a rough approximation of which schools manage to bring their children up to a high level. The thing to remember is that the state standards represent a political decision, not necessarily an academic one. Test scores go up and down from year to year depending on decisions in Albany about how hard to make the tests.

For this book, we assigned each school 1 to 5 stars based on their 2016 reading and math scores. Schools ranked in the top fifth citywide have 5 stars (*****), the second fifth have 4 (****), the middle fifth 3 (***), and so on. Schools with "NA" had no test scores available because the schools are so new they had no 3rd-graders in 2016. Test scores can be a useful guide, but they can be deceptive and shouldn't be the only criterion by which you make a decision. For example, schools with a large proportion of children receiving special education services may have scores that are deceptively low—that is, the children in general education do well, but those with special needs don't score well on tests. Schools with a gifted program may have scores that are deceptively high—that is, the children in the gifted program do well, but the others do not. In schools with a large immigrant population, children sometimes score poorly in the lower grades but improve as they get older. Some schools have high test scores because parents are paying for after-school tutoring (and the quality of teaching is only so-so). And some schools with very high test scores rely on lots of tedious test preparation.

When a new principal improves a school dramatically, it takes a few years for the changes to be reflected in the test scores. To be fair, you should look at the scores after the principal has been in a school for at least 4 years, because children who started kindergarten under that new principal will be tested for the first time in 3rd grade.

Two other useful sources of information: The city conducts annual surveys of hundreds of thousands of teachers, parents, and students. These give valuable insights into a school's climate. The Quality Reviews, conducted by a trained administrator, offer clues about teacher quality. Both are available on the DOE website; we've quoted pertinent bits in our school profiles.

You'll also want to consider a school's demographic makeup. In each profile, we include the percentage of children from **low-income** families, that is, those who receive public benefits or who qualify for the federal free lunch program. (Some schools offer free lunch to all children regardless of income; for those schools, we don't have a breakdown of the number of low-income children, so we labeled them "NA.") The citywide average is 76.5%. Schools with a high free-lunch rate qualify for federal anti-poverty money. Some schools with very high poverty rates function well, but many of the best schools have a core of middle-class parents who are able to volunteer and raise money to offset budget cuts and pay for special programs.

The Department of Education classifies children according to race and **ethnicity**: white, black, Hispanic, Asian, and multiracial or other. The school system as a whole is 15% white, 27% black, 41% Hispanic, and 16% Asian. I've listed the percentage of each group represented at each school, "W" for white, "B" for black, "H" for Hispanic, "A" for Asian and "O" for multiracial or other. Sadly, many of the city's schools are deeply segregated by race and class.

We particularly sought out racially and economically integrated schools to include in this book because we believe that learning to get along with others is part of a good education.

At the turn of the 20th century, philosopher John Dewey wrote that schools must teach children to be "social beings," trained for leadership as well as obedience, trained so they can be voting citizens in a multiethnic democracy, not passive subjects. Teaching them to be social beings without letting them mingle with other children, Dewey wrote, is like teaching them to swim without letting them go in the water.

Consider **class size** when you visit a school. Under the contract with the United Federation of Teachers, most New York City public schools have a maximum of 25 children in kindergarten, 28 in grades 1–3, and 32 in grades 4–6. That's too big, in my opinion, but a skillful principal will bring those numbers down, at least for part of the day, by getting extra grown-ups in the classroom— parent volunteers, retired people from the neighborhood, or student teachers. Some classes, called team-teaching classes or Integrated Co-Teaching (ICT) classes, have two teachers, one of whom is certified in special education.

The skill of the classroom teacher is more important than the size of the class. Better to be in a big class with a good teacher than in a small class with a bad one. And some of the best schools have large class size precisely because they are so popular and parents move into the zone to enroll their children.

What to Look for When You Visit

It's important to visit to get a sense of a school's atmosphere, tone, and philosophy. Call the "parent coordinator" to find out when there are tours for prospective parents. See if you can attend a school fair, a musical performance, or a social event to get a feel for the school. Talk to parents dropping their children off in the morning or picking them up in the afternoon. Try to attend a meeting of the Parent–Teacher Association (PTA). You'll get a good idea of parents' concerns and worries.

You want a school where children love to spend their days. The nicest schools make you slightly envious of your child. You'll wish you were 5 years old again so you could start kindergarten. The physical look of a classroom will tell you a lot. And so will the sounds. For a crib sheet on what to look for, see the "What to Look for on a School Tour" section at the end of the book.

You don't want anarchy, and you don't want a police state. You don't want total silence, and you don't want an incessant din. Look for classrooms in which kids are focused and engaged in their work—not staring out the window or wandering aimlessly. Look for children's work (not just decorations made by the teacher or provided by a textbook company) displayed on the bulletin boards and walls, preferably not identical shapes cut from construction paper, but work that shows individual thought and creativity.

You want a place where parents are welcome. Fresh paint and general cleanliness are a plus, but the school doesn't have to be fancy to be good. Don't look for expensive equipment; what you really want is a good principal who hires good teachers. The best schools have a coherent philosophy, articulated by a strong principal and carried out by a unified staff. The philosophy may be traditional, progressive, or a mixture of the two, but the best schools have teachers and a principal with similar goals and a common vision of how to reach them. Avoid schools with warring factions, or a mishmash of ideologies where teachers shift for themselves.

The principal is the most important person in the building. A good principal can transform a mediocre school into a gem in just a few years. A bad principal can dismantle good programs and demoralize a competent staff just as quickly. Not all good principals are personable, and some who are charming as people aren't great as educators. What good principals have in common is an abiding respect for the pupils in their care—a respect that is obvious even on a brief tour. It's fine to be strict, but watch out for principals who yell at kids or who regularly use a bullhorn to keep order. A principal should be not merely an administrator, but an educational leader who can articulate his or her vision for the school and help the staff carry it out. A principal should spend time in classrooms regularly and shouldn't be holed up in the office pushing paper. Ideally, the principal knows the name of every child in the school—not just the stars and the troublemakers.

Look for interesting, fun-to-read books. Good schools, whether traditional or progressive, don't rely exclusively on textbooks to teach reading, math, history, and science. The more progressive schools have no textbooks at all, but teach all subjects from "real" books that you might read for pleasure. Other good schools use textbooks to make sure everyone gets the basics of how to read, but move quickly to picture books, novels, books about historical events, biographies, and science discovery books. Good schools have a rich class library in each classroom, and each child may well be reading a different book, depending on his or her ability and interest. If everyone in a class spends most of the day reading the same textbook, I'd be worried that a lot of kids are bored.

You should see examples of children's writing in the very youngest grades. Good schools ask children to keep journals and to write their own stories using their experiences and their imagination. Watch out for schools where most of the writing is material copied from the blackboard, or where every child's essay is almost exactly the same.

Little kids (and a lot of adults) have trouble with the abstract concepts of mathematics. They need something concrete they can see and hold. That's why so many kids count on their fingers. Good schools provide children with small objects to count with, called manipulatives, such as tongue depressors or buttons, or specially designed small blocks or rods. Little kids use them to learn how to add and subtract; older kids use them to calculate decimals or multiply fractions.

Look for evidence that the school teaches history, geography, and science—and not just reading, writing, and arithmetic. Look for classrooms with live animals, plants, fish tanks, and materials such as magnets and electric motors. Look for globes, maps, and atlases; timelines with dates in history; and projects such as study of the Brooklyn Bridge that may combine lessons in engineering and history.

Trips are an important part of the curriculum. Concerts, museums, the zoo, the beach—all can be incorporated into what children are studying in the classroom. Trips expand children's general knowledge of the world, build their vocabularies by showing them new things, and indirectly improve their reading skills.

Many schools that are good in other respects give up the cafeteria and playground as lost causes. The cafeteria food is terrible, the din is deafening, and the playground is chaotic. Those that refuse to acknowledge defeat manage to rein in the bedlam. Some have children eat family-style in their classrooms, or have someone read aloud in the cafeteria. Recess can be a time for organized circle games. These schools believe every minute of the day can be used for instruction.

Very few schools manage this, so don't get frazzled trying to find one. And perhaps noisy lunchrooms are preferable to the gloomy silent lunches that a few schools insist upon. But I wish more schools would let children out to play in cold weather—rather than having them watch videos in the auditorium.

Many schools have after-school programs to help families whose work schedules require it. Alas, these programs vary in quality as much as the schools themselves. Most charge a fee. Some after-school programs are on school grounds. Others are at nearby community organizations or houses of worship. The members of the community organizations generally pick up children up at their schools and walk them to a nearby after-school center.

The best public schools have all the brains, variety, and excitement of the city itself. They help make this complicated, multiracial city work, by teaching people of different backgrounds to live together. Neighborhood by neighborhood, they build communities of people who care about one another. And they'll give your child a first-rate education—for free.

If Your Child Needs Extra Help: Special Education

If your child has a physical disability, you were probably aware of it before he or she started school. However, there are other, invisible disabilities that only become apparent later. If your child is having unusual difficulty learning to read, or struggles to control his or her behavior in class, or is unable to make friends, he or she may have a learning disability or an emotional issue that requires extra help from a specialized teacher. This help is called special education, and your child is entitled to it by law.

All children with disabilities are entitled to "free and appropriate" education until they turn 21 or graduate from high school. A wide range of services is available (at least in theory): smaller classes for part of the day, speech therapy, psychological counseling, and individual attention from a specially trained teacher in a regular classroom for a few hours each day. Visually impaired students may have extra-large computer keyboards and screens. Hearing-impaired children may participate in a regular class in which the teacher wears a microphone with an FM radio unit that transmits to a child's hearing aid. An impulsive child may be assigned an aide to help him learn to control his behavior. A child with unusually bad handwriting may receive occupational therapy to learn to hold a pencil and form letters better. A dyslexic child may receive tutoring from a specialist. More than 180,000 New York City children receive special education services.

If your child is having difficulty in school, he or she is entitled to extra help, whether or not he or she has a diagnosed disability. Your first step is to ask your teacher for special help—such as tutoring with a learning specialist. Schools are supposed to try various strategies, called "response to intervention," before referring a child for special education services.

If these strategies don't work, the next step is to have your child evaluated. A formal evaluation will give you a better sense of what your child's issues are and what the best way to address them might be. An evaluation will also give you the legal clout you may need to get appropriate services. Your district's Committee on Special Education will conduct a free evaluation, but if you can possibly afford it, consider paying for a private evaluation. Although it's very expensive, a private evaluation will probably be more thorough and will give you significantly more information about what your child needs.

If your child's disability is mild, the evaluators may recommend a plan with inexpensive, commonsense changes in classroom routines to help him or her succeed in school. For example, a child with a learning disability may need extra time on tests. A child who is visually impaired may need books with large print.

These simple changes are called 504 accommodations, named after Section 504 of the Rehabilitation Act of 1973, which bans discrimination on the basis of physical or mental disability in federally funded programs. Every school has a 504 coordinator, charged with implementing these plans.

If the evaluators determine that the child needs special services, a team that includes the parents will draw up an Individualized Education Program, or IEP. In most cases, these services will be provided in your child's neighborhood school during the regular school day. Your child may be assigned to a class with two teachers, one of whom is certified in special education. These classes, called Integrated Co-Teaching or ICT, have a mix of children in general education and those with special needs. Children with severe or rare disabilities are referred to District 75, an administrative entity that supervises highly specialized programs. Some District 75 programs are contained within regular schools. Some have their own school buildings.

The quality of special education programs varies tremendously from school to school. Some excellent programs manage to give children with complicated special needs the extra help that allows them to participate fully in regular classrooms. Others consign disabled children to dingy, segregated classrooms in a school basement—even if their learning problems are fairly mild. We've described noteworthy special education programs in the school profiles that follow.

It's important to know your legal rights and to find someone to help you navigate the special education bureaucracy. Both 504 plans and IEPs are legal documents, and schools are required by law to follow them. For advice about your child's rights, call the Advocates for Children hotline Monday to Thursday from 10 a.m. to 4 p.m.: (866) 427-6033; or check their website, www.advocatesforchildren.org.

For help navigating the byzantine special education bureaucracy, you also can call INCLUDEnyc (www.includenyc.org, formerly known as Resources for Children with Special Needs), a nonprofit advocacy and referral agency: (212) 677-4660. For parent-to-parent advice and hand-holding, call Ellen McHugh at Parent-to-Parent at (800) 405-8818 (www.parenttoparentnys.org). She will put you in contact with a parent whose child has a disability similar to your child's. Good luck.

District 1
1. New Explorations Into Science, Technology & Math (NEST+m)
2. Children's Workshop School
3. East Village Community School
4. PS 364: Earth School
5. PS 363: Neighborhood School
6. PS 63

District 2
7. PS 276, The Battery Park City School
8. PS 89
9. PS 234
10. Peck Slip School, PS 343
11. PS 126
12. Spruce Street
13. PS 150
14. PS 124
15. PS 130
16. PS 3
17. PS 41
18. PS 11
19. PS 33
20. PS 40
21. PS 116
22. PS 51
23. Midtown West
24. PS 59
25. PS 267
26. PS 183
27. Ella Baker
28. PS 158
29. PS 6
30. PS 290, Manhattan New School
31. PS 151
32. Hunter College Elementary School
33. PS 527, East Side School for Social Action
34. PS 198/PS 77: Lower Lab School
35. PS 217

District 3
36. Special Music School
37. PS 199
38. PS 452
39. The Anderson School, PS 334
40. PS 87
41. PS 9
42. PS 166
43. PS 84
44. Manhattan School for Children
45. PS 75
46. PS 163
47. PS 180

District 4
48. PS 12: Talented and Gifted
49. Central Park East
50. Central Park East II
51. PS 171
52. River East

District 5
53. PS 125
54. Harlem Village Academy West Charter Elementary School
55. Teachers College Community School
56. Neighborhood Charter School
57. Thurgood Marshall Academy, PS 318

District 6
58. Castle Bridge School, PS 513
59. Dos Puentes, PS 103
60. PS/MS 187
61. PS 178
62. Muscota New School, PS 314
63. Amistad Dual Language School, PS 311
64. PS 278

Manhattan Schools

MANHATTAN

The real estate mantra "location, location, location" applies doubly to public schools in Manhattan. The quality of education your child receives depends a lot on where you live, and the gap between good and bad is dramatic. Although there are some opportunities for school choice, most children attend their zoned neighborhood school.

Manhattan is divided into six school districts. Of these, District 2, serving the Upper East Side, midtown, and downtown, has the most consistently strong leadership and the most successful schools. Sky-high real estate prices, of course, mean that most families can't afford to move into District 2. Parents priced out of the high-rent districts will find good schools in less expensive neighborhoods as well. District 1, serving the Lower East Side, and District 4, serving East Harlem, have a long history of school choice. The schools in District 3 on the Upper West Side are of uneven quality, but a few are among the best in the city. The schools in District 6, north of 135th Street, are improving under the effective leadership of Supt. Manuel Ramirez. There are even signs of life in District 5 in Central Harlem, which has long had some of the worst schools in the city.

Manhattan is home to three schools for the gifted that accept children from all five boroughs (NEST+m, Talented and Gifted Young Scholars, and the Anderson School); and one that accepts children who live anywhere in Manhattan (Hunter College Elementary School). Most of the districts have their own gifted programs. Admission to these is determined by a test. The Special Music School accepts children from all five boroughs based on their musical talent.

There are other options as well. Charter schools—tuition-free schools that operate independently of the Department of Education—admit children by lottery. Unzoned or "option schools"—schools with no defined attendance zones—accept children from an entire district. Some schools have dual-language programs—designed to make children fluent in two languages—that admit children outside their attendance zone.

District 1: Lower East Side

Once known for its squatters in vacant buildings and for shantytowns built on vacant lots, the Lower East Side is now home to trendy bars and boutiques with a sprinkling of luxury apartments tucked amidst towering blocks of public housing. The area north of Houston Street has been renamed the East Village—a name more befitting the high rents now being charged.

The public school parents represent a funky and eclectic mix of working-class Puerto Ricans; new immigrants from India, Bangladesh, and China; artists; "bohemian" types with tattoos and pierced noses; and more than a few accountants and lawyers. There are no attendance zones; parents are encouraged to shop around and must submit an application choosing from the schools in the district. All have tours for prospective parents. Some have admission policies designed to ensure a mix of families of different income levels. Soon to open: a Family Resource Center where parents can learn about school choice. Check out the website of the Community Education Council, the elected parent body that advises the superintendent on policy, for updates: https://cecd1.org. The school district office is at 180 Essex Street, New York, NY 10002, (212) 353-2948.

Many of the school buildings, just a block or two from one another, were constructed to serve the teeming immigrant population at the turn of the 20th century. Not long after they were built, new subway lines to the Bronx allowed people to move to less congested areas. The schools built for another era remain, and many are still half-vacant.

The luxury of space has allowed the district to experiment and, as a result, the district has an unusual number of alternative schools. Every school in the district has **prekindergarten** classes (except the charters). And, since there are no zoned schools in the district, once you are accepted into the prekindergarten, you are automatically "in" for kindergarten too.

Worth watching: Tiny **PS 15**, at 333 East 4th Street, has a district gifted program as well as some terrific teachers and administrators. The test scores are low, partly because the school serves a lot of homeless kids and it's hard for teachers to get traction with such a transient population. But the school offers lots of opportunities: Children study dance with Mark DeGarmo teaching artists and acting with Rosie's Broadway Kids. Students grow plants, hatch chicks, and take frequent fieldtrips.

Outside of the public schools, **Bank Street Head Start**, 535 East 5th Street, is a delightful, play-based program, led by thoughtful and caring adults; it gives preference to low-income families. See http://insideschools.org/component/schools/school/8410?Itemid=79 for details.

District 2: Downtown, Midtown, and Upper East Side

District 2 is a huge district that includes some of the most expensive real estate on the planet: the Upper East Side, Sutton Place, Gramercy Park, Greenwich Village, and Tribeca, as well as some more modestly priced neighborhoods in Chinatown, Hell's Kitchen and a tiny corner of East Harlem. The schools are uniformly strong, not just for the elementary years but for middle and high school as well. While most city high schools are open to children from all five boroughs, District 2 is unusual in that it has developed its own high schools with admission limited to children who live in the district—a privilege parents elsewhere in the city envy. Many of the schools have formidable Parent Teacher Associations (PTAs) that raise hundreds of thousands of dollars annually for books, supplies, and assistant teachers.

The district's great strength has been the teaching of writing—lively, engaging poetry and prose that give children a sense of power and a voice. The schools have long experience with the Reading and Writing Project developed by Teachers College, Columbia University, and its principles are deeply ingrained. Children learn to write for a purpose, for a response, for a real audience beyond the classroom. In kindergarten a child might write to the school custodian telling him a coat hook is broken. By 5th grade, a child might write to the *New York Times* to complain that a rental lease excludes pets. Children learn that writing is not something you do just because your teacher tells you to, but something you want to do because it gives you a sense of confidence and control over your world.

District 2 has gifted and talented (G&T) programs at PS 124 and PS 130, both in Chinatown; PS 11 and PS 33 in Chelsea; PS 217 on Roosevelt Island, **PS 111** in Hell's Kitchen; and the Lab School (PS 77) and PS 198 on the Upper East Side. But many parents of high-achieving children are quite content with their neighborhood schools and don't apply to the G&T programs. Call the district office at 333 Seventh Avenue for details: (212) 356-3811.

Enrollment has boomed in recent years, and a number of new schools have opened to accommodate the new pupils. The only drawback to the schools' popularity (besides occasional wait lists for kindergarten) is large class size and a shortage of space for **prekindergarten** classes.

There are some good options for prekindergarten, however. **PS 6** and **PS 183** on the Upper East Side added Pre-K classes in 2016. **Ella Baker School**, also on the Upper East Side, accepts children from all five boroughs. There are freestanding Pre-K centers—that is, schools your child will attend for only one year—housed at PS 51 in Hell's Kitchen, at Peck Slip School, and at the Department of Education headquarters at 52 Chamber Street (see http://insideschools.org/component/schools/school/9543).

PS 126, a sweet, engaging school, has room to spare for children outside the school attendance zone. PS 2 at 122 Henry Street, (212) 964-0350, has a stellar prekindergarten program for little scientists. PS 33 accepts Pre-K kids from across the district. PS 124, a large school in Chinatown, has 90 Pre-K seats and typically has space even for out-of-borough children.

Two new schools that are worth watching: **PS 340, Sixth Avenue Elementary School**, 590 Sixth Avenue, in Chelsea, (917) 305-1000, has lots of classroom pets, fieldtrips, and hands-on experiences for little ones. Started in 2014 to ease overcrowding at nearby PS 41, the school occupies several floors of a modern building that was formerly the Foundling Hospital. Kindergartners studying restaurants take fieldtrips to several in the neighborhood and then create their own in the classroom. When a prekindergarten class became enthralled by a construction project on the building next door, teachers helped them track the building's progress with photographs and stories, culminating in a fieldtrip to the actual site and a tour by a construction worker. PS 340 is a new zoned school, but houses a Pre-K center that's open to children outside the zone.

Another new school, **PS 281**, 425 East 35th Street, (212) 251-6640, serves a polyglot population including the children of diplomats at the United Nations nearby. Classrooms are colorful, neat, and stocked with supplies and books. Pre-K and kindergarten rooms have play areas, and teachers make sure the youngest students have easy access to developmentally appropriate materials such as chunky markers and thick pencils that are best suited for tiny hands. Teachers collaborate to write their own curriculum, and in all grades there's a nice mix of independent and groupwork. PS 281 is a zoned neighborhood school. The building also houses a Pre-K center open to children outside the zone.

District 3: Upper West Side

The politics of race and class are as vexing in District 3, which covers the West Side from 59th Street to 122nd Street, as they are anywhere in the city. The southern end of the district is mostly white; the northern end, mostly African American (although it has become more mixed in recent years). Parents in the northern end of the district have long been angry that the quality of their schools is mostly inferior to those in the south.

Class plays a role as well. With posh brownstones and luxury high-rises right next to public housing projects throughout the district, rich and poor live close together. Soaring real estate prices in the luxury market have only widened the gap between rich and poor: As one father put it, the millionaires are being forced out by the billionaires. What this means for the schools in the coming years is difficult to predict.

The growth of charter schools has added another layer of complexity to the equation. Designed primarily to serve low-income black and Latino children who had no good public school options, charters have proliferated in the northern end of District 3. Particularly popular are the Success Academies. By attracting the most motivated parents, the charters have left some of the district schools even more burdened with the neediest students.

A few of the schools profiled here are models of racial and economic diversity, where people of different backgrounds get along well and cherish learning from one another. Others have internal divisions between the haves and the have-nots, when, for example, a gifted program disproportionately serves prosperous children. Perhaps not surprisingly, the highest-performing schools in the district are oversubscribed, while the low-performing schools have room to spare.

The District 3 Community Education Council, the elected panel of parents charged with setting school attendance zones, has been wrestling with ways to deal with overcrowding, while also addressing the racial and economic segregation in the district. The solutions are difficult, but at least the problems are being raised.

Most of the schools in District 3 have far more applicants than seats for **prekindergarten,** but a few schools have some space.

PS 145, 150 West 105th Street, (212) 678-2857, is an up-and-coming school with plans for a new Russian dual-language program. It has a sunny atrium that doubles as a community garden. The principal is popular with parents and the prekindergarten classes are particularly strong. The school mostly serves a needy population, including many homeless families. **PS 191**, long housed at 210 W. 61st Street, (212) 757-4343, is moving into a new building nearby. It has a well-established Pre-K program with plenty of seats. The principal, Lauren Keville, has brought order to a school once known for discipline problems and has introduced the Teachers College Reading and Writing Project.

(If you're willing to travel, the Pre-K center at PS 51, listed above, has well-equipped classrooms and room to spare, possibly a result of the out-of-the-way location on 44th Street, west of 10th Avenue.)

District 4: East Harlem

District 4 in East Harlem (also called Spanish Harlem) includes public-housing blocks as well as some posh Fifth Avenue apartments near Mt. Sinai Hospital. An uncrowded district, it was one of the first in the country to allow parents to choose their child's public school, and there are some important and interesting schools here. District 4 extends from roughly East 96th Street and Second Avenue to East 125th Street and the Harlem River.

Philosophies vary a great deal from school to school. Some are firmly in the progressive camp—where kids call teachers by first names and sprawl on rugs or sofas—and others are more traditional—with kids in uniforms and a formal tone.

Unfortunately, the district's 40-year history shows that "choice" is not a cure-all for failing public schools. Many schools in the district still have very low levels of achievement, and the system of choice may have exacerbated the gaps between the best and the worst. The district accepts applications from children who live outside its boundaries; however, space has been tight in recent years. The district office is at 160 East 120th Street, Room 401, New York, NY 10035, (212) 348-2873. Most of the schools profiled here have **prekindergarten.** An under-the-radar choice for Pre-K: safe, joyful **PS 112,** 535 East 119th Street, (212) 860-5868, led by longtime principal Eileen Reiter. Tiny, progressive **River East**, open districtwide, has had Pre-K seats to spare in recent years.

District 5: Central Harlem

District 5, in Central Harlem, has long had some of the most poorly managed schools in the city. We found a few bright spots and listed them here. One promising sign: Parent activists are organizing to improve the schools, and their efforts are bearing fruit at one school, at least, PS 125. The district office is at 425 West 123rd Street, New York, NY 10027, (212) 769-7500.

For **prekindergarten,** besides PS 125, we recommend **Addie Mae Collins 3**, 2322 3rd Avenue, (212) 831-3144, where kids go on trips to the New York Aquarium and the American Museum of Natural History. This child-care and Head Start center gives preference to low-income families.

District 6: Washington Heights and Inwood

Over the years, upper Manhattan has changed from mostly Irish and Jewish to predominantly Dominican. More recently, Russian immigrants moved to the area, along with artists and musicians escaping sky-high rents downtown. The most prosperous families live in large co-op apartments surrounded by formal gardens on Cabrini Boulevard and in Castle Hill Village overlooking the Hudson River.

District 6, serving northern Harlem, Washington Heights, and Inwood, was once one of the most crowded districts in the city. School construction didn't keep pace with the waves of immigrants who moved to the neighborhood in the 1980s and 1990s, and hundreds of pupils were bused to less crowded schools downtown and in the Bronx.

Now, gentrification has led to a decline in the school-age population: An apartment that once might have housed a grandmother, three grown daughters, and their six children might now have two hipsters and a dog. Schools that were once seriously overcrowded now have space to spare.

A popular superintendent, Manny Ramirez, is bringing new life to some long-neglected neighborhood schools. Some creative dual-language programs designed to make children fluent in English and Spanish have opened. Schools that were once overwhelmingly made up of children of Dominican ancestry now serve a mix of Spanish speakers and English speakers. The district office is at 4360 Broadway, 4th Floor, New York, NY 10033.

Many of the schools profiled here have **prekindergarten.** However, some of the most sought-after schools in District 6 have far more Pre-K applicants than seats.

For Pre-K, consider: **PS 173,** 306 Fort Washington Avenue, (212) 927-7850. It has huge, bright, well-stocked classrooms, clean furnishings and equipment, and a new principal who is popular with parents and keen to turn the school around.

Kym Vanderbilt, an early childhood expert from Lehman College, recommends **Fort George Head Start**, 1525 Saint Nicholas Avenue, (212) 795-9184, for low-income families, and the **Children's Aid Society** Pre-K programs at PS 5, 3703 10th Avenue, (212) 567-5787, and PS 8, 465 West 167th Street, (212) 740-8655.

New Explorations into
Science, Technology & Math (NEST+m)

111 Columbia Street
New York, NY 10002
(212) 677-5190
www.nestmk12.net

Who gets in: kids in 99th percentile on gifted exam
Grade levels: K–12   **Reading scores:** * * * * *
Enrollment: 1,753   **Math scores:** * * * * *
Low-income: 27%   **Ethnicity:** 42%W 9%B 11%H 33%A 5%O

One of the most sought-after schools in the city, New Explorations into Science, Technology & Math (NEST+m) has a demanding curriculum, hyper-involved parents, and children who love to come to school. It is one of five schools for the gifted that accept applicants from all five boroughs, and the only one to serve grades K–12.

Teachers in grades K–5 have a progressive approach, with opportunities for children to work independently, to express themselves by speaking and writing, and to explore their own interests. Each class in kindergarten through 2nd grade has a play area with lots of blocks. Lessons are woven around interdisciplinary themes such as transportation (the different types, how quickly or slowly they move) and Central Park (how to read maps or build bridges, or what kind of wildlife lives there).

The elementary school (also called the Lower School) has weekly "enrichment clusters" in which children from different classes work together on projects such as cooking, puppetry, or street hockey. All elementary school students study Mandarin once a week. One nice, old-fashioned touch: Children have good handwriting, the result of much practice.

NEST+m uses Singapore Math in grades K–7, a curriculum that combines quick recall of arithmetic facts with a deep understanding of math concepts. For parents who are frustrated by the slow pace of math in many of the city's schools, Singapore Math is one of NEST+m's great strengths.

Parents are invited to read with kindergartners at the start of the day. On one of our visits, mothers and fathers sat with groups of children on the corridor floors, reading aloud.

The school is housed in a sunny two-story building with wide halls and classrooms arranged around a central courtyard.

Both elementary and middle school children play outside in the pleasant courtyard after lunch. Children in grades 3–8 have a dress code: shirts of various colors emblazoned with a NEST+m logo. In the winter months, many swap the polo shirt for purple sweatshirts with the school logo. Kids seem happy to be here, and attendance is very high. On one of our visits—a snowy day when most schools had poor attendance—nearly all the NEST+m kids showed up.

A hyperactive PTA raises a substantial budget to pay for teacher assistants in the lower grades, dozens of laptops and computers, ballroom dancing lessons for 5th-graders, after-school enrichment programs, and sports teams.

Mark Berkowitz, who became principal in July 2015, was former assistant principal at NYC Lab School for Collaborative Studies. Berkowitz recognizes that gifted children, like all children, need social and emotional support. "We want to create a space where it's safe to make a mistake," he said.

Berkowitz moved his office from the ground floor main office (where it was protected by secretaries) to the third floor, where students may walk in without an appointment. He shares the office with his secretary, and students stop to chat informally or even share a joke. He seems to know every child by name.

Children with disabilities such as dyslexia and ADHD receive SETSS (special education teacher support services). Occupational, physical, and speech therapists assist children, and a psychologist is on hand 2 days a week.

The admissions process is daunting, and there are far more applicants than seats available. Kindergartners must score in the 99th percentile on the city's gifted and talented exam to even be considered. (Siblings of current students may apply if they score in the 97th percentile.)

For kindergarten admissions, parents must submit a Request for Testing in November; children are tested in January. See the Department of Education's gifted and talented handbook for details on admission to grades K–2, including practice tests. Only parents whose children score in the 97th percentile may attend the elementary school open house held in the spring. Current elementary students are guaranteed admission into middle school.

NEST+m attracts children from all five boroughs. Free yellow bus service is available for some children in grades K–6 who live in Manhattan. Others are eligible for free Metrocards for city buses or subways. Many parents pay for a private bus service, which costs about $3,000 a year. (Clara Hemphill)

PS 63

121 East 3rd Street
New York, NY 10009
(212) 674-3180
www.staracademyps63.com

PK

Who gets in: District 1 choice, with room for out-of-district kids
Grade levels: PK–5   **Reading scores:** ****
Enrollment: 203   **Math scores:** ****
Low-income: 84%   **Ethnicity:** 10%W 20%B 65%H 4%A 1%O

PS 63, also called the STAR Academy, is one of those schools whose strengths aren't obvious from the data. Test scores are only average, and attendance is below average—a reflection of its needy population, including some homeless children. But the school has a warm environment, a smart approach to math, and teachers who are willing to invest time to learn new techniques.

A few years ago, faced with new, tough Common Core State Standards, teachers confronted their own anxiety about math, and, over the course of two summers, re-educated themselves and wrote their own math curriculum. Each day, children have one 45–60-minute period of teacher instruction and group-work in math, plus a second 20-minute period of math games and skills.

Teachers use the Teachers College Reading and Writing Project. Older students are encouraged to write about weighty topics such as immigration and the Holocaust. Literacy is the focus of the first half hour of each day in small groups. Advanced students may also use that morning time to learn the ukulele or computer coding.

Most classes have two teachers, one of whom is certified in special education. A child with writing difficulties might have a designated "scribe" to help her express ideas. "You may have a kid who can only write at a kindergarten level, but who can think at a very high level," Assistant Principal Jodi Friedman said.

"Whenever I had a problem or was struggling in a family crisis," a graduate wrote on the InsideSchools website, "staff members were always there by my side."

There is a free after-school program for grades K–5. The school shares the building amicably with The Neighborhood School. Admission is open to District 1 children, but the school also has room for out-of-district children. There is a small fee-based after-school program for kindergarten. (Aimee Sabo)

PS 361: Children's Workshop School

610 East 12th Street
New York, NY 10009
PK
(212) 614-9531
www.childrensworkshopschool.org

Who gets in: District 1 lottery
Grade levels: PK–5
Enrollment: 267
Low-income: 47%

Reading scores: *****
Math scores: ****
Ethnicity: 38%W 11%B 39%H 10%A 2%O

One of four small, progressive schools in the East Village, The Children's Workshop School prides itself on the fact that the racial, ethnic, and economic diversity inside the building closely reflects the population outside the building. The staff makeup is also noticeably diverse in terms of gender, ethnicity, and race.

Hallmarks of Children's Workshop include semester-long themes on topics like water, immigration, and the city. Children delve into artsy, hands-on projects. First- and 2nd-graders are mixed together but separated into age-level groups for math. No other grades are "bridged" in that way, but teachers stay with the same children for 3th and 4th grade, a strategy called "looping."

Principal Maria Velez-Clarke co-founded the school in 1993 and based it on the principles of Dr. Martin Luther King Jr. There are no Christmas or Halloween parties, but every January the kids put on a big celebration and performance to commemorate the late civil rights activist.

Children call teachers by their first names and teachers relate to children in an easygoing, matter-of-fact way. Many lessons have an active component: Addition is explored using beads and pipe cleaners in one room and colored wooden rods in another. Teachers use expressive voices and kids lean forward to watch and listen: "I like that!" said a boy, spontaneously, after a math demonstration.

Art, music, technology, drama, and music teachers connect what happens in their classes with social studies themes and classroom work. Much of the student work incorporates art. Children draw food chains and water cycles. They make colorful charts in math showing how many ways you can add two numbers to make 10, for example.

Fieldtrips are significant here: 2nd-graders went to the Central Park reservoir, Lake Tear of the Clouds, the NYC watershed, Highbridge Park, and other places related to their study of water.

"These kids know more about New York City than I do," said Joyce Borden, the school's longtime secretary, who remembers carrying mace in her bag on her walk to school when the East Village was more crime-ridden than it is now.

To maintain the school's diversity, teachers spread flyers and visit Pre-K programs and public housing developments. The school gives scholarships to anyone who can't afford the after-school fee, and each child has a designated "special day" hosted by the child's family. A father who lives across the street in Campos Houses said children (including his own) are happy, "and if they're happy everything else is taken care of."

Children's Workshop shares a 100-year-old building with the progressive East Village Community School and PS 94, a District 75 school for children with special education needs who attend classes at Children's Workshop. (Lydie Raschka)

PS 315: East Village Community School

610 East 12th Street
New York, NY 10009
(212) 982-0682
www.evcsnyc.org

PK

Who gets in: District 1 lottery
Grade levels: PK–5
Enrollment: 299
Low-income: 21%

Reading scores: ****
Math scores: *****
Ethnicity: 55%W 9%B 21%H 9%A 6%O

At East Village Community School, schoolwide morning meeting begins with a few dads, moms, and teachers strumming banjos and guitars leading an audience sing-along of "This Land Is Your Land." It's a family affair, with long-haired dads bouncing infants; toddlers clapping along with the kids on the stage; and one tyke even crying inconsolably after the show ended because he wanted to stay at school with his older sibling.

EVCS can seem almost like a throwback to the 1960s, even down to the singing of the 1972 song "Free to Be You and Me." Kindergarten still looks like kindergartens of old, where children learn through play to read, write, and get along with one another. The block corner doesn't disappear after Pre-K—it's an active place used even in 1st-grade lessons about community buildings.

There is joy in the classrooms, and plenty of exploration. Each class goes on as many as 10 fieldtrips a year, not counting the many neighborhood walks. Prekindergartners consider the question: "Where does food come from?" and then visit the Union Square Farmers Market. Even the youngest children help plan what they are going to do or study.

The atmosphere is informal: Teachers and administrators go by their first names and students may pull out snacks if they're hungry. Freedom does not lead to chaos, however: Classrooms are tidy and all items, from books to blocks, have clearly defined homes in color-coded bins and on brightly labeled shelves.

Homework isn't assigned until 2nd grade and there are no consequences for not doing it. Test scores are among the highest in the district, although about one-third of the families decided in 2015 to opt their children out of taking state exams.

The neighborhood's changing demographics are seen in the faces of the children: Pre-K, kindergarten, and 1st grade are largely white; there are more Hispanic and black children in the upper grades. Only 28 percent of families qualify for free lunch, far fewer than at many of the neighborhood's more traditional public schools.

EVCS shares a 100-year-old building with the Children's Workshop School and PS 94, a District 75 school for children with special education needs.

District 1 lottery: There was a wait list of about 100 students for admission to prekindergarten in 2015. There is never space for out-of-district students in Pre-K or kindergarten; occasionally slots may open up in older grades. (Pamela Wheaton)

PS 364: Earth School

600 East 6th Street
New York, NY 10009
(212) 477-1735
www.theearthschool.org

PK

Who gets in: District 1 lottery (set aside for low-income kids)
Grade levels: PK–5
Enrollment: 340
Low-income: 46%

Reading scores: ★★★★★
Math scores: ★★★★
Ethnicity: 37%W 13%B 35%H 7%A 7%O

At the Earth School, children grow vegetables for the cafeteria on a rooftop garden, tend to a fig tree in the back yard, and learn to compost scraps and recycle. Through hands-on arts and science projects, they learn to be good citizens and stewards of the planet. The quality of teaching is high and students are engaged.

Parents bring their children to the classroom each morning and are welcome throughout the day. Parents may attend weekly Town Hall meetings and chat with one another at "coffee Fridays."

Abbe Futterman, a science teacher who has been at the school since its founding in 1992, became principal in 2014. Most classes mix children of different ages: Prekindergarten and kindergarten are grouped together, as are 1st–2nd and 4th–5th grades. Only 3rd grade is a stand-alone year. Teachers say they get to know children well because they have them for two years. And students feel comfortable in the room, making for a smooth transition. The grouping also means older children get the chance to be "elders" and may help younger ones, the principal said. Many of the classrooms have at least two teachers. Older children are separated by grade for math.

Social studies topics may last an entire year, such as the 4th–5th grade study of immigration. Children visited Ellis Island, the Tenement Museum, and Museo del Barrio to learn about immigration movements in the past as well as today's migrants from war-torn countries such as Syria. Children were asked to zero in on individual immigrant stories, and to tell a person's story with a drawing, poem, or map.

Many art projects incorporate science, social studies, and even math. A detailed mural and timeline about the lead in the water in Flint, MI, took up much of a corridor. In another project, 1st- and 2nd-graders took fieldtrips around the city, interviewed community workers, and made models of landmarks from cardboard and papier-mâché.

Classrooms are large, full of light and plants. There's a full-time cooking teacher and a room dedicated to cooking—a great hands-on way to learn math. The smell of gingerbread baking filled the corridors on our visit.

The large building is shared amicably with PS 64 and Tompkins Square Middle School. Earth School occupies the first floor and ground floor. All have access to the rooftop garden.

The Earth School has long had a mix of children of different income levels and races, and the school community is determined to maintain that even as the neighborhood gentrifies, Futterman said. In 2015, the city allowed the Earth School to set aside 45% of its seats for students learning to speak English and those who qualify for free or reduced lunch.

The Earth School staff and parents have been in the forefront of the movement to opt out of state tests for 3rd- to 5th-graders. In recent years more than half of the students did not take the state exams.

There is sometimes space for out-of-district students in the upper grades, although not in Pre-K or kindergarten. (Pamela Wheaton)

PS 363: Neighborhood School

121 East 3rd Street
New York, NY 10009

PK

(212) 387-0195
www.tnsny.org

Who gets in: District 1 lottery (set aside for low-income kids)
Grade levels: PK–5   **Reading scores:** ***
Enrollment: 313   **Math scores:** ***
Low-income: 39%   **Ethnicity:** 45%W 13%B 34%H 5%A 3%O

At the Neighborhood School, children make towering structures of wooden blocks not only in prekindergarten, but all the way up through 2nd grade. They paint life-size self-portraits on brown paper, and decorate the classroom with them. Recess lasts for a full 50 minutes (not counting lunch) in Pre-K though 2nd grade.

Dyanthe Spielberg, who became principal in 2013, has worked with teachers to forge a thoughtful, interdisciplinary curriculum that's influenced by Bank Street College of Education, where she received her master's degree.

The curriculum changes each year, depending on current events and on children's interests. Every year, 3rd-graders study immigration to New York City, but when refugees from the war in Syria flooded Europe, children learned about that crisis as well. In one homework assignment, they were asked to imagine they had to leave home taking only the belongings that would fit in a brown paper grocery bag.

Fourth- and 5th-graders study the civil rights movement, as they do in many schools. But at the Neighborhood School, they also learned about the Black Lives Matter protests and compared them to the protests of the 1960s. Children learn to write from different points of view: They write essays imagining they are the civil rights hero Rosa Parks, or the man who drove the bus when she refused to give up her seat, or a white person or a child on the bus.

Science is not taught only as a once-a-week "special" but integrated into regular classroom lessons. In a unit on the human body, for example, children made a skeleton out of cardboard (using torn egg cartons as a spine). One child asked, "Is there blood in a bone?" and the teacher brought in a beef bone so children could see the marrow firsthand. Young children learn about simple machines on a trip to a playground with a merry-go-round and an old-fashioned teeter-totter. Older children learn how penguins protect themselves from the cold.

Reading is taught with fun-to-read picture books, novels, and science discovery books. There is plenty of emphasis on phonics and spelling as well.

The school, which shares a building with PS 63, has a passionately committed, multiracial parent body. Parents are welcome in the classroom and many volunteer in the library.

The school has embraced the "opt-out movement," as the parent-led rebellion against standardized testing is known, and most children sit out the state tests. Children receive "evaluations" or narratives written by their teachers rather than report cards with grades.

Most classes mix children of different ages: Pre-K and kindergarten in one, 1st and 2nd grades in another, and 4th and 5th grades in another. Teachers get to know children well because they have the same pupils for two years. Each year, half the children in the class are old hands; because fewer children need to learn new routines, less time is spent settling in.

Children are separated by their grade for math lessons—a recognition that in math, more than other subjects, it's difficult for teachers to reach children of different ages and abilities in one class. Here, too, children learn through projects. For example, 5th-graders measure the exterior of the school building in meters several times, and learn that they come up with a slightly different measurement each time. Through this lesson, they learn in concrete terms the difference between average, mean, and median.

A possible downside: The school has a higher than average rate of absenteeism. Spielberg said some new immigrants take their children out of school for extended vacations to their home countries.

The school has long prided itself on serving children from different racial and ethnic groups as well as different income levels. As part of a pilot project to maintain socioeconomic diversity, priority for up to 45% of kindergarten seats goes to children who qualify for free or reduced lunch or who have limited proficiency in English. Children who live in District 1 are eligible. (Clara Hemphill)

PS 276: The Battery Park City School
55 Battery Place
New York, NY 10280
(212) 266-5800
www.bpcschool.org

Who gets in: kids in zone, some wait lists
Grade levels: K–8   **Reading scores:** * * * * *
Enrollment: 872   **Math scores:** * * * * *
Low-income: 7%   **Ethnicity:** 56%W 4%B 11%H 21%A 8%O

PS 276, The Battery Park City School, boasts splendid views of the Hudson River and the Statue of Liberty from its home inside New York's first "green" public school building. Opened in 2009 to alleviate overcrowding in nearby schools, PS 276 has quickly established itself as an extremely popular neighborhood school with a strong science program, lots of extra enrichment activities, and Spanish instruction starting in 1st grade.

The school is, unfortunately, a victim of its own success. It has had wait lists for kindergarten in recent years, even among children who are zoned for the school.

The vibe throughout the school is cheery and relaxed. Students call their teachers and principal Theresa Ruyter by their first names. During group and independent work, particularly in the lower grades, it's common to find students spread out across the classroom, some on the rug or in a corner and others at their desks.

Writing is emphasized in all subjects and there seems to be a nice balance between nonfiction and more creative writing. The hallways are lined with student work, ranging from reflections on math equations and engineering problems to student-authored fantasy stories and poetry.

All elementary school students have science instruction twice a week, though teachers also weave in science during other times. Hands-on learning is emphasized in all grades and teachers do a good job of tying science into other subjects. Kindergarten students have fun sorting dinosaur models into carnivores and herbivores; older children build model roller coasters with cardboard and paper towel tubes.

As part of a 3rd-grade social studies unit on Africa, students read about a Malawian boy who built a windmill to power his family's home in *The Boy Who Harnessed the Wind*, and then built their own windmills as part of a study of engineering and sustainable energy. Three science teachers hold classes in the well-equipped labs. By 8th grade, students study challenging topics such as genetics and learn to write detailed lab reports in preparation for the demands of high school science.

Students also plant vegetables in a rooftop garden, convert their leftover food scraps to compost, and separate recyclables from garbage in clearly marked bins throughout the building.

The school relies on a variety of math programs that they tailor to different grades and different children. It's common to find two or three adults in a room during a math lesson, each working with a small group of students. Students are expected to learn multiple methods for solving problems and to explain their work in detail. Twice-weekly Spanish instruction begins in 1st grade.

The lower and middle school grades are mostly kept apart, with different lunch periods, and most classes on separate floors. Class sizes are large in the middle school and there are no lockers, so middle school students store their coats in their homeroom class. The school's gym is large enough to be used for practice by nearby high schools and there is an outdoor track and a small play area with climbing equipment. The large, airy library is open to students during lunchtime recess. A soundproof music room is used exclusively by the lower school.

Manhattan Youth runs a fee-based after-school program that goes until 6 p.m. Students may participate in a variety of lunch clubs such as chess, drama, and puzzles for the lower school and TED talks, improvisation, community service, and chorus for the middle school.

Children with special needs are integrated into regular classes. In some grades, a special education teacher splits her time between two classes, each led by a general education teacher and each serving a mix of general education students and small groups (five or six) of students with special needs. In other grades, special education teachers work with students in classrooms and on a pullout basis as needed. (Laura Zingmond)

PS 89

201 Warren Street
New York, NY 10282
(212) 571-5659
www.ps89.org

PK

Who gets in: kids in zone
Grade levels: PK–5
Enrollment: 425
Low-income: 4%

Reading scores: * * * * *
Math scores: * * * * *
Ethnicity: 62%W 2%B 14%H 17%A 5%O

At the heart of PS 89, The Liberty School, are the big social studies and science investigations that take place in the fall and spring. These explorations of urban farm markets, the five boroughs of New York City, or the Revolutionary War help "even the playing field for all kids," according to experienced principal Veronica Najjar. "It brings kids together in a way just having a strong reading program does not. Learning, wondering, inquiring, asking questions—it gives everyone that equal chance."

The school is housed in a modern, comfortable building in Battery Park City with a beautiful cafeteria, gym, library, dance studio, art studio, and science room. Classrooms are large, and each has a sink and ample storage.

First-graders make eight trips to urban farm markets in Union Square and Tribeca. There they spot honey, leading them to a conversation with beekeepers. They notice wool, meat products, and root vegetables. They pickle asparagus and cucumbers, and preserve carrots and fruit. They taste ramps and goat cheese. At the end of the unit they hold a busy farm market in the schoolyard. Second-graders study birds in the same rich, all-encompassing way; 3rd-graders take on New Amsterdam, dressing up as tradesmen of old, and visiting Wyckoff House in Flatbush. Fourth-graders study the American Revolution. Fifth-graders explore Westward expansion. First-graders take home books, but regular homework only begins in 2nd grade.

A 2015 Quality Review by the Department of Education suggested the school could do more to challenge high-achieving children. Najjar, principal since 1998, says a goal for staff is to find ways for kids to "make their learning a little bit deeper." Nonetheless, test scores are high, and parents and teachers almost unanimously recommend the school, according to school surveys. (Lydie Raschka)

PS 234

292 Greenwich Street
New York, NY 10007
(212) 233-6034
www.ps234.org

Who gets in: kids in zone
Grade levels: K–5   **Reading scores:** * * * * *
Enrollment: 704   **Math scores:** * * * * *
Low-income: 3%   **Ethnicity:** 70%W 1%B 8%H 11%A 10%O

Just a 10-minute walk from the Hudson River, PS 234 has long been a magnet that has drawn and kept families living happily in Tribeca. Children explore the rich waterways, bridges, and parks outside the school door, and enjoy sparkly city views from one of the prettiest playgrounds in the city.

Children explore the city with trips to Central Park, local restaurants, or the Brooklyn Bridge—and have opportunities through reading, writing, and the arts to reflect on what they learned. Science lessons focus on discovery and include a study of snails, watching eggs hatch, or learning all about birds. Older students examine the theme of "revolution," through women's suffrage, civil rights, and other historic events. In 5th grade, they pick and research an ongoing revolution, such as the American gay rights movement. "It's all part of being in a democracy," Principal Susan Ripperger said. "The idea that unrest never ends."

Recess is sacrosanct—kindergartners and 1st-graders go outside twice a day; 2nd–5th-graders go out once or twice a day. The Parents' Association raises money for the well-regarded music program. Children dance with instructors from the National Dance Institute. Studio in a School provides art lessons.

PS 234's three-story, beige brick building, built in 1988, has large, sunny rooms, light oak tables and chairs, brightly lit corridors, and floors with shiny beige tiles.

Friction between Ripperger and the staff has shown up in annual surveys. Ripperger said she made some "tough" staffing decisions that she says benefits the kids. The vast majority of parents and teachers responding to the surveys say they recommend the school. (Lydie Raschka)

PS 343: Peck Slip School

1 Peck Slip
New York, NY 10038

PK

(212) 312-6260
www.peckslip.org

Who gets in: kids in zone
Grade levels: PK–5
Enrollment: 279
Low-income: 12%

Reading scores: * * * *
Math scores: * * * *
Ethnicity: 59%W 3%B 13%H 16%A 8%O

The newest of the downtown schools, Peck Slip School has the luxury of space, with large windows with stunning views of the Financial District; airy, well-equipped classrooms; and well-lit halls.

Children play outside on a rooftop playground on all but the most frigid days. One room, adjacent to the cafeteria, is set aside for children to play in with large rubber blocks. Classrooms for Pre-K through 1st grade are equipped with wooden blocks and LEGOs, which help children understand shapes and sizes as they learn arithmetic. There is a lovely library but no textbooks: Children read exclusively from books you might read for fun.

Principal Maggie Siena, who started her teaching career at PS 234 and was the principal of PS 150, has significant experience with the progressive, project-based curriculum for which the downtown schools are known. Children might study birds or the subways, with lessons that integrate reading, writing, history, and science.

Third-graders study the Brooklyn Bridge, beginning by posing their own questions: "Who thought of the idea of a bridge?" "How did they get it on the water?" "How many people died building it?" "Was it worth it?" "How does it stay up?" They then study the history of the bridge, reading picture books but also contemporary accounts from magazines like *Harper's Weekly*. They learn about the frigid winter of 1866 when ferries couldn't cross the frozen East River. They take a ferry to Brooklyn, and they walk across the bridge to see the difference. They learn basic principles of engineering.

Children call the teachers, including the principal, by their first names. Routines are clear and children move from one activity to another without a lot of wasted time. Children are free to move around the classroom and stand and stretch. The school prides itself on its vegetarian lunchroom. A typical meal: vegetarian chili, rice, corn, and salad. (Clara Hemphill)

PS 126

80 Catherine Street
New York, NY 10038
(212) 962-2188
www.ps126mat.com

PK

Who gets in: kids in zone, District 2 kids for middle school
Grade levels: PK–8   **Reading scores:** * * * * *
Enrollment: 759   **Math scores:** * * * * *
Low-income: 80%   **Ethnicity:** 8%W 11%B 21%H 59%A 2%O

A sweet, engaging place, PS 126/Manhattan Academy of Technology (MAT) is a combined elementary and middle school with strong academics, an impressive sports program, and a dynamic community spirit.

The elementary school serves neighborhood children from Chinatown and the Lower East Side, representing a range of races and ethnicities—including children from nearby housing projects. The school does a wonderful job teaching English to kids who speak Spanish or Chinese at home. Kids were happy and well-behaved in every class we visited.

PS 126 is a place where teachers can perfect their craft, and in doing so they offer children of different backgrounds thoughtful, rigorous, progressive education. The level of teacher collaboration and planning is impressive. Reading, writing, and science come together in an investigation of birds in 2nd grade, for example, and 5th-graders spend 2 months studying prairie ecosystems to support their Westward Expansion unit. The school uses Math in Focus, a Singapore-based math program, and a math consultant works with teachers, who also visit each other during math lessons to offer feedback.

The middle school, called MAT, is open to children from across District 2 and middle-class parents from neighborhoods like Tribeca clamor for admission. Teachers' excitement for their students' progress is palpable, and they do a good job giving extra help to the children who need it while offering a challenge to the top students, even though students aren't grouped by ability. For example, a strong reader may be assigned a complex book about World War II, while a struggling reader may be assigned an easy one—but all can take part in the same class discussion. Eighth-graders may take the algebra and earth science Regents exams. Most classes have two teachers. Teachers may work with a small group of students, or even one-on-one.

PS 126 prizes the arts and has two art teachers and two music teachers that serve all grades. The music program is very strong and kids seemed to clearly enjoy the change of pace. On the day of our visit, we saw a music student from NYU leading 8th-graders in a lively warm-up, using their own bodies as percussion instruments to work on rhythm and beat. In 6th grade, children choose to "major" either in visual art or band.

The physical education teacher, John DeMatteo, has assembled 51 teams in 27 sports to create the largest middle school sports program in the country—including exotic sports like surfing and more traditional ones like soccer and basketball. The fitness room has exercise bikes attached to video games—making exercise fun even for kids who might otherwise prefer to be couch potatoes. Students are not cut from teams; instead, there is a range of levels for each sport and most middle schoolers participate. (DeMatteo also helped create the city's CHAMPS Middle School Sport and Fitness League and continues to oversee its management.)

The building, constructed in the 1970s, has wide, shiny corridors, clean white walls, and doors trimmed in yellow, red, blue, lavender, green, and purple. Large windows let in plenty of sunlight, and there are views of the Brooklyn Bridge just a few blocks away. A climbing wall (with fake rocks) on the back of the stage in the auditorium gives kids a fun way to build strength.

Carlos Romero became principal in 2016 after serving as assistant principal of the middle school since 2004. He replaced seasoned administrator Jacqueline Getz, who called Romero's promotion "well-deserved."

One possible downside: The PTA isn't as rich as at most District 2 schools, and cannot raise as much money for extras. Still, that hasn't stopped staff from securing an impressive array of programs and specialized equipment through grants and personal appeals to donors. (Aimee Sabo)

PS 397: Spruce Street School

12 Spruce Street
New York, NY 10038
(212) 266-4800
www.sprucestreetnyc.org

PK

Who gets in: kids in zone
Grade levels: PK–8
Enrollment: 443
Low-income: 11%

Reading scores: * * * * *
Math scores: * * * * *
Ethnicity: 58%W 3%B 12%H 14%A 13%O

Housed in the first five floors of a dazzling skyscraper designed by architect Frank Gehry, Spruce Street School has a cafeteria that could be mistaken for a trendy Tribeca eatery, a padded rooftop playground, and a state-of-the-art auditorium.

Teachers use effective techniques to promote independence: In a Pre-K class, the teacher asked a child to dismiss his classmates to clay, blocks, dress-up, and watercolor activities. Students take turns leading assemblies and teach their peers how to stay safe in cold weather or how to compost, among other topics.

Children's ability to work independently frees the teachers up to work with individuals and small groups.

Math and science are particularly strong. The core math session is 45–60 minutes, but math is taught "across the day," according to Principal Nancy Harris. Morning "tabletop" math games build problem-solving speed or help kids understand concepts. "Number talk," often after lunch, is geared toward helping children strengthen their ability to do "mental math"—computing in their heads.

Every child visits the science lab weekly to participate in studies of the teachers' own design, such as a 1st-grade bird study and a 3rd-grade paleontology unit. Reports on classroom walls were refreshing for the fact that they were handwritten, had "voice," and highlighted ideas rather than gimmicky computer fonts.

As a group, the staff seems to place a priority on generating discussion. During a discussion of the novel *The Little Prince*, a 5th-grade teacher asked, "Can you thirst for things other than water?" A child answered, "You can thirst for invisible things, like friendship or love." Another said, "You can thirst for power and money."

Parents pay for dance lessons from the National Dance Institute and more. They say they appreciate that they are invited into classrooms on a regular basis. (Lydie Raschka)

PS 150

334 Greenwich Street
New York, NY 10013
(212) 732-4392
www.ps150.net

PK

Who gets in: District 2 residents, downtown preference
Grade levels: PK–5   **Reading scores:** * * * * *
Enrollment: 184   **Math scores:** * * * * *
Low-income: 14%   **Ethnicity:** 55%W 5%B 14%H 16%A 10%O

Tucked away at the top of a steep flight of stairs in Tribeca, tiny PS 150 offers a demanding math program, hands-on science, and plenty of fieldtrips. The school's small size (with just one class per grade) sets it apart from many Manhattan schools.

PS 150 uses Math in Focus, a sophisticated and fast-paced approach that encourages students to solve multistep problems. Math in Focus is based on the math curriculum used in Singapore, the island nation in Southeast Asia known for high levels of math achievement. Teachers say the program challenges strong students while offering lots of support to those who are struggling. We saw a class in which children worked on the same math problem but received different amounts of guidance: Strong students attacked the problem on their own, others received clues to help them get started, and still others worked closely with the teacher, who offered more step-by-step help.

Children have semester-long projects (called units of study) that integrate science, social studies, reading, and writing. For example, 2nd-graders study snakes—visiting the Central Park Zoo, observing snakes housed in a tank in their classroom, and reading books and writing essays about snakes. Other classes study bakeries, farm animals, New York City transportation, immigration, bridges, Colonial New York, and Lewis and Clark's expedition.

Children travel to Frost Valley to take a closer look at animals, rocks, and minerals; they sail on the *Clearwater* to learn more about the water cycle.

There is no lunchroom, but kids eat a delicious family-style lunch in the classrooms. The outdoor courtyard of the complex serves as the gym, and this space provides a welcome central gathering spot for families in the morning. Priority goes to students zoned for downtown schools. Remaining seats are filled by lottery with District 2 preference. (Clara Hemphill)

PS 124

40 Division Street
New York, NY 10002
(212) 966-7237
www.ps124.org

Who gets in: kids in zone, plus District 2 kids who pass gifted exam
Grade levels: PK–5   **Reading scores:** *****
Enrollment: 810   **Math scores:** *****
Low-income: NA   **Ethnicity:** 2%W 0%B 3%H 95%A 1%O

PS 124 reflects the close-knit immigrant community it serves. Many children speak Chinese at home, and most come from low-income households. By 5th grade, most have a good command of English and a lot go on to selective middle schools. Student attendance is among the best citywide.

In classes we visited, children seemed happy and engaged. Children move around for various activities, rather than sit for long stretches of time. It's common to walk into a room and hear student chatter. In a school full of English language learners, group-work that fosters conversations among peers is critical for language development, says Principal Alice Hom.

Class sizes run as high as 32, but teachers do a good job of making sure their students stay on task. Teachers walk around the room and work with small groups of children while other students focus on individual or group assignments.

We observed an impressive range of writing as early as 1st grade. In all grades students write and revise multiple drafts on a wide range of topics such as snakes and planes (2nd grade); life and food in Kenya (3rd grade); and essays arguing for and against structured play during recess (4th grade).

Math and science instruction are strong. Some projects blend social studies and science. For example, as part of a unit on Brazil, 3rd-graders learned about Brazilian waste management and landfills and then researched and designed waste reduction plans for their own families. One student timed his parents in the shower daily to assess how much water was being wasted.

The school is home to a districtwide gifted and talented (G&T) program. G&T students may plow through a unit of study quickly, leaving more time to tackle additional topics and lengthier projects. (Laura Zingmond)

PS 130

143 Baxter Street
New York, NY 10013
(212) 226-8072
www.ps130m.org

PK

Who gets in: kids in zone, plus District 2 kids who pass gifted exam
Grade levels: PK–5   **Reading scores:** * * * * *
Enrollment: 970   **Math scores:** * * * * *
Low-income: NA   **Ethnicity:** 3%W 1%B 5%H 88%A 3%O

Located on the edge of Chinatown, PS 130 has strong leadership, a robust arts program, and one of the highest attendance rates in the city. Many children speak Chinese at home, and most come from low-income households.

Walk into any classroom at PS 130 and you will find calm, focused kids. Teachers speak in quiet, conversational tones; students listen to instructions, move quickly from one activity to another, and quiet down when asked. Classrooms are neat and thoughtfully arranged, with areas for students to gather as a class as well as work in groups. Supplies are plentiful and every room is stocked with a generous selection of grade-appropriate books arranged neatly on shelves.

Math instruction follows a challenging curriculum called Math in Focus (the American version of Singapore Math), which teaches children to solve problems and show their findings in multiple ways. Strong students may tackle a problem on their own, while others get hints to help them get started, and still others get more step-by-step guidance from the teacher.

For English, students read many books of their choosing and at their skill level as well as write and revise multiple drafts of work on a variety of topics. By the upper grades students can write lengthy essays and stories on a range of topics.

There is one G&T (gifted and talented) class per grade. The main differences between G&T and general education classes lie in the pacing of instruction and types of projects. G&T students may plow through a unit of study quickly, leaving more time to tackle additional topics and lengthier projects. In general education classes, teachers spend more time on the fundamentals, though we observed plenty of challenging work and engaging projects in those classes, too.

PS 130 has an impressive roster of partnerships with arts organizations such as Dancing Classrooms, Rosie's Theater Kids,

Inside Broadway, National Dance Institute, Third Street Music School Settlement, and Young People's Chorus of NYC. There are also homegrown options including lion dance club, the fife and drum corps, and chorus.

Renny Fong became principal in 2014 after working for nearly two decades at the school as a classroom teacher, technology program director, and assistant principal.

There is a rooftop play space, which is impractical to use for lunch recess. However, teachers schedule time during the week to take their classes to the roof for activities and free play, said Fong. (Laura Zingmond)

PS 3

490 Hudson Street
New York, NY 10014
(212) 691-1183
www.ps3nyc.org

PK

Who gets in: kids in zone
Grade levels: PK–5   **Reading scores:** * * * * *
Enrollment: 789   **Math scores:** * * * * *
Low-income: 17%   **Ethnicity:** 70%W 5%B 12%H 7%A 5%O

A charming reflection of the progressive Greenwich Village community it serves, PS 3 has an involved parent body, happy kids, and a relaxed feel. Parents may bring their children to the classroom through 1st grade, classes often take midday neighborhood "walkabouts" to "clear their heads," and students caught running in the hallways are gently, but firmly, told to walk—or skip.

Classrooms have mixed grades, designed to encourage older and younger children to work together. The class discussions we saw during our visit were thoughtful—and respectful. Kindergartners learned about Giving Tuesday, the global day for donating time, goods, and money, and were encouraged to mirror fellow students by repeating each other's thoughts, a technique we also saw used in a 5th-grade class exploring character motivation in a novel called *The Landry News* by Andrew Clements.

For math, teachers use Investigations, a curriculum that emphasizes conceptual understanding, supplemented with other programs such as Math in the City and the much-lauded Math in Focus, a Singapore-based math program.

Live pets and plants are abundant throughout the school. In various classrooms we saw a rubber tree, stick bugs, a terrarium, and an aquarium full of swordtail fish that the students had watched spawn. Literacy and math specialists provide intervention for struggling students and coaching for teachers.

The arts are strong, with a particular focus on dance. On the morning of our visit, families gathered in the first-floor auditorium to watch 4th- and 5th-graders perform a "flash-mob" and a structured improvisation called a "tangle dance." Principal Lisa Siegman, a former dancer herself, says all classes dance once or twice a week with one of the school's two full-time dance teachers. Fourth-graders have a residency with Alvin Ailey American Dance Theater, and students have even performed off-site at spaces such as the Dia:Beacon. (Aimee Sabo)

PS 41

116 West 11th Street
New York, NY 10011
(212) 675-2756
www.ps41.org

Who gets in: kids in zone
Grade levels: PK–5   **Reading scores:** * * * * *
Enrollment: 721   **Math scores:** * * * * *
Low-income: 4%   **Ethnicity:** 69%W 2%B 10%H 9%A 10%O

Nationally recognized for its writing program, PS 41 also has a thoughtful curriculum for science and social studies, a cohesive and experienced staff, and a principal who is responsive to both parents and teachers. PS 41 serves the children of artists, entertainers, bankers, lawyers, and other professionals, who raise more than half a million dollars a year for the PTA.

The strong synergy among the staff and the administration's determination is inspiring. Visiting educators from around the world come for workshops on topics such as special education and STEM (Science, Technology, Engineering, and Math). PS 41 has lovely facilities, standout teachers, and a strong vision built on fostering student reflection and engagement in the world.

Families are active and welcome in the school. On one of our visits, kindergarten parents gathered for coffee in the cafeteria while Principal Kelly Shannon gave tips on how to best chaperone a class trip. Second-graders showed off the homemade books they had written, while parents read them and posted thoughtful comments. In the library, teachers and administrators from other cities gathered for a workshop on how to teach writing using methods developed at PS 41 in collaboration with the Teachers College Reading and Writing Project.

The school combines a warm and relaxed tone with serious academics. Children may sprawl on the rug or in a beanbag chair to read a book. Some teachers are called by their first names. But the classes are focused and attentive and the work seems to be challenging. While a 2nd-grader might write about why he loves LEGOS or how she spends a family holiday, by 5th grade children analyze the U.S. Constitution or discuss current events. The social studies curriculum begins with a study of the school community, continues with a neighborhood study, and ends with a study of the United States. Other units focus on China, or Mexico, or restaurants.

The math curriculum, called Investigations, encourages children to find different ways to solve problems. In science, children might learn about erosion by running water through boxes of sand, or learn how sound travels through water and air.

Children also carry out science experiments on the green roof, which was 10 years in the making. Unlike some rooftop science centers, this is a true green roof covered almost entirely in patches of vegetation with solar panels. Strategically selected native plants attract rare birds, like a red cardinal students recently spotted.

A renovated playground has a nature garden area with plants and seats for quiet activities. Pre-K has its own lovely side yard with climbing equipment and room for more free play.

The lunchroom is calmer and less chaotic than a typical school cafeteria. The food is better, too. A chef from Gramercy Tavern comes (as part of a restaurant study) and shares recipes with the kitchen staff. The social studies curriculum informs the menu: blackberries when the kids are studying Native Americans, dumplings when they are studying China. Even the playground is pleasant: the school hires young people who are trained as summer day camp counselors to organize games during recess. The National Dance Institute offers dance lessons.

The staff takes pride in identifying learning issues early and providing extra support for children with special needs without stigma. The school has three speech therapists (whose work includes helping children with reading).

Music instruction is very limited. There is an introduction to violin starting in 2nd grade and a choral program with Greenwich House.

The school was once severely overcrowded, with persistent wait lists for kindergarten. The opening of a new school, The Sixth Avenue School, has eased the problem and wait lists are "manageable," the parent coordinator told us. (Aimee Sabo)

PS 11

320 West 21st Street
New York, NY 10011
(212) 929-1743
www.ps11chelsea.org

Who gets in: kids in zone, plus District 2 kids who pass gifted exam
Grade levels: PK–5   **Reading scores:** *****
Enrollment: 921   **Math scores:** *****
Low-income: 28%   **Ethnicity:** 49%W 7%B 25%H 14%A 4%O

PS 11 knits together a wide-ranging population that includes children who live in the Fulton Houses public housing development and those growing up in Chelsea's lofts, condos, and brownstones. The gifted and talented program draws students from Battery Park City to the Upper East Side. Parents raise money to pay for specialists in every grade to work with struggling students and high achievers, and help fund the arts.

The school has grown by more than 350 students since Principal Robert Bender arrived in 2005, and is now barely able to accommodate all the kindergartners in its zone. Bender has taught in an elementary school and run a theater company and a family restaurant. When he took the helm at PS 11 he found it to be starkly segregated, with mostly black and Latino kids in general education classes, and white and Asian students in G&T. The division was "so glaring," he recalls. "We started with the arts and food to get families to talk to each other more."

The school has had unusual success in forging one big happy family. Now students with special needs, those in general education classes, and children in G&T mingle in a variety of ways. They perform in musicals together, go camping, and travel to Washington, DC. On Thursday afternoons children join together and take part in fun classes they choose, such as ballet, photography, tap dancing, or airplane-making. The ballroom dance team and the chess team mix children from different classes. The science teacher shares his passion for bird-watching in an after-school program open to all. Parents told us there is little academic or social division between children in G&T and those in the regular classes.

Parents turn out in large numbers to visit classrooms on Family Fridays, and attend an evening where they pick workshops of interest to them, and then kids share a meal. Potluck dances, attended by 600–700 people, are held in September and June on the playground with a DJ.

The school has tried to balance academics with exploration and directed play in kindergarten and 1st-grade classes. Children choose topics, which they explore two or three times a week during a 50-minute period. For example, a small group of children explored space and made planets out of papier-mâché; another group made a castle and dressed up as kings and queens.

The faculty receives regular training in literacy instruction and visits from a math coach. There is one reading specialist who works with struggling 1st-graders. On our previous visit the parent coordinator said graduates "are brighter and more prepared for middle school," due to increased consistency in instruction.

In place of report cards, portfolios are sent home with children's work samples, teacher and student reflections, goals, and a variety of assessments.

The school has a big yard, a small yard, a rooftop place, and a dance room but no real gym—two classrooms with a wall removed serve the purpose.

On cold days kids dance, play soccer, enjoy arts and crafts, or watch a movie inside. Second- through 5th-graders have swim lessons in the pool once a week. (Lydie Raschka)

PS 33

281 9th Avenue
New York, NY 10001
PK
(212) 244-6426
www.ps33chelseaprep.org

Who gets in: kids in zone, plus those who pass gifted exam
Grade levels: PK–5   **Reading scores:** * * * * *
Enrollment: 639   **Math scores:** * * * * *
Low-income: 46%   **Ethnicity:** 26%W 12%B 30%H 25%A 7%O

The enrollment of PS 33 has more than doubled in the past decade, a sign of its growing popularity. The school once served mostly low-income children from nearby housing projects, but now attracts children from townhouses nearby as well as children from across District 2.

The school has a gifted program, open to children who score in the 90th percentile on the exam administered by the city, as well as a general education program for anyone who lives in the attendance zone. Some parents say the programs seem to be divided by race and class: The gifted program has mostly middle-class white and Asian children, while the general education classes have mostly working-class blacks and Latinos.

Kids from the different programs take trips together to museums or the zoo as a way to build community, and the quality of teaching is strong throughout. The city rated PS 33 "well developed" (the highest ranking) on its Quality Review. The school has made progress closing the so-called achievement gap between rich and poor, the review said. Teachers encourage children to work both independently and collaboratively, to become resilient, and to develop work habits needed to succeed in college.

Student teachers assist classroom teachers in most classes, offering individual help to children. A recess coach uses music, songs, and games to help children learn how to develop self-regulation skills during their free time. Local hospitals provide psychology interns who work closely with students with special needs.

Cindy Wang became principal in 2015, replacing longtime principal Linore Lindy.

The school offers spring tours of the gifted and talented program. (Clara Hemphill)

PS 40

319 East 20th Street
New York, NY 10003
(212) 475-5500
www.ps40.org

PK

Who gets in: kids in zone
Grade levels: PK–5
Enrollment: 631
Low-income: 8%

Reading scores: *****
Math scores: *****
Ethnicity: 64%W 3%B 13%H 9%A 12%O

Many residents view PS 40 as a vital part of their close-knit neighborhood. A local Starbucks features student artwork, and new teachers get an orientation tour of the neighborhood. Several parents said they moved in order to live in the PS 40 zone, where family-sized apartments cost far more than nearby identical units just outside the zone.

Students perform at high levels, and the administration has an open-door attitude that fosters a positive vibe. Teachers have 10 years of experience on average and are by many accounts unusually committed. "They come early. They stay late. They collaborate with each other over lunch," said Susan Felder, who has been principal since 2004. Parents approached outside the building one morning called teachers "well organized," "unbelievable," knowledgeable," "bright," and "terrific."

The staff is also open to continued learning. Teachers in an already strong literacy program receive about 20 visits a year from a coach at the respected Teachers College Reading and Writing Project at Columbia University. "It's lifting the level of work," said Felder.

In music, art, and physical education classes we saw long-time teachers exude the kind of self-assurance that makes teaching look like a joy. Additionally, every year kids enjoy a special arts residency paid for by parents, ranging from circus arts from Marquis Studios for the littlest ones to dance for the older ones.

PS 40 takes up the bottom three floors of a historic five-story building shared with the Salk School of Science, a middle school. (Lydie Raschka)

PS 116

210 East 33rd Street
New York, NY 10016
PK
(212) 685-4366
www.ps116.org

Who gets in: kids in zone
Grade levels: PK–5
Enrollment: 638
Low-income: 34%

Reading scores: * * * * *
Math scores: * * * *
Ethnicity: 44%W 9%B 22%H 20%A 6%O

PS 116 in Kips Bay places a high value on independence, choice, and project-based learning. Achievement is high in all areas, particularly in the area of reading and writing. Students live in a range of settings, from luxury apartments along 5th and Park Avenues to low-income housing developments on East 28th Street. Proudly serving children in temporary shelters and the children of United Nations diplomats, PS 116 earned the highest possible marks, "well developed" on the city's Quality Review.

Teachers strive to be sure every child is challenged and supported; during a math lesson, for example, some students will use easier methods to solve a problem than others. Relationships are tended thoughtfully here, both within and across classrooms. Working in small mixed-class groups, 5th graders tackle daily "community challenges," such as using marshmallows and toothpicks to build the tallest structure possible, and different ages eat lunch together.

In 2015, staff and parents decided to eliminate traditional homework assignments and "rebrand" what students do after school. "PDF" (play time, down time, family time), as it's called, is flexible in that children may choose from a wide range of activities. Students design their own homework from a menu of choices. A younger child might play a game of chess with a parent, for example, or visit the park with a friend. An older child may write a poem about snow or measure the perimeter of a household object.

"My son was the kind of student who used to 'phone it in' when it came to homework," one 5th-grader's mother was quoted as saying in the Quality Review. "Now, he begins each week by mapping out his required activities, planning his schedule, and showing a true commitment to his own experiences."

One downside: Some classes are large. (Lydie Raschka)

PS 51

525 West 44th Street
New York, NY 10036
(212) 315-7160
www.ps51manhattan.com

PK

Who gets in: kids in zone, plus a few out-of-zone kids
Grade levels: PK–5   **Reading scores:** ***
Enrollment: 370   **Math scores:** ***
Low-income: NA   **Ethnicity:** 20%W 12%B 42%H 24%A 2%O

PS 51 has a joyful atmosphere, a strong focus on the arts, and an experienced staff that works together as a team. The administration manages to make parents of different races, income levels, and nationalities feel welcome with events like family basketball games, movie nights, and international potluck suppers. The student body includes children whose parents work at the nearby Chinese consulate, as well as children who speak Arabic, Korean, Spanish, or Bengali at home.

The seven-story building, opened in 2013, is unusually bright and well equipped, with two science labs, two outdoor play yards, two gyms, an art studio, a library, a music room, and a health clinic.

Children were happy and engaged in the classes we visited. Longtime principal Nancy Sing-Bock believes young children learn through exploration and play. Every Pre-K–2 classroom has blocks in addition to books and objects for learning math. Sing-Bock received her master's degree in administration from Bank Street College and has visited Reggio Emilia, Italy—a mecca for teachers interested in cutting-edge ideas in education. She has brought some of those ideas to PS 51.

The younger grades pick two big themes each year such as architecture or transportation, and within these themes children explore their questions. One class became interested in blueprints brought in by an architect and so kids drew their own blueprints; another became fascinated by the pipes running belowground when they visited the 2nd Avenue subway construction. Older children may study topics such as the history of the Freedom Riders and the civil rights movement and the United Nation's Universal Declaration of Human Rights.

Kids said they like their twice-a-week science classes, where they get to dissolve M&Ms in water and vinegar, and learn about paper chromatography. The school uses the EngageNY math program, a discovery approach emphasizing different ways to solve problems. Teachers also incorporate old-fashioned math drills called "sprints."

But it's the arts programming that really sets PS 51 apart. Teaching artists from Rosie's Theater Kids lead children in song and dance at the school, and everyone takes tap-dancing lessons at nearby Maravel Arts Center. Fifth-graders attend Broadway shows like *Matilda*. A music teacher leads an Orff ensemble, recorder, drum, ukulele/violin ensembles, and chorus. An art teacher incorporates themes from academic units into children's work; for example, children studying trees in science and social studies made drawings of trees.

Families are embraced at PS 51 and increasingly active. Every month they are invited to watch their children at work in school. This way the school has been able to educate parents and alleviate worries they may have about unfamiliar-looking math homework or other aspects of the school's creative curriculum.

Sing-Bock and the staff have worked hard to build a community among parents and children of different backgrounds, by, for example, asking parents who speak different languages to serve as "cultural ambassadors" at PTA meetings and including both newcomers and old-timers on the School Leadership Team. Parents are invited to share their skills and knowledge with their children's classmates: A bus driver talks about his work when children study transportation; a busboy talks about his work when children study restaurants. The school offers parent workshops on topics such as how to deal with sibling rivalry.

Speech and occupational therapists work with children in their regular classrooms, rather than removing them from class. A separate District 75 program for children with severe disabilities shares the playground space and lunchroom with grades K–2. "We believe in mainstreaming and having all schools in the building work and collaborate together," said Sing-Bock.

Children who live outside the school attendance zone are sometimes admitted in the late summer or early fall. The school also houses a "Pre-K center," administered separately, whose seats are open to children regardless of where they live. The school has an after-school program for Pre-K. (Clara Hemphill)

PS 212: Midtown West School

328 West 48th Street
New York, NY 10036

PK

(212) 247-0208
www.midtownwestschool.org

Who gets in: kids who live in District 2
Grade levels: PK–5   **Reading scores:** * * * * *
Enrollment: 378   **Math scores:** * * * * *
Low-income: 21%   **Ethnicity:** 48%W 6%B 23%H 10%A 13%O

Located on the edge of the theater district, Midtown West is a small and welcoming school that attracts students from across District 2. It has a neighborhood feel, even though fewer than half of the children live within walking distance. The school has a significant number of male teachers and teachers of color. In addition to moms, large numbers of dads drop their kids off in the morning. Gay parents, interracial families, and families formed through adoption feel comfortable here.

Parents are welcomed in the classrooms and at the cozy Family Center, where the busy PTA has its headquarters. Every child receives a full set of school supplies each fall as well as five free books for summer reading courtesy of the PTA. Many parents participate in a Book Club, reading current and classic children's literature, followed by workshops on what to do at home to foster a love of reading. Families are strongly encouraged to volunteer a few hours a month.

The curriculum remains progressive, with continued close ties to Bank Street College of Education. Projects are nicely interconnected, weaving writing and reading into science, social studies, and math. The school uses Investigations for math, but supplements with Contexts for Learning, a series of practical, child-friendly math problems that take days to complete. Kids may determine, say, how many truffles fit into different-sized boxes, a unit introducing patterns (arrays) to help kids visualize multiplication and division in 3rd grade. These rich problems require kids to apply skills, not just memorize facts.

Ryan Bourke, formerly an assistant principal at popular PS 321 in Park Slope, became principal in 2013. Bourke, who has a master's degree in literacy from Columbia University, has been working to strengthen math and science, an area perceived by parents and staff as needing growth, he said, despite strong test scores.

Midtown West classrooms are filled with plants and animals, and while some verge on cluttered, and feel cramped with 28 kids, most are exciting places to be. It is also an advantage that the kids get outside a lot. First-graders peek behind the scenes at area theaters as they become set and costume designers in preparation for their own class play. They also learn about electricity and the simple machines they find backstage such as pulleys, wedges, and levers.

Classes are "looped," so that children spend two years with the same teacher. Teachers adjust for faster and slower learners with varying degrees of success: Sometimes faster kids are asked to help classmates, but in a 3rd-grade class we saw near the end of the school year, a group of four advanced math students were taking a test so the teacher could evaluate their skills and better prepare to challenge them right away in the fall. (Lydie Raschka)

PS 59

233 East 56th Street
New York, NY 10019
(212) 888-7870
www.059m.r9tech.org

Who gets in: kids in zone, some from wait lists
Grade levels: K–5   **Reading scores:** * * * * *
Enrollment: 573   **Math scores:** * * * * *
Low-income: 11%   **Ethnicity:** 59%W 2%B 13%H 15%A 10%O

PS 59 combines a strong academic program with an approach to teaching that values play as the foundation for learning. Kindergarten classrooms have dress-up corners for dramatic play, easels for drawing, and plenty of wooden blocks. Older children, too, use blocks as part of their study of architecture and bridges.

The school is not far from the United Nations, and children come from many countries and speak about 40 languages. Parents are welcome: One Friday a month parents are invited to stop by their children's classrooms. Kindergarten parents bring children right to their classrooms each day.

The modern building has two science labs, a state-of-the-art auditorium, and a spacious library. It is shared with the High School of Art and Design and PS 169—a District 75 program for children with special needs, many of whom join PS 59 students for gym, lunch, library, and science. The only drawback of the building is that children's voices ricochet around the cement-block stairwells, the entryway, and in the gated yard so loudly that it can be difficult for two people standing side-by-side to hear each other speak.

Longtime principal Adele Schroeter gets high praise from parents, who also rave about the fabulous teaching. Teachers develop their own lessons with great freedom to reach a complicated population—without resorting to too much test prep. "We have many English language learners," Schroeter said. "We do our most thoughtful, conscionable job without compromising how kids learn. We can't give over any more time to test prep."

The lessons we saw were open-ended, exploratory, and playful. In a kindergarten class with incubating eggs, a teacher projected a picture on the wall of blood vessels inside an egg and showed children how to place two fingers on their necks to feel their own blood vessels pulsate. The writing in all grades looked strong and we saw solid note-taking with page number references and highlighting. Students are encouraged to ask questions and engage in discussion and debate to an unusual degree. Older kids pair with younger ones for science experiments. They explore their curiosities about plants, the water cycle, and simple machines. The walls are filled with student-made charts, drawings, reports, essays, and photos in every subject area. Fieldtrips augment their studies.

A math consultant works with teachers on a regular basis, helping them hone lessons each year from a variety of sources. "The construction of a unit [requires] a lot of teacher understanding," said Schroeter. "We keep holding investigations up to each other—it really empowers teachers to be thinkers and doers in the process of designing units." Teachers invite families in to learn more about math and send home a customized plan in June for each child with reading level and math strengths, plus suggestions for games parents and kids can play together to improve skills at home.

The tone is very nurturing. Students even create mottos and chants to support one another during testing. If there is a downside it may be that teachers are so good at cushioning difficulties and helping students manage long-term assignments, emotions, and social relations that the transition to middle school is, as one parent put it, "a shock."

Fifth-grade teachers try to ease this transition by giving kids planners and long-term projects. In the last month of school they offer rotating mini-courses such as "making good choices," "executive functioning," and "managing relations."

For middle school, some of the strongest students opt for Wagner, a large middle school with a band and many team sports. East Side Middle, Clinton, and Salk are also popular choices.

Many teachers are certified in special education, and it is common practice to rotate their assignment every few years between grades. This has been beneficial particularly for students with disabilities, who have shown recent improvement on standardized test scores in English and math. The school has integrated co-teaching, or ICT classes, that mix children with special needs and those in general education. These classes have two teachers, one of whom is certified in special education. (Lydie Raschka)

PS 267: East Side Community School
213 East 63rd Street
New York, NY 10065

PK

(212) 888-7848
www.ps267.org

Who gets in: kids in zone, some from wait lists
Grade levels: PK–5   **Reading scores:** *****
Enrollment: 365   **Math scores:** *****
Low-income: 7%   **Ethnicity:** 78%W 2%B 7%H 11%A 2%O

Midway between Bloomingdale's and the 59th Street Bridge, East Side Community School is well placed for children to explore the city and its museums. Children go on frequent class trips, and The Friends of the Upper East Side and the New-York Historical Society help teachers craft lessons about the city and its neighborhoods.

Founding Principal Medea McEvoy greets children by name as they arrive near the main door each morning. She grew up next door, and her parents still live in an apartment overlooking the building. ("They literally watch over me every day," she jokes.) McEvoy taught for 10 years at PS 6, where her classroom was a Teachers College research and demonstration site.

Teachers are well organized and lessons in the older grades build thoughtfully on work done in younger grades. Teachers have a good system for working together. For example, teachers created a special checklist to help struggling writers better evaluate their own work.

Opened in 2010, PS 267 is housed in the former Manhattan Eye, Ear, and Throat Hospital. The eight-story structure features a roomy lunchroom, large gym, and elevators big enough to hold an entire class. Modern classrooms are equipped with Smart Board projectors, as well as sinks and water fountains. There is a music room, but the school lacks an auditorium; assemblies are held in the gym. The only outdoor spaces are a small courtyard off the cafeteria and a rooftop play area.

Student teachers, volunteers, paraprofessionals, and literacy interns help out in classrooms. Children learn to play chess and study computer science.

There is only one Pre-K classroom, which tends to fill with siblings of older students. (Lydie Raschka)

PS 183

419 East 66th Street
New York, NY 10065
(212) 734-7719
www.ps183.org

PK

Who gets in: kids in zone
Grade levels: PK–5
Enrollment: 555
Low-income: 8%

Reading scores: * * * * *
Math scores: * * * * *
Ethnicity: 66%W 4%B 11%H 17%A 3%O

PS 183 has a multicultural, international student body: Many of the parents are research scientists and doctors from around the world working at nearby Rockefeller University and Sloan-Kettering Memorial Hospital. Among the student body, nearly 40 different languages are spoken.

The vibe is welcoming and creative, which is apparent as soon as one enters the century-old building. Photos of smiling staff and a display celebrating the languages spoken at the school flank the main office entrance. The narrow hallways are lined with student artwork and projects. Classrooms are lively spaces where students move around with purpose. It's common to walk into a room and find children sprawled out on the rug or couch, reading and writing, while others work at tables or in a cozy corner of the room. Class sizes run large in the upper grades—roughly 32 in the 5th grade—but class routines are well established so kids move smoothly from one activity to the next with little time wasted.

"We want students to take ownership of their learning," said Tara Napoleoni, the school's principal since 2010. Teachers are very adept at meeting children's individual needs. In the younger grades students keep folders with personalized teacher notes such as what level books they should be reading, which areas they're strong in, which skills they need to practice more, and suggestions for challenge work.

The school uses the Teachers College Reading and Writing Project curriculum, which encourages students to read a wide array of books of their choosing and at their skill level as well as write and revise multiple drafts of work on a variety of topics. They read serial stories, mysteries, and historical fiction as well as biographies, memoirs, and books on social issues and science. Teachers also connect readings to topics studied in other subjects. For instance, 4th-graders learn about soil erosion in science at the same time they are reading and writing about floods and environmental themes in class. Fifth-graders read historical fiction such as *Across the Wide and Lonesome Prairie* when learning about westward expansion in social studies.

Typical of many District 2 schools, PS 183 uses Investigations math, which emphasizes conceptual learning and multiple approaches to problem solving. Teachers balance this with some drilling of math facts. A part-time math coach works with teachers to develop lessons and visits classrooms to help with instruction.

In 5th grade, classes are departmentalized—essentially a modified middle school format. Each 5th-grade teacher specializes in one of three areas—reading, writing, or math—and students travel with their class to different rooms for instruction in those subjects. The benefit is that students are taught by a specialist in a classroom filled with resources to support that subject. Students spend roughly two periods a day in their homeroom class, where they learn social studies and science (in addition to their twice-weekly visits to the science room) and get extra instruction in reading, writing, and math, too.

Every Friday, students in all grades participate in small-group electives. Teachers, staff, the principal, and even parents volunteer to run one of more than 40 clubs that cover a range of interests such as storytelling, singing, knitting, cooking, and STEM (science, technology, engineering, and math). Students get to try a new club every 5 weeks.

Parent involvement is strong. In addition to raising money to pay for teaching assistants and to support school programs, parents volunteer in a variety of ways: grant-writing, leading school tours, running events such as the school carnival, helping out in art and music classes, and much more.

Outside organizations such as Wingspan Arts, ChessNYC, Yorkville Sports, and Drama Kids run a range of on-site activities after school. PS 183 added prekindergarten classes in 2016. (Laura Zingmond)

PS 225: Ella Baker School
317 East 67th Street
New York, NY 10065
PK   ### (212) 717-8809
www.ellabakerschool.org

Who gets in: citywide lottery
Grade levels: PK–8   **Reading scores:** ★★★★
Enrollment: 335   **Math scores:** ★★★
Low-income: 39%   **Ethnicity:** 35%W 19%B 37%H 4%A 6%O

Founded on the model of Central Park East in East Harlem, Ella Baker is a happy, informal place where children call grown-ups by their first names and there's plenty of time to build with blocks, to dance, or to explore the neighborhood on class trips. Two grades of kids are taught together—PK/K, 1/2, 3/4, and 5/6— so students have the same teacher for two years. Children are encouraged to explore their own interests and work at their own pace.

Although the school is located in District 2, it is open to children citywide. Tours are offered from October through February. It is one of the few schools in the neighborhood that offers pre-kindergarten classes.

Both the student body and the faculty are racially diverse, and there are an unusual number of men. The staff, led by Principal Laura Garcia, is stable and experienced. We heard no raised voices on our tour, and kids seemed reassured by clear classroom routines.

As other public schools have increasingly focused on preparing children for standardized tests, Ella Baker has maintained its commitment to learning through play and discovery. The school has no textbooks, only fun-to-read picture books and novels, science discovery books, and historical fiction. There are weekly trips to museums, parks, and ice skating rinks.

The school is part of the Julia Richman Educational Complex, a large building that houses several alternative high schools. Ella Baker shares the complex's two gyms, pool, auditoriums, ballet studio, library, and Mount Sinai health facility.

The homework load is light and the tiny middle school does not offer Regents-level math or science—a plus or minus depending on your point of view. The school won high marks on the Department of Education's Quality Review, with a rating of "well developed" in every category. (Clara Hemphill)

PS 158

1458 York Avenue
New York, NY 10075
(212) 744-6562
www.ps158.org

PK

Who gets in: kids in zone
Grade levels: PK–5
Enrollment: 763
Low-income: 12%

Reading scores: * * * * *
Math scores: * * * * *
Ethnicity: 71%W 4%B 10%H 11%A 4%O

PS 158 is a high-performing neighborhood school with strong leadership, engaging instruction, and lots of arts enrichment across all grades. It's easy to know what students are learning, as the colorful hallways are lined with projects, essays, and artwork.

Housed in a large building constructed in 1898, PS 158 has long, winding corridors, high ceilings, large windows, and original details such as oak coat closets. It has two gyms, a small but adequate auditorium, and an elevator.

Dina Ercolano, who became principal in December 2014, has fostered a "friendlier, more kid-centric vibe," according to one parent. The previous principal, who left midyear, sometimes clashed with staff and parents, according to annual surveys. Under the leadership of Ercolano, a former literacy coach and assistant principal, the school's atmosphere is calm and cheery, and instruction is consistent from class to class and grade to grade.

Full-time specialists in math, literacy, special education, and technology work with teachers to help them develop and revise lessons and practices. For instance, during independent reading time—especially in the older grades—it's common to find teachers engaged in what Ercolano calls "spinning plates." While most students are quietly immersed in their books, the teacher bounces between two or three small groups of students, monitoring their work on a focused reading task. Ercolano says the practice lets teachers check in with students' progress more frequently than when relying on brief, weekly conferences with individual students.

Some classrooms can feel cramped, especially in the older grades, but teachers arrange their spaces thoughtfully to encourage students to move around. On a typical day, students will spend some time gathered on the rug for class-wide lessons and a lot of time working on their own and in small groups at their tables, in cozy corners, or sprawled out on the rug.

Teachers use technology judiciously. "We don't do technology for its own sake," said Ercolano. Each class has a large television monitor, similar to an overhead projector. Laptop computers are available for research and writing. During our visit we found the rich classroom libraries and hands-on materials such as blocks, dice, and counters to be the most heavily used resources.

The school uses the Teachers College Reading and Writing Project curriculum, which encourages students to read a wide array of books of their choosing and at their skill level. Starting in kindergarten, students write and revise multiple drafts of work on a variety of topics. In the younger grades they may write and illustrate stories and "information books" drawn from personal experiences and books they read. By 5th grade, students write complex essays on a range of topics as well as more creative pieces such as fiction and poetry.

Typical of many District 2 schools, PS 158 uses Investigations math, which emphasizes conceptual learning and multiple approaches to problem solving, as well as Math in the City. Teachers balance this with some drilling of math facts.

The school has long been known for its extensive special education services, and test scores for special-needs children are higher than in some other schools in the neighborhood. PS 158 offers occupational and physical therapy; speech, vision, and hearing services; and adaptive physical education. Team-teaching classes mix general education and special education pupils and have two teachers, one of whom is certified in special education. Special education teachers also visit classrooms daily during math and English instruction to work with students who need extra support but don't require a class with two teachers.

In addition to visual art, music, gym, and science classes, all students have enrichment activities that vary by grade and are funded by the very active PTA. For instance, Marquis Studios provides movement classes to prekindergartners and circus arts to 1st-graders; 5th-graders study drama with the New Victory Theater and stage a mock appellate hearing with the help of the nonprofit organization called Constitution Works.

Instructors from E3Sports organize sports and games during lunch recess to encourage students to get more physical activity.

The school runs its own after-school program. Students may participate in a range of activities for a fee.

The school has four full-day Pre-K classes. The school fills its Pre-K seats with zoned students, mostly siblings. (Laura Zingmond)

PS 6

45 East 81st Street
New York, NY 10028
(212) 737-9774
www.ps6nyc.com

PK

Who gets in: kids in zone
Grade levels: PK–5
Enrollment: 700
Low-income: 6%
Reading scores: * * * * *
Math scores: * * * * *
Ethnicity: 75%W 2%B 7%H 13%A 3%O

Just off Park Avenue, less than two blocks from the Metropolitan Museum of Art, PS 6 has a strong writing program, a thoughtful approach to math, and a devoted parent body, many of whom easily could afford private school.

There is plenty of excitement in classes and kids seem to be interested in their work, whether it's playing a telling-time memory game, writing political essays, or painting clay butterflies.

The quality of student writing is very high. From the earliest grades, children learn to write with a voice. Even kindergartners write persuasive essays. For example, one child told classmates why it's important to cross the street carefully. Children learn to speak clearly as well as write. First-graders put together multimedia presentations—narrated slideshows—explaining why some bugs are helpful (ladybugs eat other bugs, bumblebees pollinate flowers) and others are not. (Nobody had anything good to say about cockroaches.)

By 5th grade, topics are quite worldly: One child waxed poetic about "the genius of Karl Rove" and described despairingly "the breakdown of the Republican Party."

A shade more traditional than some other District 2 schools, PS 6 has a focus on spelling, grammar, cursive handwriting, and phonics. At the same time, children may pick books that interest them from bins in their classrooms and write about topics of their own choosing. There are plenty of class discussions, lots of small-group work, and virtually no lecturing by teachers.

The school has taken steps to improve the rigor of math instruction without "tracking" children into fast and slow groups. Teachers use the progressive Investigations math curriculum, which emphasizes the conceptual understanding of math, but they supplement it with other approaches, such as Singapore Math. The school has a good balance between traditional and progressive methods: Children learn the formulas or algorithms that characterize old-fashioned arithmetic lessons, but they also learn creative approaches to problem solving. Math-loving children may take part in a lunchtime "math team" to prepare for the Math Olympiad national competition.

Teachers have created an accelerated math group for particularly strong 5th graders, who may study topics more commonly mastered in 6th or 7th grade, such as volume of rectangular prisms, ratios, rates.

Children grow vegetables on the roof garden and learn about nutrition and the human body. They grow rock-candy crystals, watch caterpillars turn into butterflies, and observe the growth of silkworms. In a more challenging experiment, teams of kids had to design their own solar cookers, keeping in mind the principles of reflection, absorption, and insulation. After watching a *National Geographic* video about heating water to kill microorganisms, children placed two thermometers in their boxes, which were partially filled with water, and aimed for a target of 65 degrees Celsius. Cooking and eating their own s'mores was a well-earned bonus.

Lauren Fontana, principal since 2006, received her masters in education at Bank Street College. Fontana and her two assistant principals, Amy Santucci and Jane Galasso, ensure that teachers get plenty of support.

A hyperactive PTA raises some $800,000, which pays for full-time teaching assistants in every grade and a wide array of activities such as the National Dance Institute, Arts Connection, and chess. The PTA suggests that parents make an annual $1,200 donation for every child—a request that some find off-putting.

The school offers speech, occupational, and physical therapy, as well as team teaching classes and special education teacher support services (SETSS). The school also provides counseling, art therapy, and a support group for children whose parents are separating. Kindergarten and 1st-grade teachers receive training in Reading Reform, a method designed to help all children, including those who are struggling, based on the Orton-Gillingham techniques. PS 6 aims to be flexible in how it provides extra help, whether or not a child has an Individualized Education Program, the legal document that outlines the services to which a child is entitled.

The school added Pre-K classes in 2016. (Aimee Sabo)

PS 290: Manhattan New School

311 East 82nd Street
New York, NY 10028
(212) 734-7127
www.ps290.org

Who gets in: kids in zone
Grade levels: K–5   **Reading scores:** ✲✲✲✲✲
Enrollment: 627   **Math scores:** ✲✲✲✲✲
Low-income: 10%   **Ethnicity:** 73%W 1%B 9%H 11%A 7%O

At Manhattan New School, the best ideals of progressive education meet structure, experience, and a true love of the craft of teaching. Tour the school, and you may see kindergartners squish blueberries as part of a study on pigment and then move seamlessly into a lesson on phonics; 4th-graders may study the Greek myth of the fallen hero Icarus and then design and build their own parachutes.

Kids are happy and engaged, and staffers seem eager to go the extra mile, whether that means a weekly walk to the Metropolitan Museum of Art to supplement a social studies unit or working together on detailed plans to reach kids with different levels of skills in the same class. The quality of teaching is superb throughout, and teachers share an intellectual excitement about their work. Many staffers have written books that are used in university education courses.

MNS has long been known for its strong writing program and has a well-deserved reputation as one of the best schools in the city. Doreen Esposito, who became principal in 2014 after working at the school for 15 years as a teacher and assistant principal, is well qualified to carry on its legacy. While she maintains a clear sense of continuity, she has also brought in fresh ideas—a practice that in and of itself is highly valued at MNS. "Reflection is a huge part of what we do here," she said.

Under Esposito's watch, the school has introduced Mindfulness Mondays, where 4th-graders lead 2nd-graders in meditation to ease the transition from the weekend. Another addition is a special "maker" room, filled with natural materials and recycled household products such as toilet-paper tubes and yarn, where kids can tackle hands-on projects and learn teamwork. During our visit, a group of 4th-grade boys eagerly showed off their latest creation: a recycled robot that sprays seeds from its feet and water from its nose, tied to their study of sustainability in social studies.

In response to parents' request for more rigor in math instruction, the school has worked hard to make sure students have strong arithmetic skills as well as an understanding of underlying mathematical concepts. Posters about math strategies abound, as do small counters in all shapes and sizes across grades. We saw a class of 5th-graders get down on the floor with their teacher to tackle a particularly tricky fraction problem with small shapes, while another group converted milliliters to liters in their heads. A coach works with teachers to hone instruction and supplement the math programs—a combination of Investigations and the City College program called Math in the City. Kids who excel may join Math Olympiad.

The parent body is extremely active both off- and on-campus. Last year, parents successfully petitioned to have a Citi Bike station next to the school moved after arguing it was a safety hazard. On the day of our visit, we saw moms in the main office cutting out labels for the school auction, a fundraiser that supports extra programs like chess, National Dance Institute, and Wingspan Theater. We also saw several part-time staffers who were former school parents, including a choral and band instructor leading a group of vivacious 4th-graders and a dance teacher helping kindergartners get their wiggles out in the makeshift auditorium.

While the old building is charming and very well kept, space is tight. Staffers make it work: The cafeteria doubles as a gym, complete with brand-new foldaway tables and a basketball hoop, and 5th-graders have recess on a closed-off side street, while younger kids play in one of two enclosed side yards. Plans are in the works for a green roof, which will serve as both an extra play space and a science center.

The school suffered from overcrowding for a number of years, but it has not had wait lists since the attendance zone was reduced a few years ago. However, there is no room for prekindergarten. (Aimee Sabo)

PS 151: Yorkville Community School

421 East 88th Street
New York, NY 10128
(212) 722-5240
www.yorkvillecommunityschool.org

Who gets in: kids in zone
Grade levels: K–5
Enrollment: 548
Low-income: 40%

Reading scores: ★★★★★
Math scores: ★★★★★
Ethnicity: 47%W 14%B 27%H 7%A 6%O

In a city that's divided by race and class, PS 151: Yorkville Community School has a healthy mix of children who live in luxury high-rise buildings, expensive brownstones, modest five-floor walk-ups, and public housing. It's a warm school with strong leadership, a cohesive staff, and lots of parent involvement.

The vibe throughout the school is cheery and laid-back. Students address teachers and staff by their first names. (The principal, Samantha Kaplan, is called "Miss Samantha.") Large classrooms with high ceilings in the 100-year-old building are arranged so kids have lots of opportunities to move around. There are colorful rugs for classwide gatherings, low tables for group-work and cozy corners for quiet reading. There is a tiny gym, and the cafeteria doubles as an auditorium, but the building is pleasant despite these limitations.

Teachers put a lot of effort into crafting interesting lessons, with many emphasizing the schoolwide theme of community. Students take walking tours of the neighborhood, advocate for causes, raise money for charity, and learn to acknowledge good qualities in others. First-graders study restaurants by visiting local eateries, writing about what they learn and observe, and crafting their own menus. For their study of marine life, 2nd-graders drafted persuasive pleas for causes such as saving coral reefs, whales, and walruses. To foster good social and emotional development, students are often asked to write about the good qualities and kind acts of their fellow students.

Art, science, and gym are offered to all students. Students learn music and attend concerts through a partnership with the 92nd Street Y. Visiting instructors from the Salvadori Educational Center teach students about architecture and city infrastructure. Lunchtime sports and games are overseen by visiting instructors from the fitness nonprofit Asphalt Green.

The PTA raises money to support the school and parents volunteer to conduct school tours. Kaplan makes sure there are lots of opportunities, like publishing parties and performances, for parents to come in. Once a month, parents are invited to Family Fridays, where they visit their child's classroom to observe lessons and participate in activities.

Perhaps the most noteworthy part of PS 151 is the story of how it came to be. Formerly housed in a dilapidated building at 91st Street and First Avenue, the old PS 151 served mostly children from the nearby housing projects before it was torn down in 2001 to make way for a high-rise residential building and a new school that would become East Side Middle School. Elementary school children who lived in the zone were dispersed to other schools in the neighborhood for years.

But parents in the community campaigned hard to have the school reopened. Kaplan, who attended PS 41 in Greenwich Village as a child and taught there before becoming assistant principal of PS 217 on Roosevelt Island, met with activist parents at an Upper East Side nursery school regularly for more than a year, sharing her vision for a new school and listening to their dreams for their children. Kaplan built relationships with the community organizations that would offer enrichment classes and built support among elected officials. She gave the school a new name—Yorkville Community School—to help give it a fresh start. Parents of different backgrounds embraced the new school when it opened in temporary space in an old parochial school on 91st Street on 2009. Several members of the City Council provided money for renovations of a former high school building, and children moved into the current building in 2011. (Clara Hemphill)

Hunter College Elementary School
71 East 94th Street
New York, NY 10128
(212) 860-1292
www.hunterschools.org

Who gets in: Manhattan residents who score very high on IQ test
Grade levels: K–6 **Reading scores:** NA
Enrollment: 339 **Math scores:** NA
Low-income: 1% **Ethnicity:** 42%W 7%B 4%H 16%A 31%O

Hunter College Elementary School for intellectually gifted children is one of the most sought-after schools in the city. Nearly 2,200 families request an application for their children to take an IQ test to be considered for admission (at a cost of about $350, plus $70 for an application fee). Of those, between 250 and 300 meet the cutoff necessary to be interviewed, which has been in the 99th percentile in recent years. A total of 50 are chosen for the kindergarten class.

The school offers lots of intellectual stimulation, a fast-paced curriculum, and a peer group in which very bright children can feel at home no matter how unusual their abilities. Kids can talk about atomic theory or Greek mythology without being labeled a "nerd" and can bounce ideas off other children who are just as bright.

At first glance, the classrooms look much like those in any other elementary school, with piles of blocks, bins of picture books, and children's artwork posted on the walls. But look more closely and you'll see the block structures are more elaborate, the books are more difficult, and the level of sophistication is higher than in a typical elementary school. During one of our visits, kindergartners not only played chess, they played an Ancient Egyptian board game. A 3rd-grader gave a presentation on Chinese geography and history and taught her classmates a few phrases in Mandarin. Fifth-graders discussed the philosophies of Plato and Aristotle as well as the roots of American democracy in the Magna Carta.

Children not only learn complex ideas, they also learn to explain them to others. On another visit, 6th-graders created Rube Goldberg machines—elaborate contraptions of cardboard, pulleys, chutes, balls, and dominos—designed to perform the simple task of zipping a zipper. The children were then asked to use the devices to explain the principles of force and acceleration—Newton's Laws of Motion—to 3rd-graders.

Lisa Siegman became interim acting principal in 2016, replacing Dean Ketchum. She was assistant principal of Hunter College High School for 10 years.

Hunter Elementary School is firmly in the progressive camp, with an emphasis on teaching children to work independently, to discover their own interests, and to develop academic skills through hands-on projects. There is no homework in kindergarten and up to 1½ hours a night by 6th grade. Although the work is demanding, the focus is not on acceleration so much as delving into topics in depth.

"There's increased focus on writing mechanics and it seems like it's starting to show positive results," one mother told us. "The math curriculum, while still not up to my standards, is more aligned with what is taught in the high school and there is now a chance for elementary kids to get on an advanced math track."

Some parents complain there isn't enough room for outdoor exercise. "The kids don't get to go outside enough in the winter because the grounds are controlled by the college and clearing the snow and ice seems to be a monumental task that can take days to complete," this mother said, adding that kids aren't allowed on the playground's artificial turf when it's wet.

On the positive side, the physical education teacher is "young and very engaged and interested in really improving the health and fitness of the elementary students." He planned to add junior varsity sports.

The school has two "learning specialists" for children who have very high IQs but who may have other special needs.

Only Manhattan residents may apply. Parents must submit an application online via the Hunter College Elementary School website in September the year before your child starts school. Children who have their 4th birthday before December 31 are eligible. Admission is determined by an IQ test, a written application, and a "simulated classroom experience." Notifications are sent in February.

The only entry point for the elementary school is kindergarten. Hunter College High School, which begins in 7th grade, is open to children in all five boroughs who pass a demanding exam. (Clara Hemphill)

PS 527: East Side School for Social Action
323 East 91st Street
New York, NY 10128
(212) 828-2710
www.ps527.org

Who gets in: kids in zone
Grade levels: K–5   **Reading scores:** ✴✴✴✴✴
Enrollment: 231   **Math scores:** ✴✴✴✴✴
Low-income: 10%   **Ethnicity:** 59%W 2%B 20%H 15%A 5%O

Opened in 2012 to ease overcrowding at other Upper East Side schools, PS 527 has quickly developed its own personality and culture. There is a lot of emphasis on being nice—and on being a good citizen. The school is orderly but not rigid. Children move smoothly from one activity to another without a lot of wasted time.

PS 527 is a shade more traditional than some of the other schools in the neighborhood. It uses the Core Knowledge curriculum, based on the work of E. D. Hirsch, which includes classics like *The Tale of Peter Rabbit* and *The Wizard of Oz*. Every child takes part in a "guided reading" group every day, and there is explicit phonics instruction.

At the same time, teachers adapt Core Knowledge to include "more child-friendly stuff" and activities—like making paper-bag puppets about nursery rhymes, said Principal Dan McCormick. He added that Core Knowledge texts are "too challenging" and lessons are "too teacher-centered, with too much passive learning and not enough activity." On our visit, we heard children talk about the difference between fiction and nonfiction—how Balto was a real, live dog, but Alice in Wonderland was a character in a book.

Housed in a former parochial school with seven floors and no elevator, PS 527 had lavishly equipped rooms—including many that were empty—at the time of our visit. Unfortunately, it does not offer prekindergarten, because city officials decided small children could not easily climb the stairs.

The theme of the school is "social action," and children are encouraged to take part in community service, such as making sandwiches for a local food pantry, or raising money for a charity such as the ASPCA or a campaign to save the rain forest. (Clara Hemphill)

PS 198/PS 77: Lower Lab School
1700 3rd Avenue
 ## New York, NY 10128
(212) 289-3702
www. ps198m.org/www.ps77lowerlab.org

Who gets in: kids in zone, plus District 2 kids who pass gifted exam
Grade levels: PK–5/K–5   **Reading scores:** ★★★★/★★★★★
Enrollment: 498/345   **Math scores:** ★★★★★/★★★★★
Low-income: 42%/4%   **Ethnicity:** 45%W 10%B 27%H 16%A 1%O/
                              59%W 0%B 5%H 27%A 9%O

The low-slung, white-brick building with blue-trimmed windows on 95th Street houses two schools and three programs. PS 198 is a zoned neighborhood school that also has a gifted program. The Lower Lab School, also known as PS 77, is a separate school for gifted education with its own principal and staff.

Inevitably, the arrangement leads to a feeling of haves and have-nots among the three programs: Lower Lab, with a hyperactive Parents Association, seems to have more resources and faster-paced instruction than the gifted program at PS 198, which in turn has stronger students and more involved parents than the ordinary zoned neighborhood school. Lower Lab serves mostly white and Asian children, only a few of whom are poor enough to qualify for free lunch; PS 198 serves a mix of children of different races and about half qualify for free lunch.

That said, all three programs have a lot going for them. Assistant principal Katherine MacManus replaced Nancy Cabrero Emerick as principal of PS 198 in 2016. MacManus worked as a special education coach at PS 59, one of the city's strongest schools. Sandra Miller, who became principal of Lower Lab in 2015, has experience in gifted education, having served as head of the lower school of NEST+m, a citywide school downtown.

The schools have worked to build friendly cooperation in the building. Students from both schools serve on a joint student council, the schools' PTAs sponsor a joint fund-raiser, and it is a goal to have teachers from PS 198's G&T program and Lower Lab share practices by visiting one another's classrooms, said Miller.

The vibe throughout PS 198 is cheery and calm. Hallways are lined with colorful displays of student work. Classrooms are nicely decorated and well stocked with books and supplies. Each one has space where the entire class gathers for lessons and discussions; at other times students in all grades sit in groups, either around tables or at desks clustered together.

Lower Lab, founded in 1987, was modeled after two progressive private schools: Manhattan Country School and Bank Street School for Children. More than two decades later, Lower Lab remains true to its roots, providing creative instruction and lots of groupwork.

First-graders learn about architecture with the Center for Architecture; 2nd-graders study buildings, bridges, and landmarks in their local community with The Salvadori Center; 3rd-graders take a look at different cultures through dance and music at Symphony Space; and 4th-graders work with Wingspan Arts to develop dramatic presentations based on lessons in New York history. Lab teaches students to debate in conjunction with persuasive writing in 5th grade and an author-in-residence works with 3rd-graders as they learn the art of revision in realistic fiction.

Teachers draw from several approaches to math, including Investigations and Math in the City. Lower Lab encourages participation in clubs and competitions including Math Olympiads for grades 4 and 5, the NYS Math League, the National Science Competition, and CML coding (computer science).

A parent said she was surprised at the speed with which her kindergarten-aged son learned to read when he started at Lab. Most kindergartners are reading by December, according to the administration. In general, children work about one-half to one full grade level above their age. All students receive instruction in art, music, and gym. Children study Spanish (grades K–2) and Latin (grades 3–5). Grades 2–5 learn keyboarding, coding, digital literacy, and more in a new technology program.

Sporting a shock of Albert Einstein hair, veteran science teacher Katerina Klaf meets with all students two to three times a week in her tidy classroom complete with live pill bugs, earthworms, and hornworms. "Larvae are beautiful!" she told us with enthusiasm.

Fifth-graders have a modified middle school schedule. They have math and science instruction from one teacher and English and social studies from another. Small-group advisories help students manage the middle school–level intensity of their studies, and to juggle expectations from two teachers. Math lessons are rooted in problem-solving activities as a group.

Any child who lives in the attendance zone may attend PS 198. Children who live in District 2 may apply to Lower Lab and the gifted program at PS 198. Admission is determined by the city's gifted exam; Lower Lab is more selective. (Lydie Raschka and Laura Zingmond.)

PS 217: Roosevelt Island School
645 Main Street
New York, NY, 10044
PK
(212) 980-0294
www.217pta.com

Who gets in: kids in zone, kids who pass gifted exam
Grade levels: PK–8   **Reading scores:** ****
Enrollment: 587   **Math scores:** ****
Low-income: 35%   **Ethnicity:** 36%W 16%B 14%H 29%A 5%O

Roosevelt Island, a long, narrow strip of land in the East River between Manhattan and Queens, has the feel of a small town. It's connected to the Upper East Side by an aerial tramway, and the F train connects the island to Manhattan and Queens. Housing prices, while rising, are still affordable compared to other parts of District 2.

PS 217, the only public school on the island, is housed in a modern building with large windows, glass bricks, wide hallways, an airy lobby, and a cafeteria with a commanding view of Manhattan. Many employees of the United Nations live on Roosevelt Island and the school has children from 60 different countries.

Cornell Tech, the technology-focused campus of Cornell University under construction on the Island, has an unusual collaboration with PS 217: The university is training the school's teachers in computer science. Children take class trips to places like Google's Manhattan offices and may study digital media and game design as part of a program sponsored by the Museum of the Moving Image in Queens.

Enrollment has grown steadily in the past decade, a sign of the school's growing popularity. One mother said she loves the "community vibe." Another said her son's teachers "inspire him every day to be respectful, to be curious, to work hard, and to love school." The Department of Education's Quality Review called the school "well developed" in all five categories, the highest ranking.

Children from District 2 in Manhattan may apply to the school's gifted and talented program. In recent years, children from District 30 in Queens have been admitted as well. (Clara Hemphill)

PS 859: Special Music School
129 West 67th Street
New York, NY 10023
(212) 501-3318
www.kaufmanmusiccenter.org/sms

Who gets in: kids citywide who display unusual musical talent
Grade levels: K–12   **Reading scores:** * * * * *
Enrollment: 277   **Math scores:** * * * * *
Low-income: 18%   **Ethnicity:** 43%W 13%B 14%H 16%A 13%O

The Special Music School offers intense musical training along with rigorous academics. It's tough to get in—some 400 children audition for just 15 kindergarten seats—but for those who are admitted the opportunities are extraordinary.

The school has evolved from its original mission—to replicate the strict focus of the music schools of the former Soviet Union—into a school that balances musical training with academics, music theory, and music history, said Principal Katherine Banucci-Smith. The school's academic test scores are among the highest in the city.

Banucci-Smith, principal since 2010, graduated from Oberlin Conservatory, where she studied voice. As a child she played violin. She was formerly assistant principal at River East Elementary School.

The New York City Department of Education is responsible for the academic classes, while the Kaufman Music Center provides students with full music scholarships. The curriculum includes two private instrumental lessons each week and group classes in music theory, solfège (ear training), music history, and chorus. At the end of 5th grade all students must audition to be readmitted to the middle school, and only a very small percentage leave.

Originally serving grades K–8, the school has expanded to include grades 9–12. The high school is housed in the Martin Luther King Campus nearby. For admission in grades K–2, no previous musical training is necessary. However, parents are supposed to ensure that their children practice 2 or 3 hours a day.

Open houses are offered four times a year. Testing for kindergarten begins in September. Children are asked to clap, sing, and move to music; they are assessed based on their pitch, sense of rhythm, and musical memory. Applications are available online at www.kaufman-center.org/sms or by calling the school. (Lydie Raschka)

PS 199

270 West 70th Street
New York, NY 10023
(212) 799-1033
www.ps199pta.org

Who gets in: kids in zone; long wait lists in recent years
Grade levels: K–5   **Reading scores:** * * * * *
Enrollment: 903   **Math scores:** * * * * *
Low-income: 7%   **Ethnicity:** 63%W 2%B 13%H 14%A 7%O

A unified staff with a shared vision of education; an active parent organization; and a long history of stable, effective leadership make PS 199 one of the most sought-after schools in the city. Walk into the school at any time, and you're likely to see lively instruction and happy, engaged kids in every class.

The school leadership and staff are self-confident enough to resist the latest education fads. Instead, they rely on their long experience to offer a sophisticated approach to teaching writing and math. Student teachers from Teachers College perfect their craft here—and some are hired as regular teachers when they finish their graduate work.

Children learn to read from picture books and children's literature—not textbooks. The Everyday Math curriculum incorporates math games and paper-and-pencil work. Science involves hands-on projects and exploration. In one class we visited, 3rd-graders learned about adaptation by stroking a live rabbit and pondering why it had eyes on the sides of its head (to better spot predators) and strong back legs (to better escape).

The depth and volume of student writing is impressive. Posted on the walls were thoughtful essays on topics such as "Columbus: Hero or Villain" and lesser-known explorers like "Amazing John Cabot and Jacques Cartier."

The school boasts big, bright classrooms, a gym with soaring windows, a music room, a wheelchair-accessible playground, two art rooms, and a well-equipped library. All classrooms are well equipped and kid-friendly. Kindergarten classrooms have blocks and play areas; one 5th-grade classroom has comfy sofas. The PTA, which raises more than $800,000 a year, pays for teaching assistants in the lower grades.

"The reason we are able to fill the classrooms with all of these wonderful materials is the PTA," said longtime parent coordinator Allison Sansoucie, who gave us our tour.

The school has partnerships with several arts organizations, including the New York Philharmonic, Vital Theatre, Lincoln Center Institute, and National Dance Institute, whose teaching artists work with each of the 4th-grade classes once a week. A "Special Forces" class combines general education pupils with special-needs students, including some in wheelchairs, in a dance collaboration.

New construction in the area has caused overcrowding at the school, and some classes have ballooned to 31 children. In 2015, the Department of Education proposed shrinking the school's attendance zone and sending new pupils to nearby PS 191. Hundreds of parents protested, and the DOE withdrew the proposal. Nonetheless, rezoning seems inevitable. The school has had wait lists in kindergarten and 1st and 2nd grades in recent years, and some children who live in the zone have been assigned to nearby PS 452 instead.

One of the city's first barrier-free schools, PS 199 has a legacy of serving students with physical challenges. The playground is wheelchair-accessible.

In recent years, not all children who live in the zone have been offered seats because of overcrowding. (Clara Hemphill)

PS 452

100 West 77th Street
New York, NY 10024
(212) 496-1050
www.ps452.org

Who gets in: kids in zone
Grade levels: K–5   **Reading scores:** * * * * *
Enrollment: 325   **Math scores:** * * * * *
Low-income: 13%   **Ethnicity:** 64%W 8%B 13%H 11%A 4%O

Opened in 2010 to ease overcrowding on the Upper West Side, PS 452 has quickly become one of the best schools in the district. Principal David Scott Parker, former assistant principal at nearby PS 199, has built a school with a thoughtful approach to writing, math, social studies, science, and the arts.

The National Dance Institute, a nonprofit organization, offers weekly classes to every student in grades K–4. Music is woven into history and geography lessons; children learn why one part of the country gave birth to bluegrass, another to jazz and blues. Children not only sing in the chorus and learn to play instruments, they also learn about the physics of sound.

In every class we visited, children seemed happy and engaged in interesting projects. Children move efficiently and quietly from one activity to another, with little wasted time. There's a tolerance for quirky kids: A child who has trouble sitting on the floor may sit on a "wiggle seat" (an inflated cushion that allows him to wobble without distracting others) or be assigned active tasks such as wiping down tables or taking the attendance sheet to the office.

Like PS 199, PS 452 has a very active PTA that raises a substantial budget to pay for teaching assistants in some classrooms as well as the extra arts programs. "Almost everything we have that sparkles comes from the PTA," Parker said. Almost every classroom has two adults, including teachers, teaching assistants, teachers' aides, and student teachers from Teachers College.

Also like PS 199, PS 452 has a well-developed writing program as part of Teachers College Reading and Writing Project. Children's work we saw posted was quite sophisticated, including persuasive essays (with topics such as "Trains are the best form of transportation," and "Dogs are better than cats") and "literary essays" analyzing character development in picture books. The Everyday Math Program, developed by the University of

Chicago, encourages children to understand the conceptual foundations of math.

Social studies and science are integrated in thematic units such as the "bridge study," in which children learn the history of how the Brooklyn Bridge was built and the science of what makes bridges stand up. Children make paper models of skyscrapers with the help of Salvadori, a nonprofit group that offers lessons in architecture and engineering.

In 5th grade, children have one teacher for math and science and another for English and social studies. The arrangement allows teachers to specialize in their subjects and has the effect of putting more emphasis on math and science than many elementary schools manage.

The school has a flexible and thoughtful approach to special education. A special education teacher may work with individual kids and serve as one of two teachers in a team-taught class part of the day. There are no self-contained special education classes, but there is a commitment to team-taught classes on each grade level, and there are occupational, physical, and speech therapists.

The school shares the William O'Shea Complex, a former junior high school, with the Anderson School and MS 245, the Computer School. PS 452's spacious, sunny rooms are well equipped with colorful rugs, classroom libraries, blocks, and book bags. There are no prekindergarten classes.

In 2016, the administration proposed moving the school to the building that houses PS 191 at 210 West 61st Street, if that school moves, as expected, to a new building nearby. Parker said the plan would allow PS 452 to expand and serve more children, but some parents objected, saying their children would no longer be able to walk to school. (Clara Hemphill and Aimee Sabo)

PS 334: The Anderson School
100 West 77th Street
New York, NY 10024
(212) 595-7193
www.ps334school.org

Who gets in: kids who score in 99th percentile on gifted exam
Grade levels: K–8   **Reading scores:** * * * * *
Enrollment: 559   **Math scores:** * * * * *
Low-income: 10%   **Ethnicity:** 53%W 4%B 9%H 28%A 6%O

One of the most demanding and selective schools in New York, PS 334, The Anderson School, attracts children from all over the city. Engaging instruction, imaginative projects, and a stellar record of getting children into top high schools (both public and private) has made Anderson one of the most sought-after schools anywhere.

Don't set your heart on sending your child here, however. The competition for admission is unbelievably tough. Nearly 15,000 4-year-olds take the city's gifted and talented test each year; of those, 1,500 score high enough to qualify for Anderson and four other citywide gifted programs. Just 50 are admitted to Anderson's kindergarten and a handful in 1st through 3rd grades. The odds are ever so slightly better in the middle school, particularly in 7th grade (when one-third of the class leaves for Hunter College High School, which begins in 7th grade).

The school has a particularly strong math program. Rather than relying on one set of textbooks, teachers skillfully blend different approaches that combine fast-paced instruction with deep conceptual understanding. Teachers encourage children to look for different ways to solve problems and the kids seem to take joy in discovery—not just in getting the right answer. By 8th grade, nearly all have passed the high school algebra Regents exam.

While kindergarten classrooms elsewhere have removed blocks and dramatic play areas, at Anderson children enjoy "center time," when they may shop at a play store (and learn to make change), squeeze and flatten bits of clay (strengthening fine motor skills), or roll marbles down ramps made from wooden blocks. On our visit, we saw a kindergartner put together "base ten blocks" usually used by older children to learn addition, subtraction, and place value. As the boy used the blocks to construct a house, the teacher encouraged him to count them—which turned into a three-digit addition problem.

First-graders often read books more typical for 3rd-graders. (See the school website for summer reading lists.) Third-graders' essays about where they spent their summer vacation reflect both sophistication and the good luck of being world travelers at a young age, with stories about a trip to China; a country house in Woodstock; Cancun, Mexico; and Disneyland in France. Fourth-graders' essays showed an understanding of complex ideas, such as a report one child wrote about the air quality in New York nail salons.

A beloved science teacher, Charles Conway, asked 5th-graders to determine how changing the length of a pendulum affects the number of swings in a given time period. Sixth-graders use a rooftop weather station to predict the weather. Eighth-graders take the high school Regents exam for living environment, as biology is called.

In an 8th-grade U.S. history class, we heard a lively discussion comparing the debate over the Fugitive Slave Act to today's gridlock in Congress. In 8th-grade English, children were asked to write a "coming-of-age memoir—when your perspective on the world changed and you grew up a little," using as models authors such as Jeannette Walls, Ernest Hemingway, and David Sedaris.

The homework load is heavy but not oppressive. Kindergartners have weekly homework packets. By middle school, children may spend 2 hours a night on homework. Kids compete in the math team or the Science Olympiad, but aren't cutthroat, says Principal Jodi Hyde. "They say, 'Yes, we're competitive because we want to do well.' But they aren't mean to each other. They are competitive with themselves."

The school is committed to giving extra academic and emotional support to all. Despite this help, a handful of children can't keep up with the work and perhaps one a year leaves the school as a result. Graduates go on to the top high schools in the city, including elite public schools like Stuyvesant and Bronx High School of Science and private schools like Trinity.

The school has a very active PTA that raises more than $1 million a year for assistant teachers in every class as well as programs such as dance, chess, sports, and fieldtrips. The PTA has a "suggested contribution" of $1,300 per child. Some are put off by the Type A crowd, but many appreciate such intense participation.

A handful of children who have disabilities such as dyslexia receive extra help. A guidance counselor works on social skills with children with conditions like Asperger's syndrome.

Yellow bus service is available for Manhattan students who live more than half a mile from school. Students outside Manhattan arrange their own transportation. (Clara Hemphill)

PS 87

PK

**160 West 78th Street
New York, NY 10024
(212) 678-2826
*www.ps87.info***

Who gets in: kids in zone, wait lists
Grade levels: PK–5   **Reading scores:** *****
Enrollment: 852   **Math scores:** *****
Low-income: 7%   **Ethnicity:** 64%W 5%B 15%H 7%A 10%O

PS 87 has long been one of the most popular schools in District 3, known for its passionate teachers, active parents, and commitment to the arts. Parents chip in to plan fund-raisers and help out on the playground, and they advocate for improving the quality of the food.

Hallways are filled with creative and inspired student work. Social studies units begin with the child and expand outward from "me" and "my family" to the neighborhood, city, state, country, and world. Kids take trips to the Central Park Zoo, the botanical gardens, and area museums. The school has a popular dual-language Spanish-English program, designed to make children proficient speakers and writers of both languages.

Alas, the quality of teaching is uneven. Depending on the luck of the draw, your child may get a fabulous teacher—or one who is not ready for prime time. The staff is famous for its independence, or, depending on your point of view, its resistance to supervision. The school had five principals in a decade; one told us she left because the teachers acted as if they didn't need a principal.

Monica Berry, principal since 2010, has a rocky relationship with some of the staff; according to school surveys, many teachers mistrust her.

That said, nearly all the parents who responded to the survey say they would recommend the school. "In a school this big you are bound to come across a few less-than-impressive teachers, parents, kids," a parent wrote on the InsideSchools website. "The classes are big, lunchroom is crowded, and the auditorium gets noisy—but this is a NYC public school. The experience for kids and parents, I think, mirrors real life. I highly recommend this school for families looking for a well-rounded education in life and in academics." (Lydie Raschka and Clara Hemphill)

PS 9

100 West 84th Street
New York, NY 10024
(212) 678-2812
www.ps9.org

PK

Who gets in: kids in zone
Grade levels: PK–5
Enrollment: 611
Low-income: 21%

Reading scores: * * * * *
Math scores: * * * * *
Ethnicity: 59%W 5%B 21%H 9%A 6%O

PS 9 is an unusually quiet and orderly school, with little of the restlessness and chatter that often override classroom decorum. Teachers have clear expectations and children seem happy to follow the classroom routines. It has demanding academics, creative arts, and an active Parents Association.

The teaching is a bit more traditional than at some other Upper West Side schools, with more emphasis on skills like handwriting and spelling. Although there are blocks and dress-up corners in the kindergarten classes, there is a focus on academics and early reading skills rather than play. For example, in diagrams for a unit on penguins, kindergartners spelled words like "beak" and "flipper" correctly.

At the same time, children go outside for recess every day, and there is room to explore music, art, and dance. Classrooms clearly have personalities, and creativity is valued; one 5th-grade class named all their group tables after Hogwarts dormitories, while a kindergarten class had a cache of bright ukuleles they are learning to play, inspired by their guitar-loving teacher. Children's artwork covers the walls; 5th-graders learn square dancing and work with visiting teachers from the New York City Ballet. Essays posted on the walls show both creativity and care—such as 3rd-graders' letters imagining they were immigrants to Ellis Island or Civil War soldiers.

Social studies projects bring history to life. Children made their own documentaries about the age of exploration, learning about Christopher Columbus or Giovanni da Verrazano while mastering the art of video editing on shiny new Macintosh computers. As part of their study of American history, 4th-graders go to Philadelphia and 5th-graders go to Gettysburg.

Even recess is orderly: Children line up on the playground to listen to instructions from school aides before they are permitted to play. Still, maintaining calm doesn't come at the expense of caring; when a boy with a history of behavioral issues had a tantrum during our visit, administrators and teachers swiftly and sweetly helped him work through his feelings outside the room and within minutes he was back inside participating with his friends. Parents are welcome to volunteer, but must undergo training by the Learning Leaders organization that includes a background check.

In 2015, Katherine Witzke, the former assistant principal, replaced Diane Brady, who had been principal since 1997. Parents we spoke to outside the school gushed about Witzke. "She's very approachable and has really improved communication with parents," one mom told us. Enrollment has grown by more than 50% in the past decade, a sign of the school's increasing popularity. Class size ranges from 25 in kindergarten to 30 in 5th grade, and a few classes feel a bit cramped.

The Parents Association raises a significant amount of money for assistant teachers in all classrooms, and for chess, Spanish, class trips, art, and music programs. They also installed tennis balls on the bottoms of all classroom chair legs to minimize those distracting screeches.

The school works to ensure that academic problems are identified and corrected early. For example, all teachers in grades K–2 have been trained in Orton-Gillingham, a multisensory approach to reading that has been successful with children with dyslexia. The school serves a range of children with special needs, including those with significant disabilities who would normally be assigned to segregated or self-contained classes. Instead, Witzke assigns these children team-teaching classes in which a special education teacher and a general education teacher work together in the same classroom. The school offers speech, occupational, and physical therapy. It is not wheelchair-accessible.

Tours are held in December and January. (Aimee Sabo)

PS 166

132 West 89th Street
New York, NY 10024
(212) 678-2829
www.PS166.org

Who gets in: kids in zone, plus District 3 kids who pass gifted exam
Grade levels: K–5   **Reading scores:** *****
Enrollment: 614   **Math scores:** *****
Low-income: 20%   **Ethnicity:** 59%W 6%B 17%H 11%A 8%O

PS 166 has the most popular gifted program on the Upper West Side, big song and dance performances, and an active parents association that raises a ton of money. Fine examples of children's art and writing are posted on bulletin boards throughout the school. One example: a 10-page guide to the school for prospective parents, written by a 1st-grader.

The beautifully renovated building, constructed in 1897, has high ceilings and bright and sunny classrooms that are lavishly equipped with books and supplies. Children go outside even on cold days and recess takes place before lunch to encourage children to eat more slowly and to create a calmer transition back to the classroom. The lunchroom is one of the more civilized ones we've seen.

The rich arts programs can be heard and seen throughout the building. On one of our visits, we watched 3rd-grade girls twirl in red skirts as they practiced a Mexican folk dance. In the science lab, children plucked kalimbas—African thumb pianos—to explore pitch and amplification. In the music room children sang a lively spiritual. On another visit, we saw dance and music teachers collaborate to put on a musical production. Children made paintings in the style of Frida Kahlo—one of a series of lessons designed to teach art history as well as studio art.

Children were engaged in every class we saw. During "center time," kindergartners may choose to play with blocks, write, read, or put together plastic cubes that build math skills.

The quality of writing is particularly high and Teachers College Reading and Writing Project works closely with teachers at PS 166. Kindergartners write "personal narratives" that may include New Year's resolutions. ("My resolution is to clean up my toys.") Older children write persuasive essays on topics such as "Should chocolate milk be banned in school?"

Debra Mastriano, who became principal in 2012, has won high marks from district administrators for the rigor of the curriculum. The annual teacher survey, however, gives her mixed reviews for her leadership, and we heard some grumbling that she can be abrupt. She told us that some pushback from staff is inevitable as she steps up demands.

The school was once starkly segregated, with mostly black and Latino children in general education classes and mostly whites in gifted and talented. But on our visit we couldn't easily tell the difference between the classes. That's because more white families from the zone are opting for general education classes, which offer smaller class size than the G&T and the same wonderful art, music, and drama that everyone enjoys. The quality of instruction is high throughout the school.

We did speak with one mother who said that black and Hispanic parents sometimes feel marginalized. Another mother said working-class parents sometimes feel left out. The PTA, which raises nearly $300,000 a year, can be cliquish, this mother said. The parent coordinator, Deborah Markewich, told us the school organizes events that everyone can take part in, such as an international dinner and family fitness night. She said parents whose children qualify for free lunch may receive free tickets to the annual auction, which raises much of the PTA budget.

PS 166 has an unusual partnership with the Stephen Gaynor School, a private school nearby that serves children with learning disabilities. Some PS 166 students with reading difficulties go to the Stephen Gaynor School for extra help several afternoons a week. Like most public schools, PS 166 also has team-teaching classes with two teachers, one of whom is certified in special education.

All children who live in the zone are admitted. Children who live in District 3 are admitted to the districtwide gifted program based on the results of an exam administered by the Department of Education; to be considered, parents must submit a Request for Testing in November. (Clara Hemphill)

PS 84

32 West 92nd Street
New York, NY 10025
(212) 799-2534
www.84web.org

PK

Who gets in: kids in zone, plus native French and Spanish speakers outside zone

Grade levels: PK–5	**Reading scores:** ****
Enrollment: 552	**Math scores:** ****
Low-income: 50%	**Ethnicity:** 38%W 13%B 42%H 3%A 4%O

On a leafy street half a block from Central Park, PS 84 offers dual-language programs in French and Spanish as well as English-only classes. The French program is growing in popularity: A second French dual-language class has been added in the lower grades; as these children grow, these classes will likely make up half the school's enrollment. Each grade also has one Spanish dual-language class and one English-only team-taught class with two teachers and a mix of general education and special-needs children.

The school has a mix of children of different races, income levels, and home languages, with no one group dominating. There are children from nearby housing projects as well as from pricey brownstones. Children of nannies and bus drivers learn alongside the offspring of architects and lawyers. Add to the mix West Indian, African, French, and Hispanic backgrounds—and the school is a microcosm of the city. Half the children in the dual-language programs are native speakers of English; half speak French or Spanish at home.

One father grumbled that the dual-language programs function as "gifted" classes, and that those parents make unreasonable demands. Cultural expectations differ from group to group. "Spanish culture is one where they are content to leave it to school administrators," said parent coordinator Anita Hauschild. "The French are more inclined to voice an opinion."

The atmosphere is relaxed. Children are free to talk and to move around the classroom. A rooftop garden provides an inviting outdoor classroom where children plant and harvest vegetables and have hands-on science lessons. The playground and lunchroom are calmer than at many schools (and the food, with lots of fresh vegetables, is better than the typical lunchroom fare). Some classrooms are a bit cluttered, and the level of student engagement varies, but the quality of children's written work is good overall. Children and staff both seem happy to be here.

The school has a wide variety of community partnerships. Volunteers from the Jewish Community Center work as "reading buddies." Enrichment programs are offered by Juilliard, the 92nd Street Y, the New-York Historical Society, and Magic Box Productions (which teaches children to use cameras). An active PTA raises several hundred thousand dollars a year to pay for teacher assistants in most classrooms and enrichment activities. The school has a well-stocked library, staffed by parent volunteers.

Longtime principal Robin Sundick, who established the French dual-language programs and made the school more welcoming to parents, retired in 2015 and was replaced by Evelyn J. Lolis, formerly an elementary school principal on Long Island. Lolis, a native speaker of French (her mother is French and her father is Greek), has a PhD from Hofstra University and had worked in the Reading and Writing Project at Teachers College. Hauschild and Assistant Principal Mary Acosta both speak Spanish, so parents can always find someone at the school who speaks their language.

The school's English-only program is made up of team-teaching classes, which mix general and special-needs children, with two teachers. There are also self-contained classes for children who need a smaller setting. Children with difficulties reading may get free after-school tutoring at the Stephen Gaynor School, a private school for special-needs children.

Children in the school attendance zone are guaranteed admission, but those living anywhere in District 3 may apply. Native speakers of French and Spanish from outside District 3 sometimes are admitted off the wait list in late summer. (Clara Hemphill)

PS 333: Manhattan School for Children
154 West 93rd Street
New York, NY 10025
(212) 222-1450
www.ps333.org

Who gets in: District 3 lottery
Grade levels: K–8
Enrollment: 742
Low-income: 14%

Reading scores: ✮✮✮✮✮
Math scores: ✮✮✮✮
Ethnicity: 62%W 11%B 17%H 7%A 4%O

Manhattan School for Children, housed in the former Joan of Arc Junior High School building, is a warm and happy place where kids call teachers by their first names and parents are welcome throughout the day. Parents come right to the classroom to drop off their children, and many stay for a few minutes to read a book or chat. A wide corridor serves as an informal meeting place for parents, kids, and teachers during the day.

Manhattan School for Children is a pioneer in including children with special needs (particularly physical challenges) in regular classrooms, and the children are accepting of one another, whether they use a wheelchair or a walker or have difficulty speaking clearly. Classrooms are sunny and cheerful, and there are plenty of books and supplies. A stunning rooftop greenhouse serves as a science lab. The school has a nice wheelchair-accessible playground surrounded by red oak trees and shrubs.

The school places as much emphasis on children's social and emotional development as it does on academics, and children seem to be unusually kind to one another. The school encourages friendships across the grades, and it's common to see older children helping younger children. Firmly in the progressive camp, the administration favors learning by doing. For example, kindergartners watch duck eggs hatch in classroom incubators—hooked up to a webcam so they can also watch them at home. Children may build a terrarium in the greenhouse or draw a timeline representing the history of the subway. They also may spend several days on a math problem, learning fractions by imagining they have to divide sandwiches among their classmates.

Some of the classrooms are a bit messy, but Principal Claire Lowenstein says that's part of the plan. "Through messiness can come genius," she said.

Lowenstein, a former assistant principal and longtime teacher at the school, was named principal in February 2014, replacing the founding principal, Susan Rappaport, who retired. Lowenstein is working to improve communication with teachers and parents by writing weekly letters and having monthly meetings. She greets children at the entrance in the morning and seems to know every child by name.

The administration believes in the importance of recess, not just as a time to run around but also as a time to develop social skills. Recess times are staggered; some children go out to play as early as 9:15 a.m. and others go out after lunch.

The arts offerings are rich, and Manhattan School for Children has full-time teachers for visual art, dance, drama, and storytelling. The school launched a music program in the lower grades in 2015, with the hope of expanding it to upper grades in coming years. Children put on an annual musical with singing and dancing.

For years, some parents have complained that the atmosphere may be too relaxed, but many others defend the school with a passion and are thrilled with the experience their children are getting. While many children once left after 5th grade, students are increasingly staying for middle school. Top students are admitted to some of the city's most selective and demanding high schools, including LaGuardia High School for Music and Art and Performing Arts.

The school, which is wheelchair-accessible, is at the forefront of "inclusion," integrating disabled children in general education classes. The school goes to great lengths to help disabled children take part in regular classes. For example, a keyboard with pictures allows a child who cannot speak to express himself. Most classes have at least two teachers. The school does not admit severely disabled children from District 75 and does not have segregated or self-contained classes.

Admissions are by lottery, limited to District 3. For details, see the school's website. (Clara Hemphill)

PS 75

735 West End Avenue
New York, NY 10025
(212) 866-5400
www.ps75pta.org

Who gets in: kids in zone, also some out-of-zone kids
Grade levels: K–5   **Reading scores:** ★★★★
Enrollment: 569   **Math scores:** ★★★★
Low-income: 70%   **Ethnicity:** 16%W 23%B 56%H 2%A 3%O

PS 75 is a gritty, idealistic place, committed to teaching children who live in expensive co-ops on Riverside Drive alongside those who live in housing projects. It has a large group of committed, enthusiastic parents who organize activities like family movie night, a Halloween party, and dances for both grown-ups and children.

With a mix of children of different races, the school is an oasis for multiracial families who fear their children would be isolated in schools where one race predominates. The tone is warm and welcoming to both parents and children. One parent said she likes the fact the school is "not too progressive, not too rigid," with a good balance between structure and freedom.

Long known for its dual-language program, in which children become fluent in both English and Spanish, PS 75 also takes pride in its rich art offerings and its ASD Nest program, in which children on the autism spectrum share an extra-small class with children in general education and two teachers.

The quality of children's writing we saw on our visit was good, with essays posted on engaging topics such as "Are zoos harmful or helpful for endangered species?" Sophisticated children's artwork covers the corridor walls, part of the collaboration with the nonprofit Studio in a School, which sends teaching artists to give every child lessons every week. Every 5th-grader studies ballroom dancing, and children from various grades take part in the Young People's Chorus.

Longtime principal Robert O'Brien works to make sure children have plenty of time to move around their classrooms, understanding that all children need exercise and no one likes to sit still all day. Children have physical education twice a week in a large gym. They go out to recess before eating lunch, which O'Brien says gives them a chance to "get their sillies out." On rainy days some children watch movies in the auditorium—but others may toss a ball around with school aides in the gym.

The building, built in 1950, is a bit drab. While some rooms are inviting—such as the well-equipped library with books in both English and Spanish—others are cluttered. The corridors are dimly lit with flickering fluorescent lights and gray- or green-tiled walls. Some floors are black, others have gray and pink squares.

The school was orderly on our visit, with children happily engaged in every class we saw. Even the cafeteria—a chaotic place in many schools—was pleasant, with children chatting quietly. PS 75 serves children from a nearby shelter for victims of domestic violence, and sometimes children with difficult home lives bring their problems to school, staff members say. O'Brien says the school works hard to get children the help and support they need. The parents we spoke to shrugged off concerns and said that a few discipline problems don't interfere with their children's education.

The school has a good record getting children admitted to their middle school choices. Most 5th-graders end up at Computer, MS 54, Mott Hall II, and West Side Collaborative (housed on the top floor of PS 75).

Children with disabilities may be assigned to team-taught classes (which serve both children in general education and those receiving special education services). These classes have two teachers, one of whom is certified in special education. The school also has an ASD Nest program for children with autism spectrum disorders (ASDs). Students with ASD learn in a classroom alongside typically developing children, taught by two teachers who have been trained in the program's specialized curriculum and teaching strategies.

PS 75 runs an after-school program that includes programs in ceramics, art, science, tennis, musical instruments, theater, dance, ice-skating, rock climbing, chess, and more. There is a fee but scholarships are available.

About one-third of the student body comes from outside the school attendance zone. O'Brien says don't be discouraged if your child isn't admitted on the first application round in the spring; seats open up. "We want people who want to be here," he said. "Call us weekly. Don't worry about pestering us." (Clara Hemphill)

PS 163

163 West 97th Street
New York, NY 10025
(212) 678-2854
www.ps163pa.org

PK

Who gets in: kids in zone, kids who pass gifted exam, plus out-of-zone kids
Grade levels: PK–5   **Reading scores:** * * * * *
Enrollment: 587   **Math scores:** * * * *
Low-income: 48%   **Ethnicity:** 27%W 16%B 46%H 6%A 5%O

PS 163 has two lively prekindergarten classes, an impressive dance program, and teachers who know how to challenge top students while giving struggling kids the support they need.

Its gifted and talented program is open to children from across District 3. PS 163 has a popular dual-language program designed to make children fluent in English and Spanish, as well as general education classes and team-taught classes for children with special needs. The Parents Association works hard to bring children in the school's different programs together with weekly clubs such as macramé, cooking, running, or filmmaking.

The attendance zone for PS 163 includes housing projects and luxury housing and, unfortunately, the school is somewhat divided by race and class. The G&T classes are mostly white and Asian, especially in the younger grades; the dual-language classes have a mix of mostly white and Latino; and the general education classes and the team-taught classes are mostly black and Latino.

The school faces a budget quandary—it's not quite poor enough for federal anti-poverty grants called Title I, but not rich enough to have the Parents Association raise a huge amount of money. There is some friction between the administration and staff: In his first years at the school, Principal Donny Lopez, who took over after longtime principal Virginia Pepe retired in 2013, got low marks from teachers on annual surveys.

Nonetheless, most parents seem satisfied. "Our girls are challenged without being stressed or overwhelmed," a mother with two children in the G&T program wrote on the InsideSchools website. "We like that the kindergarten is academic but also allows the kids center time so that they can enjoy being kids." (Lydie Raschka)

PS 180

PK

370 West 120th Street
New York, NY 10027
(212) 678-2849
www.hugonewmanprep.org

Who gets in: kids in zone
Grade levels: PK–8   **Reading scores:** * * *
Enrollment: 595   **Math scores:** * *
Low-income: 69%   **Ethnicity:** 8%W 58%B 30%H 1%A 4%O

Ask parents what they like about PS 180 and they'll tell you about the warm sense of community, the pleasure of making friends with other parents, sharing babysitting and after-school pickups, and even having holiday meals together.

It's a place where parents of different races and ethnic groups seem to get along, where families of mixed races feel at home. The PTA organizes events to encourage parents to come to the school regularly—such as an early-morning exercise class with a disco ball.

"I feel like I'm part of a community in a way I never expected," one mother said.

"You're greeted with a smile," said a father. "The teachers are accessible."

"We are traditional. We believe in homework, we have tests, a spelling bee," said another mother. "But we also have rugs and desks in groups."

PS 180 has three classes in most grades: general education, dual-language (in which children study in English in the morning and Spanish in the afternoon) and team-taught (with two teachers, one of whom is certified in special education).

Class size is small: about 20 in the elementary school and 22 in the middle school. The quality of children's written work we saw posted on bulletin boards was good. Music and art instruction are strong. Second-graders swim at Asphalt Green.

Although the school was orderly the day of our visit, Principal Lana Fleming acknowledged that a few children with behavior problems had been assigned to PS 180 after having been asked to leave nearby charter schools. To help these children, the school has a full-time social worker and 12 psychology graduate interns from Columbia University to help these children. There are frequent tours for prospective parents. (Clara Hemphill)

PS 12: Talented and Gifted
School for Young Scholars

240 East 109th Street
New York, NY 10029
(212) 860-6003
www.tagscholars.com

Who gets in: kids who score in 97th percentile on gifted exam
Grade levels: K–8   **Reading scores:** *****
Enrollment: 561   **Math scores:** *****
Low-income: 47%   **Ethnicity:** 15%W 25%B 19%H 34%A 7%O

The most diverse of the citywide gifted programs, Talented and Gifted Young Scholars (TAG) has a mix of black, Latino, Asian, and white pupils. The school also has a diverse teaching staff, so children have role models of different races. Neat red-plaid uniforms, cheery classrooms, and engaging lessons are hallmarks of this warm and orderly school. Principal Janette Cesar knows every child by name, even down to who has which allergies. Children come from as far away as the Bronx, Brooklyn, Queens, and Staten Island.

Lessons are fast-paced and demanding. All children are expected to read at home for at least 45 minutes a night. In addition, kindergartners typically have a half-hour of homework, 5th-graders have one-and-a-half hours, and middle schoolers have up to two hours each night. Homework packets are assigned on all holidays and during summer break. The quality of writing we saw was good: Children write long essays on topics ranging from Tom Sawyer to the history of the robber barons and civil disobedience.

It's long been a traditional school, with plenty of emphasis on grammar and spelling (1st-graders learn about nouns and adjectives), drills in the multiplication tables, and Latin classes (that teach children the roots of many English words).

But it's also a school where kindergartners create a restaurant in the class and learn computer coding. Everyone goes on class trips to pick apples in the countryside or to take a Circle Line Cruise around Manhattan. The school is shifting away from teacher-directed lessons and toward more class discussions.

"Whoever is doing the talking is doing the learning," Cesar told us.

Rather than relying on one math program, teachers combine the best of a number of programs, including Math in Focus (the

American version of Singapore math) and GO Math! One 6th-grade math teacher we saw had children make up their own word problems as an exercise to see if they understood a lesson on multiplying fractions. Strong math students may accelerate: A 1st-grader may go to the 3rd grade for math. Children in grades 4–8 may take part in the American Math Competitions club after school.

Most 8th-graders graduate with four Regents exams under their belt, including English, American History, algebra, and living environment. Children may choose electives such as Latin jazz percussion, band, or drama. First- through 4th-graders may study piano.

Children in kindergarten through 8th grade may attend an on-site Y after-school program that also offers all-day activities during the summer, school vacations, and holidays. TAG middle-school teachers trained with Kaplan do test prep for the specialized high schools starting in the 7th grade. A vibrant PTA raises funds to supplement electives for the after-school program.

With so much attention paid to academics and arts, however, some students (particularly the more active ones) may find that there are too few physical outlets outside of gym class.

Many 8th-graders go on to specialized high schools, while others receive financial support to attend private institutions and boarding schools such as Little Red School House, Phillips Academy Andover (in Massachusetts), and the Masters School in Dobbs Ferry, NY. Other popular choices are Talent Unlimited and Manhattan Center for Science and Mathematics.

The school, which has long attracted some of the most talented black and Latino children in the city, was founded as a small alternative program in 1989 and became a full-fledged school in 2004. It had its own admissions test until 2008, when then-schools chancellor Joel Klein centralized admissions to citywide G&T programs. Since then, white and Asian families have enrolled their children in the school, which once served almost exclusively black and Latino children.

To be eligible for admission, K–2 students must score in the 97th percentile on the city's gifted and talented exam. Parents should sign up in November for the test, given in January. Only a handful of seats are open in the upper grades. Middle-school admission is based on grades, standardized test scores, and a teacher recommendation. (Clara Hemphill)

PS 497: Central Park East
1573 Madison Avenue
New York, NY 10029
(212) 860-5821
www.centralparkeastone.org

PK

Who gets in: lottery with District 4 preference
Grade levels: PK–5   **Reading scores:** * *
Enrollment: 201   **Math scores:** *
Low-income: 31%   **Ethnicity:** 28%W 20%B 29%H 10%A 14%O

Walk into Central Park East I, and you'll see collages and card-board sculptures in the hallway, smell corn muffins baking, and hear kids chatting animatedly. For some, this flagship progressive school has too many fieldtrips and not enough math drills; for others, it is a delight and refuge—a staunch rebel taking a stand for discovery and play in a bland, standardized testing world. No matter which side you're on, this tiny school has a critical place in the New York City public school system.

Central Park East was founded in 1974 by Deborah Meier, a visionary teacher whose work has had a profound effect on education in New York City and the nation. Her belief that schools should be small, humane, democratic places where children learn how to learn and how to think for themselves helped spark a revival of progressive education in American schools.

It's hard to imagine how revolutionary Central Park East and its two sister schools, Central Park East II and River East, were when they first opened—and how much influence they've had on education in the past 4 decades.

At a time when other schools had desks in rows, Central Park East had tables and sofas. At a time when other schools tracked children into classes for smart and dumb kids, Central Park East put kids of different abilities and even different ages into the same class (kindergarten and 1st, 2nd and 3rd, and 4th and 5th grades are combined).

Instead of accepting racial segregation as a given, Central Park East has always sought, celebrated, and attracted an integrated student body.

Even today, Central Park East represents progressive education in its purest form. Children put together vast cities from wooden blocks and build covered wagons or puppet theaters with hammers and saws. They sing, dance reels, and make sculptures of the human body complete with internal organs.

Teachers say much of what is taught here can't be measured by multiple-choice tests, and most families opt out of state tests, seeing them as a crude measure of child development. What this community values is the ability to work with others, the ability to find the answers to questions of interest, and the ability to delve into projects in detail over a long period of time. "Worktime" is central to the CPE way—an open-ended period of time during which children pursue creative projects of interest to them, culminating in a fantastic museum filled with volcanoes and buildings and dioramas showing off what kids can do.

The criticism of the CPE schools over the years—and of progressive education in general—has been that too many children fail to master basic skills such as the multiplication tables, dates in history, spelling, and punctuation. Over the decades the school has clashed with new waves of standards or City Education Department mandates and new principals who want more focus on skills, more tests to measure progress, and more uniformity among classes.

Monika Garg, formerly an assistant principal at Pan American International School in Queens, was named principal in 2015 and her first year was embroiled in conflict.

Where some see CPE as a standard-bearer for progressive education, Garg saw a school entrenched in bad habits. Early in her first year, a few parents shared anecdotes about tweens not knowing fractions or grammar in middle school. In turn, Garg asked her teachers to consider curriculum, more assessments, and a checklist of skills that could follow a child from grade to grade. "If you're in a 'fish bowl,' she said—visited by educators from as far away as Denmark—"how do you say you need help or don't do this well?"

She made a series of changes that suggested she found progressive education itself suspect and the reaction from the community was swift; teachers spoke to parents, parents took sides, and before the end of her first year a petition calling for her removal had been signed by over 65% of the community, including the school's founder, Deborah Meier. "My mistake here is I've hit of a lot of 'That's not the CPE way,'" Garg said.

The conflict between Garg and the staff still raged as this book went to press, and it's too soon to say whether Garg's initiatives will strengthen the school or undermine what's still terrific about "the CPE way." (Lydie Raschka)

PS 964: Central Park East II

19 East 103rd Street
New York, NY 10029
(212) 860-5992
www.cpe2.org

PK

Who gets in: District 4 priority, some out-of-district kids admitted from wait list

Grade levels: PK–8	**Reading scores:** ✶✶✶✶
Enrollment: 346	**Math scores:** ✶✶✶✶
Low-income: NA	**Ethnicity:** 25%W 29%B 31%H 6%A 9%O

Central Park East II is a cheerful, progressive school that values exploration and discovery. Children are encouraged to speak up, think for themselves, and pursue their own interests. Teachers go by their first names and crouch down to meet kids at eye level.

The school has an eclectic approach to lessons, and teachers are equal partners with the administration in making decisions. "We have no gurus here," said longtime principal Naomi Smith.

In grades Pre-K to 5, the day begins with "work time," during which children select an area of the room to explore. (In middle school, it's called "project time.") They may construct a house with blocks, try a cooking project, or write a play. Teachers find ways to challenge top students while giving struggling kids the support they need. The level of writing varies and some of it is of high quality. Avid readers tackle fiction, nonfiction, comic books, and other genres. Children are divided into ability groups for math using a core of Engage NY lessons. In one, we watched kids rapidly jot down expressions for the number of the day (i.e., 74 = (40 x 2) – 6) using "mental math." In the next room, children used plastic counters to work through the same process.

Classrooms have a healthy buzz of movement and talk. Science takes place in the classroom with a science teacher up to twice a week. The mood during the lesson we saw was happy, verging on boisterous, as kids placed plastic cubes on balance scales, with the assistance of four roaming adults.

Many families opt out of taking state tests, and test results are not a great concern for Smith.

CPE II is creative with its physical education requirements to give kids new experiences and skills: The youngest grades ice skate weekly, 2nd-graders swim, and 3rd-graders play tennis. Grades 4, 5, and 6 visit Taconic State Park camp, and everyone has gym at least once a week. Children bundle up and play outside even in cold weather, but a child who prefers to stay inside may be allowed to do so.

In the lower school about one-fourth of the population has special needs and there are many teaching assistants to help them. At least one class per grade integrates children with special needs and two teachers in the lower and middle schools.

The school occupies one floor of PS 171, a larger school with a more traditional bent. Space is tight since CPE II has more than doubled since it opened, and this presents an ongoing problem that the community is wrestling to solve. Some kids eat lunch early; some offices are tucked in closet-size rooms.

CPE II was founded in 1981, modeled after its sister school, CPE I. It expanded to include middle school in 2015. The middle school is located four blocks away in a building shared with PS 108. Smith frequently consults her cell phone to keep in touch and visits daily. A few elementary school teachers moved up to 6th grade to provide continuity, and they exude a can-do spirit that inspires confidence.

There were two 6th-grade classrooms at the time of our visit, each with 21 children, comprising a range of skills from several children who were previously in a small, 5th-grade, "self-contained," special education class to independent high achievers, said Smith. Some children are pulled out for small-group math lessons with the likable music teacher, who doubles as a math coach and art teacher.

The classrooms have a homey feel, with plants and home-made posters. Two teachers combine science and humanities in an environmental study in partnership with Welikia Project. Students make three trips to Randall's Island to study oysters and monitor a classroom aquarium with oysters.

One downside: The middle school lacks a regular custodian, and parents have had to pitch in to help keep bathrooms clean.

CPE II invites prospective families to visit in order to help them understand its progressive stance. Pre-K and kindergarten classes fill up with younger siblings and District 4 families, in general, Smith said. If interested, "Be a squeaky wheel but not too squeaky," she said. (Lydie Raschka)

PS 171

19 East 103rd Street
New York, NY 10029
(212) 860-5801
www.ps171.org

Who gets in: kids in zone, plus some out-of-zone kids
Grade levels: PK–8
Enrollment: 734
Low-income: NA
Reading scores: * * * * *
Math scores: * * * * *
Ethnicity: 4%W 26%B 63%H 5%A 2%O

PS 171 is a bustling, orderly school where children are expected to read the minute they walk in the door: They read while eating breakfast in the cafeteria, in the hallways waiting for their teachers, and as a class heading to the bathroom, carrying books that they look at quietly while they wait their turn.

It's a formal school, where children wear uniforms and address grown-ups as "Miss" or "Mr.," but it's not rigid or harsh. Across the board, students seemed interested and engaged in their classes during our visit.

PS 171 is located in a five-story, late-19th-century building near Central Park, which it shares with Central Park East II.

In the younger grades, classrooms are cheery spaces with colorful furniture and creative work lining the walls. All have cozy reading corners with soft chairs and colorful rugs; one 1st-grade class has a bright red loft. Middle-school-grade classrooms are more subdued, but packed with resources. Each one has a neatly arranged library with a generous selection of books; laptop computers are frequently used.

Starting in Pre-K, students are primed to express ideas and learn independently. Students do lots of talking about what they are studying, and their advanced vocabularies reflect the depth of their understanding of the class material. Teachers also create resources that encourage students to answer their own questions before seeking out help. Laminated guides for vocabulary, math, and writing are placed on each table or group of desks; children check their folders and wall charts to keep track of their reading and math goals.

There's lots of attention to foundation skills—phonics, grammar, and math facts—and structure, too. Pre-K students practice writing out the entire alphabet on individual whiteboards; 2nd-graders learn to write a five-paragraph essay.

Sixth-graders stay put in one room, with the same teacher for most of the day. Seventh- and 8th-graders travel to different rooms for different subjects.

The school has a good record of graduates moving on to specialized and other well-regarded high schools such as Manhattan Center for Science, Manhattan-Hunter, Millennium, N.Y.C. Museum, Pace, Talent Unlimited, and Young Women's Leadership. Some students attend private and Catholic schools.

Dimitres Pantelidis, principal since 1999, is a stickler for data, and students in most grades take complete weekly online assessments. However, children also discuss ideas, read books of their choice, and complete projects that involve a lot of research, writing, and creative expression. In a kindergarten class, students took turns showing off their posters about the life cycle of a plant, using words like "germinate" and "seedling" to explain what they learned.

Pantelidis has amassed millions of dollars of grants for computer and science labs, laptops and tablets, and access to online learning programs from school and home.

Students benefit from an array of grant-funded programs including Studio in the School and Urban Advantage (which allows students to go on other fieldtrips to places like the American Museum of Natural History and the New York Hall of Science). The middle school has a partnership with Mt. Sinai Hospital, which offers kids the chance to meet doctors and medical students, and to dissect cow eyes and brains. The Carmel Hill Fund supports an online reading program and pays for some middle school students to attend summer programs at Vassar, Yale, and Princeton.

One downside is the school's limited space. Some teachers and staff work out of former storage areas and work with small groups of students in the hallways.

Students may participate in a wide range of after-school activities, including Chess in the Schools. Middle school sports include basketball, flag football, dance, yoga, volleyball, and soccer. Students in grades 4–8 may also participate in the Jesse Owens Track and Field Program, and a karate program is open to students and the community.

The school typically has room for children who live outside the attendance zone and even outside the district. (Laura Zingmond)

PS 37: River East

**508 East 120th Street
New York, NY 10035
(212) 348-2208**
www.rivereastelementary.org

PK

Who gets in: District 4 priority, but out-of-district kids admitted too
Grade levels: PK–5   **Reading scores:** ***
Enrollment: 203   **Math scores:** **
Low-income: 83%   **Ethnicity:** 2%W 45%B 51%H 0%A 2%O

River East is a tiny school with a progressive bent and a warm sense of community. Teachers encourage children to explore their interests and be independent; parents are invited to weekly schoolwide assemblies and get regular updates on their children's progress. The school offers a nice range of activities, such as ceramics, swimming, dance, violin, and computer coding.

Founded in 1982 and modeled after Central Park East I, River East remains true to its roots. Test prep is minimal and teachers weave lots of hands-on activities into lessons. At the same time, students are taught and expected to master foundation skills. For instance, teachers send home weekly, personalized updates for each child in their class, identifying a specific skill the child needs to work on as well as suggestions for how the family can help at home.

Mike Panetta became principal in 2016 after 5 years as assistant principal. "He's fantastic," said former principal Rob Catlin, who left the school in 2016 for an administrative job in the DOE.

Class size is low in all grades, and many classes have two teachers. Attendance and chronic absenteeism hover around the citywide average and are a challenge, because many students travel from outside of District 4, from the Bronx and West Harlem. To ensure struggling students don't fall through the cracks, each staff member, including Panetta, mentors a child who needs some extra attention—whether it's because of an academic problem or personal strife at home.

River East, which shares a building with PS 206, is a block from the East River. Despite a long walk to the subway, the school draws students from far away. (Laura Zingmond)

PS 125

425 West 123rd Street
New York, NY 10027
(212) 666-6400
www.ralphbuncheschool.org

PK

Who gets in: kids in zone, plus out-of-zone kids
Grade levels: PK–5   **Reading scores:** ***
Enrollment: 230   **Math scores:** ****
Low-income: 79%   **Ethnicity:** 7%W 44%B 42%H 6%A 2%O

A tiny school with a sweet atmosphere, PS 125 shows how a multiracial group of parents can work together to improve their neighborhood school—even in a district with few good options.

"I remember parents would get together in the park and talk about 'Where do we go?'" said Tomoi Zeimer, whose child now attends PS 125. "Either it's a super-expensive private school or a really low-rated public school. We thought, 'Is there a way that we can go into a school and make it better?'"

PS 125 has long had a popular Pre-K, but many parents left for kindergarten. That's partly because the upper grades had a traditional approach to education, not the play-based or child-centered approach that many parents said they wanted. "There were so many parents looking for a progressive choice, but one didn't exist in the district," said Daiyu Suzuki, father of two PS 125 pupils.

Parents lobbied the principal and superintendent to adopt a less scripted approach to teaching. The principal, Reginald Higgins, agreed, and enlisted Julie Zuckerman, the principal of Castle Bridge School in Washington Heights, to serve as a mentor. Higgins worked with Borough of Manhattan Community College to help revise the curriculum and coach teachers.

Higgins plans to introduce the progressive techniques one grade at a time, beginning with the youngest children. His plan seems to be working: On our visit, the lower grades had excellent teachers, engaged kids, and beautifully equipped classrooms, and the upper-grade teachers seemed excited by the prospect of change. Enrollment is increasing after a long decline.

Attendance is well below average and test scores have room for improvement. But our visits convinced us the school is moving in the right direction. "We haven't seen a final product yet," said Suzuki. "We're a community in the making." (Clara Hemphill and Mahalia Watson)

Harlem Village Academy West Charter Elementary School
74 West 124th Street
Manhattan, NY 10027
(646) 812-9700
www.harlemvillageacademies.org

Who gets in: lottery, with District 5 preference
Grade levels: K-4   **Reading scores:** ★★
Enrollment: 500   **Math scores:** ★★★★
Low-income: 79%   **Ethnicity:** 1%W 80%B 18%H 0%A 1%O

A promising new school, Harlem Village Academy West Charter Elementary School has sunny classrooms, an imaginative curriculum, and teachers who get the support they need to hone their craft.

Opened with a kindergarten in 2012, the school is one of five charter schools in the network known as Harlem Village Academies.

Although the original Harlem Village Academy once stressed strict discipline and a back-to-basics curriculum, the network has more recently embraced a progressive philosophy designed to foster independence. Children may pick the books they want to read, decide the activities they want to pursue during "choice time," and chat quietly with other children about their work—sometimes sitting on beanbags rather than desk chairs.

Deborah Kenney, the founder of the network, hopes to offer poor and working-class children of Harlem the same opportunities that rich children have. In an op-ed in the *Washington Post* she said upper-income schools typically focus on "active play," while low-income schools typically have regimented systems of rewards and punishment with little opportunity for students to talk.

The network has hired Shelley Harwayne, the founding principal of Manhattan New School (MNS) on the Upper East Side and a number of former MNS teachers to work with Harlem Village Academy West Elementary School staff. The elementary school principal, Kevin Tallat-Kelpsa, is also a former MNS teacher. New teachers have a chance to observe classes of seasoned teachers, and the staff has plenty of time to plan lessons together.

Like all new schools, the elementary school is a work in progress. On our visit, most children were fully engaged, but a few had trouble focusing. Still, the school offers a fine alternative to both the "no-excuses" charter schools and the mostly low-performing district schools that make up Harlem's District 5. (Clara Hemphill)

PS 517: Teachers College Community School

PK

168 Morningside Avenue
New York, NY 10027
(212) 316-8080
www.tc.columbia.edu/communityschool

Who gets in: lottery, with preference for Districts 5 and 6
Grade levels: PK–5   **Reading scores:** ***
Enrollment: 266   **Math scores:** **
Low-income: 46%   **Ethnicity:** 20%W 39%B 28%H 6%A 7%O

Teachers College Community School, opened in 2011, has attracted a multiracial group of parents hungry for an alternative to West Harlem's mostly low-performing schools. The school has an engaged parent body that includes both professional and working-class families. Whatever the school's struggles—and there are many—these parents are committed to making the school successful.

Founded as a partnership between Teachers College at Columbia University and the city DOE, Teachers College Community School (TCCS) is finding its way after a tough spell that included the death of the founding principal, a testing scandal, significant teacher turnover, and several dozen parents' withdrawing their children. While some parents are confident the school is moving in the right direction, others complain that neither Teachers College nor the DOE district office has offered adequate support during a difficult time.

The school has a few seasoned master teachers—and some who are still learning their craft. On our visit we saw some classes with lively projects and engaged kids. But others had drill-and-kill lessons we associate with the most rigid charter schools.

Nancy Streim, Teachers College associate vice president for community partnerships, said in a telephone interview that the university is "100% committed" to providing support to TCCS, including staff developers and graduate students who run the school's music, art, and science programs. She said staff developers are "working with the newer teachers," including some who previously taught at charter schools, to train them in the Teachers College methods.

Michelle Verdiner, named principal in fall 2015, has her work cut out for her, but if she manages to restore the trust of parents battered by the turmoil of the past years, this could be a school to watch. (Clara Hemphill)

Neighborhood Charter School of Harlem
132 West 124th Street
Manhattan, NY 10027
(646) 701-7117
www.ncsharlem.org

Who gets in: lottery, with preference for Districts 5 and 6
Grade levels: K–8   **Reading scores:** *****
Enrollment: 313   **Math scores:** *****
Low-income: 80%   **Ethnicity:** 3%W 55%B 40%H 1%A 1%O

Little is left to chance in this structured, tidy school: Books in baskets all face in the same direction, just like the children, who sit with straight backs, hands folded, and all eyes on the teacher, a practice called "tracking." "Scholars" wear uniforms and walk through hallways in boy and girl lines. Academics start early and the day is long.

Yet it doesn't feel overly rigid: Kindergartners move in and out of groups, and 2–3 times a week spend time in a spacious "learning lab" with blocks, standing easels, puppets, costumes, and toy "stores." In class, they work with math manipulatives like snap cubes, shapes, and fraction tiles.

Students at Neighborhood Charter School share their classrooms with turtles, fish, hermit crabs, a bunny, and potted plants. They study science daily. First-graders learn to type. Fourth-graders study 10 novels in depth, as a class, in addition to books they choose. Fourth-to-eighth-graders study Spanish 5 days a week.

Scholars receive points, stickers, extra gym, or other rewards for following routines. The language and structure seem a little stilted at times, but it seems to work—we watched a rebellious kindergartner roll his eyes, sigh, yank out his chair, then quickly settle down to solve a math problem, merging into the quiet order around him.

"We believe in structure, and I'm unapologetic about that," said Principal Brett Gallini.

Neighborhood Charter has made it a priority to serve children with special needs, including children on the autism spectrum, in team-taught classes.

The school offers tours from January to March. There are typically 1,000 applicants for 60 kindergarten seats. They fill empty seats that open up in all grades. (Lydie Raschka)

PS 318: Thurgood Marshall Academy
282 West 151st Street
New York, NY 10039
(212) 368-8731
www.tmals.org

Who gets in: District 5 priority; some kids start in 1st grade
Grade levels: K–5   **Reading scores:** ***
Enrollment: 219   **Math scores:** ***
Low-income: 85%   **Ethnicity:** 1%W 79%B 14%H 3%A 4%O

At Thurgood Marshall Academy, students wear crisp white shirts and red ties and raise their hands respectfully to speak in class.

A grandmother of two chose it over TAG (Talented and Gifted) Young Scholars because she told us it was exceptionally nurturing of the "whole child," particularly "black and Latino kids."

The 15 or so staff members wear several hats—the nurse sings opera to the kids, the secretary doubles as the step-team coach. Children are in school until 5:30 p.m., allowing them time for sports, drumming, dance, and more, which helps balance the serious academics that start in kindergarten. Kids meditate, and track their emotions with "mood meters." Children visit lots of museums and study dance, violin, and jazz.

The school was opened in 2005 in collaboration with the Abyssinian Development Corporation, the housing and social service arm of Harlem's biggest church, Abyssinian Baptist Church.

Principal Dawn Brooks DeCosta won a Cahn Fellowship in 2015, a reflection of her strong leadership. An educator for more than 23 years, she has watched the rise of middle-class parents in Harlem, and she and her staff hope to learn from PS 125, where parents have demanded more progressive practices such as hands-on "centers" in kindergarten. She wants to ensure her teachers have the tools to reach faster learners, too: "We've had such a focus on the struggler," she said. "We also need to focus on the advanced."

A few downsides: The old building has only two bathrooms on the third floor, with one stall in each. There is no gymnasium, but kids play in a small yard or in the cafeteria. Some children miss many days of school because of long commutes or for health reasons such as asthma.

Applications for grades 1 to 5 may be picked up at the school. There are twice as many seats in 1st-grade slots as in kindergarten, a boon to families set adrift from area charter schools. (Lydie Raschka)

PS 513: Castle Bridge School

560 West 169th Street
New York, NY 10032
(212) 740-4701
www.friendsofcastlebridge.org

PK

Who gets in: District 6 priority, set aside for low-income families
Grade levels: PK–5   **Reading scores:** NA
Enrollment: 193   **Math scores:** NA
Low-income: 59%   **Ethnicity:** 21%W 11%B 64%H 2%A 2%O

Castle Bridge is a nurturing place where kids explore, construct, sew, make snacks, take care of class pets, ice skate, and swim. The school is patterned after Central Park East I in East Harlem. Children are encouraged to read books they choose themselves and to speak as much as they listen.

The entire school offers dual-language instruction: In the lower grades, teachers spend half the day speaking English to their students and half speaking Spanish. In the older grades, teachers alternate Spanish and English days. The goal is to teach children to read, write, and speak fluently in both languages.

Classes combine two grades; kids stay with the same teacher, in the same classroom, for two years. Instead of report cards, teachers write multiple-page "narratives" for each child twice a year.

Children make decisions about what they want to study to an unusual degree. During a daily "project time," they choose from a menu that may include blocks, construction, or dress-up in the younger grades. Two children from each class take turns preparing snacks in the kitchen during this time, such as pancakes, or asparagus with garlic butter.

Projects in grades 3–5 last longer and must be accompanied by a plan. Third- and 4th-graders made longhouses, baskets, and other artifacts for their Native American unit. Projects do not always follow a theme; 2nd- and 3rd-graders interested in fashion bought fabric and made clothing for a spring show.

Project time is not a free-for-all by any means. Teachers watch carefully and invite a child to try an unexplored area of the room if they feel he or she would benefit. A kindergartner new to the block area persistently and unsuccessfully tried to stand skinny blocks on end to support a building. The teacher wanted her to practice, she said, because block-building can build a foundation for success in math in the older grades.

Principal Julie Zuckerman, formerly principal of Central Park East I, believes playtime is crucial to learning. She even participates in daily gym class, acting as both referee and playmate as her kids let off steam and run around. She keeps five warm coats in her office in case anyone needs one for daily outdoor recess in the winter.

Pre-K children nap after lunch with optional teddy bears, and even kindergartners and 1st-graders get to enjoy some downtime, during which some fall asleep, a rare respite in today's push-down academic culture.

Children practice public speaking during weekly "recitals," to which families are invited. They may sing a song, recite a poem, or tell a story. It helps the kids get to know one another better and learn to speak up, said Zuckerman.

Parent involvement is strong. Families join students in a weekly schoolwide sing-along, for which the principal plays guitar. They are invited to accompany kids on their weekly ice-skating sessions in Central Park.

Zuckerman said the school is very popular with middle-class families. Yet she is just as pleased when local, working-class parents find it, such as the bus driver who returned to inquire about it for his child after driving students on a fieldtrip.

Opened in 2012, Castle Bridge shares space with PS 128 Audubon, close to the 168th Street A, C, and 1 subway stop and across the street from New York–Presbyterian Hospital.

Children with disabilities are included in all school activities. Starting in kindergarten, every classroom has two teachers, at least one of whom is certified to teach special education or English as a new language.

Tours are held in the evening to avoid disrupting children as they work, except for families from local Head Start programs, who are invited to tour during the school day. English-dominant kids are not accepted after 1st grade. The school was one of several across the city selected to pilot admissions policies aimed at maintaining economic diversity. Beginning in 2016, Castle Bridge reserves a portion of its seats for students from low-income families. (Lydie Raschka)

PS 103: Dos Puentes

185 Wadsworth Avenue
New York, NY 10033
(212) 781-1803
www.dospuentespa.org

Who gets in: kids in zone, some others off wait list
Grade levels: K–5   **Reading scores:** NA
Enrollment: 203   **Math scores:** NA
Low-income: NA   **Ethnicity:** 17%W 2%B 81%H 0%A 0%O

Experienced leadership, a carefully crafted curriculum, and a cohesive staff that's fully bilingual in English and Spanish make Dos Puentes one of the most promising new schools to open in recent years. Dedicated to teaching children to read, write, and speak fluently in both languages, the administration and staff have fostered an unusual degree of parent involvement from both Spanish- and English-speaking parents.

Founding principal Victoria Hunt, who received her doctorate in bilingual education from Teachers College, taught for many years in the dual-language programs at PS 165 and PS 75, where she was also assistant principal. What distinguishes Dos Puentes from those schools is that the whole school is dual-language, while those schools have just one dual-language class.

The school is firmly in the progressive camp. There's time for play, with dress-up corners and toy kitchens in kindergarten. Children are encouraged to explore their own interests, to read books they choose themselves, and to speak as much as they listen. "If the teacher is the only one talking, they aren't going to learn the language," says Hunt. All children, even as they grow older, have "choice time," a time when they may choose to read, write or draw, to play with blocks or Legos, or to explore science projects.

Fieldtrips enhance children's experiences. Educators from the Bronx Zoo work with Dos Puentes teachers to create a science curriculum that includes activities not only at the zoo but also at outdoor spaces near the school.

Opened in 2013, Dos Puentes shares an old but well-kept building with PS 132. Halls are covered with children's work. Each grade has two general education classes and one ICT class (a class with two teachers and a mix of children with special needs and those in general education). Each class has an intern college student from City College or Teachers College. While the school has no track record—it only had grades K–2 at the time of our visit—it seems to be off to a terrific start.

Families (including the preschool brothers and sisters of children enrolled at Dos Puentes) are invited to sit in on classrooms for a little while every other Friday. The language of instruction alternates each day, and the day of our visit, all instruction was in Spanish. Dozens of parents came to work on projects with their children: Younger children were constructing gingerbread houses, while older ones interviewed their parents for essays about their family histories. Classroom visits were followed by a chat with Hunt, who welcomed and introduced a family who had just enrolled their children that day, having arrived from the Dominican Republic. Hunt then shared the schools' goals for the coming year.

The meeting with the principal was held in Spanish, with translators on hand for English speakers—a sign of the school's commitment to ensuring Spanish doesn't get short shrift and that Spanish-speaking parents feel welcome. One of the goals for the year was to decrease tardiness but, rather than criticizing parents for bringing children to school late, Hunt invited parents to converse with one another, then to share aloud their tips for getting children to school on time. Both Spanish- and English-speaking parents offered suggestions—such as insisting on an early bedtime, laying out school uniforms the night before, or planning to leave the house 15 minutes early.

The school offers team-taught classes as well as SETSS (special education teacher support services), occupational therapy, speech counseling, and physical therapy. A full-time reading specialist works with small groups of children.

Parents who live in the attendance zone may choose either PS 132, which has a traditional English-only curriculum, or Dos Puentes. In the school's first years, some 40% of Dos Puentes students came from outside the attendance zone. (Clara Hemphill)

PS 187

**349 Cabrini Boulevard
New York, NY 10040
(212) 927-8218**
www.187hudsoncliffs.org

Who gets in: kids in zone
Grade levels: K–8   **Reading scores:** * * * *
Enrollment: 802   **Math scores:** * * * *
Low-income: 50%   **Ethnicity:** 34%W 3%B 58%H 2%A 3%O

PS 187 has a wholesome, Norman Rockwell feel to it. It's a traditional school in a quiet, family-oriented neighborhood a short walk from beautiful Fort Tryon Park, the home of the Cloisters.

Cynthia Chory has been the school's principal since September 2006. A former teacher and assistant principal at the school, Chory grew up in the neighborhood, where she too attended PS 187 through the 8th grade. Roughly 20% of the teachers on staff are former PS 187 students, and many teachers have a long tenure there.

In the lower grades, we saw cheerfully decorated classrooms and a lot of attention to foundation skills. We saw kindergarten students working on their writing of upper- and lowercase letters. In another class, they were discussing the difference between a long and short "U" sound.

Students in all grades read and write a lot, and there's explicit instruction in grammar. Seventh-grade students were taking a pop quiz on complex sentences on the day of our visit, answering questions such as: What is an independent clause? What is the punctuation rule if the dependent clause comes first?

The school is orderly and values respect when it comes to behavior. The elementary students have quiet lunches with music playing, so they focus on eating (there is a nice salad bar) rather than talking, which allows them more time for outdoor play. Students enjoy the large, open play yard at recess, and there is a small climbing structure for the youngest children.

The school hasn't been able to accommodate Pre-K classes in several years, and class sizes can run as high as 32.

Every year some graduates move on to specialized and selective high schools such as Bronx Science, LaGuardia, and Beacon; some graduates also attend Catholic and private high schools on scholarships. (Laura Zingmond)

PS 178

12-18 Ellwood Street
New York, NY 10040
(212) 569-0327
sites.google.com/site/ps178elementary

Who gets in: kids in zone
Grade levels: K–5   **Reading scores:** ****
Enrollment: 304   **Math scores:** ****
Low-income: 77%   **Ethnicity:** 12%W 2%B 84%H 1%A 1%O

When you step into the light-filled atrium at PS 178 you are met with friendly greetings from parents, a security guard, and the largely bilingual staff. This small school excels at mixing children of all abilities and giving each the attention he or she needs. "We've always been a school of inclusion," said Principal Deirdre Budd, a Bank Street graduate who founded the school based on principles of innovative teaching in the areas of reading and writing from Teachers College.

PS 178 weaves three programs together in a remarkably cohesive way. In the dual-language program, children alternate between English-only and Spanish-only classrooms. The school also has an ASD Nest program in District 6 for high-functioning autistic children who are mainstreamed in small classes. And then there are classes that mix a variety of children with special needs with general education students.

Children get used to the special tools that abound in classrooms, like the ball chair, designed to help a wiggly child sit still. Academic abilities span many levels in one room. Because class size is small and there are many adults—we counted up to four in some rooms—teachers manage this range thoughtfully, and they send letters home so parents know how to help out, too.

Adaptations for children with special needs have occasionally been adopted by the whole school in ways that seem beneficial. Movement and music, initially a tool to help children with disabilities start the day, is now a 5-minute aerobic workout for all, with music piped in over the loudspeaker. Schedules and signs include both words and pictures so kids have more than one way to understand.

Opened as a school serving grades K–2, PS 178 has expanded to serve grades K–5. Call the school for information about tours. (Lydie Raschka)

PS 314: Muscota New School
4862 Broadway
New York, NY 10034
(212) 544-0614
www.muscotanewschool.org

Who gets in: District 6 lottery
Grade levels: K–5 **Reading scores:** ✻✻✻✻✻
Enrollment: 270 **Math scores:** ✻✻✻✻
Low-income: 33% **Ethnicity:** 42%W 3%B 46%H 4%A 5%O

Founded by a group of parents and teachers in 1993, Muscota New School offers a cheerful learning environment with an emphasis on the arts. Parents are involved to an unusual degree: On our visit, we saw parents lead a visual arts class, work with children in a drama class, and read to students.

Children learn what it means to be a member of a community. Teachers use morning meetings, closing circle, and schoolwide meetings to discuss how to solve conflicts and create shared expectations. In September, each class spends 6 weeks outlining its hopes and dreams for the year. Kids help create their own rules and come up with concrete ways to take responsibility for their actions.

Fieldtrips augment the four social studies units children study each year. Second-graders study transportation and visit the New York Museum of Transportation. Fourth-graders visit Ellis Island during their immigration unit. "They go out into the real world for authentic experiences," says Camille Wallin, principal since 2010.

All students participate in dance, music, visual arts, and drama, with performance opportunities in each. The school has partnerships with Carnegie Hall and the NYC Student Shakespeare Festival.

Under Wallin's leadership, the school has boosted its test scores while retaining the qualities it has long been known for: creative projects, a progressive philosophy, and focus on social and emotional development. This small school has two classes for every grade.

The school is housed in a four-story brick building, which it shares with Amistad Dual Language School (profiled next). Space is tight, and classrooms feel small and cramped. Parents are encouraged to tour. (Mahalia Watson)

PS 311: Amistad Dual Language School
4862 Broadway
New York, NY 10034
(212) 544-8021
www.amistadschool.org

Who gets in: District 6 lottery
Grade levels: K–8   **Reading scores:** ***
Enrollment: 431   **Math scores:** **
Low-income: 78%   **Ethnicity:** 5%W 1%B 91%H 2%A 0%O

Amistad Dual Language School has a warm sense of community and a commitment to making children fluent speakers and readers of both Spanish and English. Children seem happy and relaxed as they work together on engaging classroom projects. The curriculum is filled with music, dance, and visual and theater arts.

Class size is capped at 25, and there are at least two adults in every classroom. All teachers are bilingual. Kindergartners are taught 3 full days in Spanish and 2 in English. By 3rd grade, students spend 2 full weeks learning in Spanish, before alternating to English for the next 2 weeks. Reading instruction follows the "whole language" approach, which encourages students to recognize whole words and focus on the meaning of what they read and write, rather than decoding letters and sounds.

The PTA organizes events such as family movie night, field day, performances, and a large carnival. During our visit a group of parents were on hand to chaperone a fieldtrip, and a grandparent taught an ESL class to other parents in the school's large parent lounge. The school shares a rather cramped building with Muscota New School.

Amistad is not without its challenges. Test scores are below average. The city's new enrollment system admits students by lottery, making it difficult for the administration to control the level of language proficiency of incoming students. As a result, the kindergarten class has recently skewed to more English-dominant speakers, while the goal is to have an even mix of English and Spanish speakers. "One of the biggest strengths of language acquisition is that kids learn from each other side-by-side, but if everyone speaking English it's difficult to learn Spanish," said Principal Zoraida Hernandez.

About 300 children apply for 30 seats in kindergarten. (Mahalia Watson)

PS 278

421 West 219th Street
New York, NY 10034
(917) 521-2060
www.psms278.org

Who gets in: kids in zone, wait lists
Grade levels: K–8   **Reading scores:** ****
Enrollment: 533   **Math scores:** ****
Low-income: 65%   **Ethnicity:** 17%W 3%B 78%H 2%A 1%O

PS 278 has a gentle, caring atmosphere and an emphasis on traditional manners and values—in some ways reminiscent of the parochial schools Principal Lillian Reyes attended as a child. There's a focus on basic skills such as handwriting, phonics, and the conventions of grammar. Children wear uniforms, and some of the classrooms have desks in rows.

This high-performing school, founded in 2004, has become increasingly popular, not only with Spanish-speaking families who have long lived in the neighborhood, but also with newcomers.

Reyes, who became principal in 2015, says the policy on uniforms "levels the playing field" between well-off and working-class children. The culture of the school encourages children to get along with one another. "There's no place for hate," she says. "Everyone values everyone else."

Children take trips around the city: the Holocaust Museum, the Hall of Science, or dance performances at the 92nd Street Y. Middle-school students may attend Broadway shows.

For reading, the school has adopted ReadyGen for grades K–5 and the Scholastic Codex for grades 6–8—both scripted programs recommended by the state when the Common Core learning standards were introduced.

Once a week, a schoolwide enrichment program offers children a chance to mingle and be creative. On one of our visits, we saw students create backgrounds for a puppet show, practice a song for a musical, and build Eiffel towers out of clay.

All teachers in grades 2 through 6 have been trained in the Salvadori method, a hands-on method of teaching children about architecture using math and science. One year, students visited monuments before building monuments of their own related to their study of the Bill of Rights. Another year, it was skyscrapers.

Parents may tour in the fall. (Clara Hemphill)

Bronx
Schools

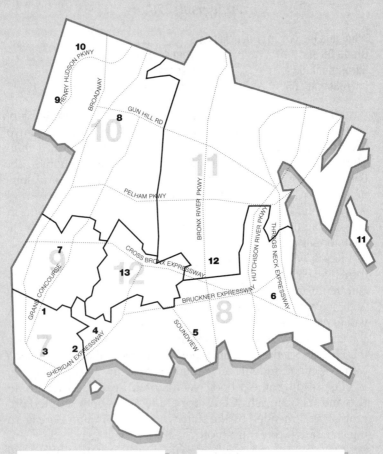

District 7
1 Concourse Village School
2 Heketi Charter School
3 Mott Haven Academy Charter School

District 8
4 Girls Prep Charter School of the Bronx
5 PS 69, Journey Prep
6 PS 304

District 9
7 Mount Eden Children's Academy

District 10
8 AmPark, PS 344
9 PS 24
10 PS 81

District 11
11 PS 175
12 Linden Tree Elementary School, PS 567

District 12
13 Samara Community School

THE BRONX

From the leafy, almost suburban neighborhood of Riverdale to the seaside community of City Island, the Bronx is filled with surprises. The quality of schools, alas, is uneven. But we found a few gems, even in tough neighborhoods; some promising schools in changing neighborhoods; and some solid, traditional schools in stable neighborhoods.

Most schools in the Bronx face enormous challenges. High rates of chronic absenteeism, whether caused by illnesses such as asthma or bouts of homelessness, make it difficult even for effective teachers to get traction with a constantly changing roster of children. On the positive side, some principals manage to offer children a high-quality education despite the challenges. Some new schools, including charters, have opened in recent years, and others have managed heroic turnarounds. With a lot of research and a little bit of luck you may be able to find a good spot for your child. There are more good options than there were even a few years ago.

Listed here are a handful of good neighborhood schools, a few charter schools, and other schools that accept children from a whole district or the whole borough. Charter schools have proliferated in the Bronx, and range in philosophy from the "no excuses" schools, with very strict discipline and a back-to-basics approach, to the progressive schools, with plenty of hands-on activities, fieldtrips, and time for play. Our favorites are included here. See also our section on charter schools in the introduction.

Unlike Manhattan, Brooklyn, or Queens, the Bronx does not have a school for the gifted. However, children who score extremely high on a gifted and talented exam are eligible for so-called citywide gifted programs in the other boroughs. Several of the Bronx districts offer their own gifted programs. In 2016 the city added gifted classes, beginning in 3rd grade, at Concourse Village School in District 7.

District 7: South Bronx

The South Bronx has long been one of the poorest areas in the city, but it has good subway connections to Manhattan, a vibrant shopping district, and brownstones that are being renovated. The District 7 Community Education Council eliminated school attendance zones in 2012; all parents must apply for their children to attend kindergarten. The district office is at 501 Courtlandt Ave., Rm 102, (718) 742-6500.

Our favorite prekindergarten programs are at **Concourse Village Elementary School** (profiled here) and **PS 157** at 757 Cauldwell Avenue, Bronx, NY 10456, (718) 292-5255. Longtime principal Ramon Duran trained at Bank Street College of Education and Teachers College. PS 157 opened a third Pre-K class in 2015 to meet growing demand.

Also recommended: **Girls Prep Bronx Charter**. Contact: (212) 346-6000 x108 or enroll@publicprep.org.

District 8: Soundview and Throgs Neck

District 8 is a racially mixed district that stretches from the edge of the South Bronx through the neighborhoods of Soundview and Throgs Neck. In recent years it has benefited from the strong leadership of Superintendent Karen Ames, formerly an administrator in the high-achieving District 2. The district office is at 1230 Zerega Ave, Bronx, NY 10462, tel: (718) 828-6653.

Prekindergarten seats are tight. Our favorites are at **PS 304** and **PS 69,** both profiled here. We also like **PS 36**, 1070 Castle Hill Ave., Bronx, NY 10472, (718) 822-5345, where children examine hermit crabs, trace letters in shaving cream, and try out Smart Boards and iPads.

Recommended for Pre-K: **Kiderific Nursery School**, 1621 Pilgrim Avenue, Bronx, NY 10461, (718) 518-7170, has respectful and nurturing teachers. Children enjoy computer time, sand and water tables, and a housekeeping area for imaginative play. After a visit, Schools Chancellor Carmen Fariña called the school "exciting, invigorating and joyful" and added, "The intensity of listening, the respect, is unusually high here."

District 9: Morrisania

District 9 is on the western edge of the South Bronx and is home to Yankee Stadium and much of the revitalization in the South Bronx. District office: 450 St. Paul Place, Bronx, NY 10456, (718) 828-6653.

Best bet for prekindergarten: Mount Eden's Children's Academy, although it has a long wait list and is hard to get into. Also consider **PS 204**, 1780 Dr. Martin Luther King Jr., Blvd., Bronx, NY 10453, (718) 960-9520. It has lots of music and science and a beautiful building.

Long a neighborhood favorite, **PS 170** at 1598 Townsend Ave., Bronx, NY 10452, (718) 583-0662, is a sweet school that serves children in K–2 and offers dance, swimming, puppetry, and theater arts.

District 10: Riverdale and Central Bronx

A gigantic district, District 10 includes the leafy neighborhood of Riverdale overlooking the Hudson River and the working-class neighborhoods of Fordham, Belmont, and Kingsbridge. In addition to zoned neighborhood schools, the district offers a number of gifted programs and several schools of choice. The district office is at 1 Fordham Plaza, Rm 835, Bronx, NY 10458, (718) 741-5852.

Pre-K expert Kym Vanderbilt, of Lehman College and the NY Early Childhood Professional Development Institute, recommends prekindergarten at a Roman Catholic school, **St. Dominic's Torch Annex** at St. Simon Stock Elementary School, 2195 Valentine Avenue, Bronx, NY, (917) 645-9117. She also enthusiastically recommends **Amalgamated Nursery School** at 3980 Orloff Avenue, Bronx, NY 10463, (718) 543-8688. **Marble Hill Nursery School** at 5470 Broadway, Bronx, NY (718) 562-7055 "remains strong," she says, and **AmPark** is "fabulous."

In the Fordham section, **PS 209**, at 313 East 183rd St., Bronx, NY 10458, (718) 364-0085, serves just 300 children in grades Pre-K–2. It's an orderly school with fun trips to places like the Bronx Zoo.

There are a couple of other options: **PS 7**, 3201 Kingsbridge Ave., Bronx, NY 10463, (718) 796-8695, which has high expectations, a principal who is well respected by staff, and a gifted program that admits children from across the district. The school, which serves more than 700 children in grades K–5, has seen its enrollment increase significantly in recent years, a sign of its growing popularity. The school was rated "well developed" on the city's Quality Review, the highest ranking. Teachers unanimously recommend the school to parents and say the principal, Frank Patterson, is an effective manager, according to school surveys. Part of a working-class community in the Kingsbridge section, PS 7 has mostly Latino children with a sprinkling of whites, blacks, and Asians.

In the Belmont section, **Bronx New School**, PS 51, at 695 East 182nd St., Bronx, NY 10457, (718) 733-0347, is a progressive school serving grades Pre-K–5. Founded in 1988 by a group of parents, Bronx New School is an informal place where kids happily immerse themselves in projects and call teachers by their first names. Ming Hong, former assistant principal, became principal in 2015. Admission is open to children from across District 10.

District 11: Northeast Bronx

District 11 in the northeast Bronx includes the high-rise towers of Co-op City; the tiny seaside community of City Island; the leafy neighborhoods of Eastchester and Pelham Parkway; and the low-rise apartments around Montefiore Medical Center. The district office is at 1250 Arnow Ave., Bronx, NY 10469, (718) 519-2620.

Prekindergarten offerings are scarce. **PS 160** in Co-Op City at 4140 Hutchinson River Parkway East, Bronx, NY, 10475, (718) 379-5951, and **PS 89** at 980 Mace Avenue, Bronx, NY 10469, (718) 653-0835, have satisfied parents and teachers, according to surveys.

Bronx Charter School for Excellence, 1960 Benedict Avenue, Bronx, NY 10462, (718) 828-7301, serves 650 children in grades K–8 in the Parkchester section. It's a high-performing school with a back-to-basics curriculum and strict discipline: Students move silently through hallways, their time at drinking fountains is measured in seconds, and stern voices can be heard inside classrooms admonishing kids who don't obey instructions. Both parents and teachers are enthusiastic and test scores are well above average. Admission is by lottery. There are far more applicants than seats.

District 12: Crotona Park

District 12 includes the area around the Bronx Zoo and the Brooklyn Botanic Garden. The district office is at 1434 Longfellow Ave., Bronx, NY 10459, (718) 328-2310.

For prekindergarten we like **Samara Community School**. In addition, **Little Scholars**, 850 Jennings Street, Bronx, NY 10459, (718) 887-2928, based on the methods developed in Reggio Emilia, Italy, is "truly wonderful," says Vanderbilt. Kids explore topics of interest through art, drama, music, and puppetry. Preference goes to low-income families.

A few blocks from the Bronx Zoo, **Phipps Neighborhoods**, 921 E. 180th Street, Bronx, NY 10460, (718) 364-2496, has a strong reputation and a long history of supporting children in one of the city's neediest neighborhoods. The organization "truly understands the neighborhoods they serve," said Chancellor Carmen Fariña after a visit. She praised teachers for handling even difficult situations well.

PS 359: Concourse Village School
750 Concourse Village West
Bronx, NY 10451
(718) 402-7503
www.cves.connectwithkids.com

Who gets in: kids who live in District 7
Grade levels: K–5
Enrollment: 303
Low-income: 95%

Reading scores: * * * * *
Math scores: * * * * *
Ethnicity: 3%W 33%B 62%H 0%A 2%O

In a few short years, Principal Alexa Sorden (who sends her own child to the school) has created a place with high expectations, clear routines, and a winning mix of high-quality art and academics. The school has made remarkable gains in a building that once struggled with poor discipline and low levels of academic achievement.

Children wear uniforms and recite the school creed in unison. They take tests at the beginning and end of each 7-week "unit of study" to measure progress and plan instruction. Despite a meticulous structure, academics do not feel stodgy or "safe." For example, in a lesson that mixed arts and math, children made collages incorporating the principles of perimeter and area.

Prekindergartners explore big themes such as transportation and connect it to everyday life. During a record snowfall, they added snowy roads and snowplows to their dramatic play, and made pretend snow in the classroom.

Kindergarten is more serious, with its focus on writing, reading, and numbers. Unlike Pre-K, there is little open-ended play or exploration. Kids annotate texts by circling key words and underlining words. Children in all grades practice 3–5 new sight words weekly—the "words of the week."

The school does a good job challenging top students while offering support to struggling students. Two bright 3rd-graders researched big cats on our visit, nimbly looking up leopards and tigers on their iPads. "White tigers are so rare!" said one. "It's a mutation." On Saturday, teachers meet with small groups of students who may be falling behind. Families head home to the Dominican Republic for holidays and often stay an extra week, a challenge for the attendance team. Sorden leads a parent workshop in which she leaves out key information, as a way to demonstrate how confusing it is to miss school. (Lydie Raschka)

Heketi Charter School
403 Concord Avenue
Bronx, NY 10454
(718) 260-6002
www.heketi.org

Who gets in: lottery, with District 7 preference
Grade levels: K–5   **Reading scores:** **
Enrollment: 247   **Math scores:** ***
Low-income: 85%   **Ethnicity:** 1%W 29%B 69%H 0%A 2%O

Heketi, meaning "one" in Taino (the language of the indigenous people of the Caribbean), is a lovely name for this cheerful school with a strong sense of unity. Teachers seek to instill pride in South Bronx children and to offer them social and emotional support along with hands-on lessons, projects, and fieldtrips. The ethnically diverse staff reflects the student population, and there is a Spanish-English dual-language program.

Children do not wear uniforms or walk silently in hallways or between activities, as they do at some charters; instead of using the term "scholars," teachers simply say "friends."

Every day, teachers lead lessons on caring about others, listening, and identifying feelings. They focus on virtues such as persistence and compassion. Aside from some novice teachers who have struggled with classroom management here (and sometimes been asked to leave), educators at Heketi find this to be an approach that works.

Kindergartens are stocked with books, math games, blocks, and dress-up areas. Test scores are above the citywide average in math but below average in English language arts, not too surprising given that more than one-third of students are new English speakers.

There was a hum of chatter as kids worked in groups or pairs. Teachers train the youngest kids to adjust to the give-and-take of working in groups. Stronger readers may join older students so they can participate in more complex conversations about books. Class size is small on purpose to reach all kids, and because many need extra help, said Principal Cynthia Rosario.

Heketi is open to all city students, but preference is given to those who speak a language other than English at home and who are residents of District 7. The school does not participate in the charter schools' common application. Applications can be found on the school website. (Lydie Raschka)

Mott Haven Academy Charter School

170 Brown Place
Bronx, NY 10454
(718) 292-7015
www.havenacademy.org

Who gets in: lottery, with priority to District 7 and kids in foster care
Grade levels: PK–5   **Reading scores:** ✳✳✳✳
Enrollment: 341   **Math scores:** ✳✳✳✳✳
Low-income: 95%   **Ethnicity:** 1%W 29%B 69%H 0%A 2%O

Mott Haven Academy is a haven for some of the neediest South Bronx children. One-third live in foster care; another third are in temporary housing or at risk of being removed from their homes. All benefit from on-site social services and teachers who encourage them to talk about feelings and to work through conflicts.

New York Foundling, one of the city's largest social service agencies, offers mental health, dental, and medical care (including asthma or pinkeye medication); family counseling; and speech and occupational therapy. There are three full-time social workers, four social-work interns, a full-time health counselor, and three academic behavior specialists.

The school day begins with a healthy breakfast at 7:45 a.m. and ends at 4 p.m. It is one of few New York City schools with its own chef. Children study science with their classroom teachers, focusing on nature and gardening.

In a relaxed yet carefully structured atmosphere, children thrive in one of two playful prekindergarten classes, where they pretend to run pet stores and nail salons and read books to cuddly stuffed bears. "I know our students love being here," said a Pre-K teacher. The staff is racially and ethnically diverse, and teachers use their own experiences to augment lessons. During an immigration lesson, for example, the director of the after-school program, who is Guyanese, told a group of 2nd-graders about sugarcane, a historic wooden church, and wedding rituals in his home country.

Principal Jessica Nauiokas has provided steady leadership since the school opened in 2008. Staff try to prevent upsetting transitions, in some instances finding a home for a child in the neighborhood so he doesn't have to change schools if his family moves. The bright, modern building is cramped but clean, with wooden floors, lots of windows, and interesting twisty hallways. The school plans to add middle-school grades. (Lydie Raschka)

Girls Prep Charter School of the Bronx

681 Kelly Street
Bronx, NY 10455
(718) 292-2113
www.girlsprepbronx.org

PK

Who gets in: lottery; priority to NYCHA residents, staff children, and District 8

Grade levels: PK–8   **Reading scores:** * * *
Enrollment: 727   **Math scores:** * * *
Low-income: 81%   **Ethnicity:** 1%W 33%B 64%H 0%A 2%O

In the life of a school, Girls Prep Bronx seems to have hit its stride. It offers lots of science, yoga, choir, and art. Teachers put thought, care, and training into their instruction rather than follow scripted lessons. Girls may now begin their schooling in one of three prekindergartens and continue through 8th grade. The best entry points are in Pre-K or kindergarten and again in 6th grade, when the middle school takes about 30 new students.

Founded in 2009, it is modeled on Girls Prep Lower East Side, the first all-girls charter in New York City. Girls Prep differs from no-nonsense charters like Success Academy and Bronx Classical by favoring more input from teachers and a more relaxed atmosphere.

Teachers look for a balance in kindergarten between academics and play. Many kindergartens in the city lack blocks and dress-up areas, but Girls Prep has block-building and girls go on fieldtrips; however, it introduces more writing and reading around these activities.

Children spend extra time in reading and writing lessons. Girls study phonics, vocabulary, and oral reading, but also enjoy fun-to-read books of their own choosing, sprawled on beanbag chairs. Fridays are reserved for handwriting and dictation. The elementary school uses CGI (cognitively guided instruction), a hands-on, problem-solving approach to math in which teachers pay attention to children's mathematical efforts and use them as a basis for instruction, rather than following scripted lessons.

Full-time math and literacy coaches help teachers choose a goal for math lessons or structure a reading lesson, the fine points of teaching that make a school not just safe and orderly but stimulating. Parts of 3rd grade and all of 4th and 5th grades are "departmentalized," like in middle school, where one teacher leads all the math lessons and another leads the language lessons.

On the day of our visit, the 5th-grade math teachers were at a workshop on fractions and decimals at Metamorphosis, a math-coaching center. Math scores are beginning to rise. "Reading scores outperform district schools but are still not where we want them to be," said Josie Carbone, who left her job as principal in 2016 to work for the Girls Prep network. She was replaced by Sharon Stephens, formerly principal of Madiba Prep Middle School in Brooklyn. Stephens grew up in Bedford-Stuyvesant and taught English at Benjamin Banneker High School.

The girls have an unusual four days a week of science with a trained science teacher. Kindergartners observe, draw, and write about trees they visit in the neighborhood. Second-graders study the water cycle and simple machines with hands-on experiments and work up to lab reports based on collected data in older grades. "Science is incredibly important for girls, and it's really difficult to make time for it in regular classrooms because of the preparation involved," said Carbone.

The school offers special education services in team-taught classes that mix children with special needs in general education classes.

The middle school is at 890 Cauldwell Avenue.

There are roughly 2,300 applications for 75 seats. Priority goes to siblings, New York City Housing Authority residents, and the offspring of teachers. (Lydie Raschka)

PS 69: Journey Prep
560 Thieriot Avenue
Bronx, NY 10473

PK

(718) 378-4736
www.ps69bronx.org

Who gets in: kids in zone
Grade levels: PK–5   **Reading scores:** ***
Enrollment: 622   **Math scores:** ****
Low-income: 86%   **Ethnicity:** 1%W 16%B 80%H 2%A 1%O

With its striking, sun-drenched library and flourishing vegetable garden, PS 69: Journey Prep is an inviting place. Teachers and the principal work hard to devise strategies to energize and engage students who live in one of the city's poorest neighborhoods.

At a time when many schools use scripted lesson plans, Principal Sheila Durant says she values spontaneity and leaves many decisions to her teachers, who pick and choose from various programs. Teachers work with two coaches—one in math and one in reading—and advise one another on what works in the classroom. In the lower grades, teachers can opt for aspects of the Reggio Emilia Approach, which seeks to harness children's curiosity to help them learn.

PS 69 developed a reputation for being a high-quality school in a tough neighborhood under the previous principal, Alan Cohen. Cohen retired in 2010, but the school's energy and commitment to its students has continued under Durant, who had been the assistant principal. It is a school where the custodian builds a bridge for students to use in science experiments and where two teachers spend an evening putting together an engaging video for the next day's class.

Writing is key, even for kindergartners. Students are expected to read independently by the end of kindergarten. Those who don't may be held back, although efforts are made to bring the child along without that. "If any child isn't learning, we need to do something different," Durant says. The school also provides extra math for high-performing students.

On the day we visited, PS 69 was marking National Kale Day. For 4th-graders, this involved a trip to the school's garden with the science teacher to record their observations of kale plants (and to discover how, when dried, the vegetable could be turned into tasty kale chips). Younger children read books about vegetables and wore silly kale hats. One class whipped up a batch of kale juice.

Durant strives to bring a range of experiences to children who might otherwise not have them. A chef comes in once a week to work with students. There is an archery program, and an etiquette class for 5th-graders culminates with a sit-down dinner in the library.

The school also has counselors and other staff to help students who may come from troubled homes. It offers peer mediation, where 5th-graders try to help students resolve conflicts. Students are repeatedly reminded to be kind to one another. "I want them to be smart but I also want them to be good citizens, good people," Durant said.

Along with the garden, the heart of the school is its vibrantly colored, well-equipped library, created with the help of a $2 million donation from the Robin Hood Foundation. But the school facility has limitations. While grades 2 through 5 are in the main building, kindergarten and 1st grade are located half a block away and Pre-K and kindergarten are in colorful trailers on school grounds. The school does not have a gym, so it has set up a fitness room.

PS 69 has team-teaching classes that mix general and special education students and two self-contained classes. Durant, a former special education teacher, says she tries to move children out of the self-contained classes, even if they require help from a paraprofessional in the more mainstream classrooms. (Gail Robinson)

PS 304

2750 Lafayette Avenue
Bronx, NY 10465

PK

(718) 822-5307

Who gets in: District 8 lottery
Grade levels: PK–5   **Reading scores:** *****
Enrollment: 519   **Math scores:** ****
Low-income: 73%   **Ethnicity:** 27%W 5%B 59%H 7%A 2%O

PS 304 in Throgs Neck has a long history of high achievement: experienced, passionate teachers and an administration that really understands how kids learn. All academic areas are strong—reading, writing, social studies, math, and science. At the same time, children have a chance to play and to build the social skills they need to be successful in both school and life.

Top students get the challenges they need while kids who are having trouble get plenty of extra help. Many classes have more than one adult—including teachers, student teachers, parents, and classroom aides—so children get individual attention. Children not only learn the written skills they need to master standardized tests; they also learn how to speak and write clearly—skills that are just as important but not as easy to measure.

Kindergarten classrooms have plenty of LEGOs, wooden blocks, trains, and dress-up corners where children may play together. "This is their time for discussion," said Assistant Principal Bonnie Boltax. "They need to speak to other students. You're not only sitting at a desk." Children go on science-related fieldtrips to the Bronx Zoo, the New York Botanical Garden, the New York Hall of Science, and the Gateway National Recreation Area in Jamaica Bay.

Longtime principal Joseph Nobile is popular with parents and staff and has an easy way with the children.

The administration doesn't go in for academic fads, but it does continuously adapt its curriculum and teaching techniques to take advantage of new books and approaches as they become available. Teachers at PS 304 understand that no single reading or math program can serve all children; rather, they carefully combine elements of various programs depending on what each child needs. The school became a full partner with Teachers College Reading and Writing Project in 2016.

Classroom teachers are responsible for reading, writing, and math, but specialists teach science and social studies two or three times a week. Only the lower grades get instruction in art. There is an after-school band. Every grade gets one period of music during the day, such as recorder for 3rd grade.

The building is shared with MS 101, a District 75 program for children with special needs. The principals get along well and share ideas.

The school offers team teaching and self-contained special education classes, as well as Special Education Teacher Support Services. Some students from the District 75 program attend PS 304 classes. The instruction we saw in a self-contained class was just as good as in general education classes, and children were fully engaged in the lesson.

Admission is limited to children who live in District 8, which covers the eastern Bronx. Preference is given first to siblings who attend PS 304 or MS 101, and then to students living in the surrounding neighborhood or those students zoned for PS 14, PS 71, and PS 72. There are about 200 children on the wait list. (Clara Hemphill)

Mount Eden Children's Academy

1501 Jerome Avenue
Bronx, NY 10452
PK   **(718) 294-8155**
www.meca555.org

Who gets in: District 9 lottery
Grade levels: PK–5   **Reading scores:** ***
Enrollment: 358   **Math scores:** ****
Low-income: 93%   **Ethnicity:** 1%W 22%B 78%H 0%A 0%O

Mount Eden Children's Academy, opened in 2012, has quickly become the most sought-after school in District 9. The modern red-brick building on Jerome Avenue stands in contrast to the scrappy auto repair shops under the elevated tracks of the number 4 subway line. The New Settlement Community Campus, which houses the school, features a dance studio, rooftop garden, and five-lane swimming pool.

Teachers and administrators greet kids outside in the morning. "From the moment my daughter entered Pre-K it's been a really amazing experience for me," said a mother of two. "I never feel shut out in any way. The principal is always around."

Principal Jessica Torres Maheia is a Bronx native. Formerly an elementary school teacher, assistant principal, and literacy coach, she and her staff worked with a literacy coach and consultant to write the language lessons used in the younger grades. She wanted the school to have four periods of science a week with a science teacher because, she said, it's hard for classroom teachers to fit it in and to "build the expertise needed for teaching science."

Children have math twice a day: First is the introduction and practice of a concept and second is practice incorporating "higher-order" mathematical thinking; for example, children may choose which strategy is best suited to solve a subtraction problem, or figure out how subtraction relates to addition. Children read four or five books, as a class, each year, in addition to books they choose. They also study phonics, grammar, and word study.

Classes are large, and children are divided into ability groups for reading lessons to make sure they get the help they need. Almost every classroom has two adults: the school hires assistants to work in larger classes and there are paraprofessionals who work one-on-one with students with disabilities.

Relations between students, principal, and staff are warm and genuine. The principal often checks in on students who struggle with behavior. These kids may take a break or eat a late breakfast if it helps them get through the day without a breakdown in behavior, she said.

We saw lots of play and activity in the younger grades. There are three prekindergartens in this still-growing school. Most children are able to move into one of the two kindergartens because class size in kindergarten is a little larger.

As for physical activity, there is a gymnasium, a pool, and outside play space. "It's been nice to have a pool," said a parent. On cold days, for recess, kids "stay inside and watch movies or go to the gym," the parent said.

The campus also houses the Comprehensive Model School Project, which serves grades 6–12. The two schools occupy a dedicated portion of the building that is managed independently from the community center.

Unlike most schools, which integrate special-needs children in regular classrooms, Mount Eden offers only small self-contained classrooms for kids with special needs. "Kids in general education can function in the big classrooms with counseling, physical therapy, occupational therapy, and/or speech services," Maheia said. "Others need a small setting." We saw a high achiever in a wheelchair in a general education room with an aide called a paraprofessional. Kids in the self-contained classrooms were lively, active, and interested.

There are far more applicants than seats available, and very few spots open in the upper grades. (Lydie Raschka)

PS 344: AmPark Neighborhood School

3961 Hillman Avenue
Bronx, NY 10463
(718) 548-3451
www.amparkneighborhoodschool.org

Who gets in: District 10 lottery, some out-of-district kids admitted
Grade levels: K–5   **Reading scores:** ****
Enrollment: 400   **Math scores:** ****
Low-income: 45%   **Ethnicity:** 20%W 13%B 60%H 5%A 2%O

On a quiet residential street, AmPark Neighborhood School is a lively, nurturing place known for its commitment to the environment, social consciousness, and the arts. The school wears its "progressive" label proudly, in the belief that children learn best by doing and engaging in issues that matter to them—like hatching and raising trout to release into the Hudson River or even advocating for a classroom democracy.

The school was started in 2006 as a joint effort between local parents and the Amalgamated Park Reservoir Cooperative Housing Project. AmPark is unzoned, and kids hail from all over the Bronx. The student body is racially integrated and includes children from middle-class families as well as those who qualify for free lunch.

Principal Christine McCourt Milton, a District 10 teacher and administrator for more than 20 years, took over in 2012 from founding principal Elizabeth Lopez Towey (who was also founder of the Ella Baker School). Like her predecessor, Milton believes firmly in a "whole-child" approach to education, nurturing a student's mind, body, and spirit. Children practice mindfulness every morning at breakfast and yoga every Monday, and teachers and students are on a first-name basis. "We wanted to create a feeling of family, but it never impacts respect," Milton said.

The lessons we saw were creative, and teachers seemed eager to think outside the box. In a science class, 4th-graders made their own comic strips about solids, liquids, and gases. As part of a study of ecosystems, children created imaginary animals with features that would help them thrive in either desert or Arctic habitats.

The level of writing and conversation we saw was very high. A 3rd-grade essay assignment focusing on social issues sparked a flurry of conversation and activity during our visit. One girl proudly shared her essay advocating for free college tuition. Two boys collaborated on a topic close to home: putting an end to littering in residential sections of the Bronx.

In the younger grades, play is key, and teachers take great pains to protect children's ability to explore sand tables, build with blocks, and act out stories—even in the testing age. "There are ways to meet [Common Core] expectations without making everyone sit and do the same thing all day long," Milton said.

In the school's first years, some teachers and parents called for more academic rigor. In response, the school has adopted Teachers College Reading and Writing Project and has shifted its math curriculum from the conceptually based Investigations program to the more skills-based Engage NY, which teachers supplement with math games and small-group center work, Milton said. The school has also hired a math coach. Fourth and 5th grades have departmentalized, meaning that teachers specialize in literacy/social studies or math/science, while students travel between classrooms for subjects.

The building, opened in 2011, is attached to neighborhood school PS/MS 95. It has brightly colored walls, large classrooms, a science lab, art room, a music room, and a library. There are full-time music and arts teachers and designated rooms for those subjects. A small side yard has a rock-climbing wall, a brand-new jungle gym, and cushioned flooring. Older kids do need more space to play, however, so teachers and kids walk one block to the spacious Van Cortlandt Park playground every day, weather permitting.

The school offers Integrated Co-Teaching (ICT) classes as needed and mixed-grade self-contained classes for children with special needs. The self-contained classes we saw were lively and warm, made up of a range of children, including many who were preparing to move to team-taught classes. There are two full-time teachers offering Special Education Teacher Support Services (SETSS) as well as speech, occupational, and physical therapies and counseling.

First priority in admissions goes to children living in the Van Cortlandt Village/Kingsbridge Community Heights area, then to others in District 10, then to others outside the district. About 250 families have applied for 50 kindergarten spots in recent years. (Aimee Sabo)

PS 24

660 West 236th Street
Bronx, NY 10463
(718) 796-8845
www.ps24school.org

Who gets in: kids in zone, plus those who pass gifted exam
Grade levels: K–5   **Reading scores:** ****
Enrollment: 1011   **Math scores:** ****
Low-income: 27%   **Ethnicity:** 40%W 6%B 42%H 9%A 4%O

PS 24 is housed in a pleasant, two-story red-brick building on a street lined with maple trees. Built in the 1950s, the building is spotless, with shiny floors and polished brass rails. It has an art studio, a well-equipped library, and a science room that even has a planetarium. Instrumental music is offered in all grades. Classrooms are large and sunny.

Long one of the highest-performing schools in the Bronx, PS 24 has suffered in recent years from significant overcrowding and squabbling between the administration and staff.

There has long been bad blood between some teachers and the administration. *The New York Post* had a field day when former Principal Donna Connelly apparently tossed teachers' desks on the street and was quoted as saying "It's the 21st century. You don't need desks!" Connelly, who replaced a principal forced out by teachers who accused him of religious proselytizing in 2009, was forced out herself in 2015.

Overcrowding has been particularly severe since 2015, when the school lost a lease on an annex that had housed 5th-graders and a lunchroom was converted into four classrooms.

The school made the news again in 2016 when a state assemblyman, Jeffrey Dinowitz, accused the PS 24 administration of contributing to overcrowding by allowing children from outside the school zone to enroll. Assistant Principal Manuele Verdi, meanwhile, filed a lawsuit accusing a Dinowitz staffer of reviewing kindergarten applications at the school with the goal of excluding low-income children and children of color.

These problems haven't diminished the school's popularity. The school has a district gifted and talented program, which is routinely filled to capacity. (Clara Hemphill)

PS 81

5550 Riverdale Avenue
Bronx, NY 10471
(718) 796-8965
www.ps81family.webs.com

Who gets in: kids in zone
Grade levels: K–5
Enrollment: 683
Low-income: 46%

Reading scores: * * * * *
Math scores: * * * * *
Ethnicity: 30%W 10%B 49%H 8%A 4%O

Housed in a stately 1925 Georgian building in the northern-most corner of Riverdale, PS 81 has a respectful, unified tone; well-structured lessons; and consistency throughout the building.

Safe, predictable routines seem particularly beneficial for calming anxious children. In a happy, well-run kindergarten class, for instance, a teacher put one such child in charge of starting the timer for reading time, and the child took on this role with pride and responsibility.

Fifth-graders serve as big brothers and sisters to younger students. When children stand to recite Shakespeare, some speak with Russian, Dominican, or Pakistani inflections, a fact this community celebrates. There are classes in dance, visual art, music, and drama.

PS 81's test scores indicate that roughly half the students meet or exceed state academic standards—a very respectable showing especially compared to other Bronx schools. Still, City Education Department evaluations of the school cite slightly below-average student progress compared to similar schools.

Principal Anna Kirrane was assistant principal at PS 81 for 9 years before taking over in October 2012. She arrives at 6:30 a.m. each day to be available to anyone with concerns, and takes time to greet parents who drop by. She meets every kindergarten family personally. Kirrane attended boarding school in Ireland as a girl, and is of Irish heritage. She urges all parents to "Share your rich heritage with your child."

After a year of getting to know children, teachers select 25 to 30 kindergartners for placement in the school's accelerated program, which begins in 1st grade. Students usually work a grade ahead and a child must keep up with the work to remain in these classes. (Lydie Raschka)

PS 175: City Island School
200 City Island Avenue
Bronx, NY 10464
(718) 885-1093

Who gets in: kids in zone, some out-of-zone kids
Grade levels: K–8   **Reading scores:** * * *
Enrollment: 327   **Math scores:** * * * *
Low-income: 37%   **Ethnicity:** 54%W 9%B 29%H 6%A 2%O

City Island, surrounded by Long Island Sound and connected to the mainland by a bridge, looks more like a New England fishing village than most people's idea of the Bronx. It has inlets filled with sailing boats, Victorian houses with big porches, summer beach bungalows that have been converted for year-round use, and one commercial street with seafood restaurants, sail-makers, and antique shops. It's the kind of place where lots of mothers stay home with their kids, where parents keep an eye on one another's children, and where kids can walk or ride their bikes to school.

PS 175 is a small K–8 school with steady leadership, small classes, and a cheery, close-knit environment. Most students who attend live on the island, but the school's reputation also draws some off-island Bronx residents who are willing to undertake the daily trek by car or bus.

Longtime principal Amy Lipson gets high marks from teachers based on their responses to the NYC School Survey Report. During her tenure she's put in place supports for teachers and students such as forgoing an assistant principal in order to hire full-time literacy and math coaches who work directly with teachers to develop and revise lessons. Lipson also brings in retired teachers to work with students who need extra help; she invites students who are having a hard time socially to play games with her during lunchtime.

Scheduling is designed to ease students into the middle-school experience. In grades K to 3, students stay with the same teacher all day—a typical elementary school format. In grades 4 to 6, students have two teachers, one for English and social studies, and the other for math and science. Seventh- and 8th-graders change classes for humanities, math, and science.

The school developed its own reading and writing curriculum. What you don't see in classes are lots of worksheets or textbooks. In the early grades, children learn to read by selecting appropriate books from the well-stocked classroom libraries. In the upper grades students learn from many sources, such as news articles, diaries, historical documents, and fiction. They also write a lot on a range of topics. In a kindergarten class we observed, the writing topic of the day was "my favorite thing to do in school." In 5th grade, students were comparing and contrasting Cinderella stories from different cultures.

We saw teachers tailoring assignments to students' skill levels. For instance, as part of their study of the Salem witch trials, 7th-graders were assigned one of two books: Advanced students tackled *The Crucible*, while others read *A Break with Charity*, a more manageable but still grade-appropriate historical novel. Students then worked together to stage a mock witch trial. In several science classes, students seemed to enjoy working together, whether it was experimenting with yeast to identify the presence of other chemicals (5th grade) or role-playing representatives from different countries—United States, Russia, China, and India—in a classwide debate on climate change (8th grade).

For math, lessons combine hands-on work to help students understand concepts, and a lot of practice and drilling to build computational fluency.

Qualified 8th-graders may take high-school-level coursework in Earth science and algebra.

Teaching artists from Bronx Arts Ensemble work with students in all grades; music and theater instruction for grades K to 3 are provided by the Lincoln Center Institute. Grades 3 to 8 have an after-school chorus. Middle-school students participate in overnight trips to places such as Greenkill Environmental Center, Philadelphia, Boston, and Washington, DC.

Students must leave the island for high school. Some graduates attend Catholic high schools, but many choose public high schools in Manhattan and the Bronx, such as High School of American Studies, Bronx Science, Beacon, Frank McCourt, Fashion Industries, TAPCO, and Pelham Lab.

There's typically no space in kindergarten for out-of-zone students, but some are admitted in the upper grades. (Laura Zingmond)

PS 567: Linden Tree Elementary School
1560 Purdy Street
Bronx, NY 10462

PK

(718) 239-7401
http://lindentreepta.weebly.com

Who gets in: kids in zone
Grade levels: PK–5
Enrollment: 272
Low-income: NA

Reading scores: NA
Math scores: NA
Ethnicity: 3%W 16%B 64%H 16%A 1%O

As snug and inviting as its name, Linden Tree Elementary, opened in 2012, has a winning mix of rigor, warmth, and discovery. Bright paper trees bloom along the corridor, kids deliver homemade scrambled eggs to the principal's office, and they visit Frizzle, a teacher's pet hen, whose fertilized eggs hatch in an incubator in the prekindergarten classroom. "Everything is steeped in science," said principal Lisa DeBonis, a former kindergarten teacher who trained at Teachers College, Columbia University.

Teachers use drama, stories, and trips to spark curiosity. "The muscles in a worm's stomach are very strong," said the Pre-K teacher as kids took turns squishing bits of apple and pebbles in a Ziploc bag to experience how a worm pulverizes its food. First-graders take trips to the boiler room, and 2nd-graders travel to Wave Hill to find inspiration for the school garden.

Parents describe the school as close-knit and supportive. "Our kids go to the playground together and have picnics and pool parties in the summertime," said a founding parent. Teachers make home visits in the summer to incoming Pre-K families. Every day new students arrive, including some from Yemen, escaping war, or from Vietnam to be with relatives. The school does a good job serving children with autism, dyslexia, and other special needs. For example, some teachers erect tents inside the classroom so autistic kids can find the isolation they may seek for work. A child dealing with aggression painted a Jackson Pollock–style mural to express his feelings. An adult took another child for a walk to let off steam, saying, with a nod, "He earned it."

The school shares a building with a middle school, JHS 127. More than 100 children applied for 18 Pre-K spots in 2016. (Lydie Raschka)

Samara Community School
1550 Vyse Avenue
Bronx, NY 10460
PK
(718) 860-5332
www.samaracommunityschool.org

Who gets in: kids in zone, some out-of-zone kids
Grade levels: PK–5   **Reading scores:** NA
Enrollment: 125   **Math scores:** NA
Low-income: 92%   **Ethnicity:** 1%W 22%B 78%H 0%A 0%O

Located in a rapidly changing neighborhood in the South Bronx, Samara Community School is a joyful, nurturing place where children learn about the environment on weekly nature walks and fieldtrips to cultural institutions. Long an industrial zone, the neighborhood has seen new housing construction and more parks in recent years. This dual-language school is designed to make children fluent in both Spanish and English.

Samara opened in 2014 with one Pre-K and two kindergarten classrooms. The school will expand by one grade each year until it serves Pre-K through 5th grade. Some lessons are built around a theme and based on children's interests. For example, children wanted to learn more about pigeons after teachers read a book about them. So, after trips to the zoo and the park, they studied what pigeons eat, counted and graphed pigeons, and created pigeon-themed art projects. "Our purpose is to provide children with vocabulary-building experiences even beyond the classroom," said Principal Danielle Derrig.

Derrig says the best way to learn a language is through song; children chant and sing letters and sounds in English and Spanish every day. "We sing in the mornings, we sing when we go swimming, and we sing on fieldtrips," she said.

Many students enter kindergarten without having attended Pre-K, so teachers work to build skills and enhance vocabulary in the early grades. Kids listen to books on tape and take books home to read and share with their families.

Prekindergartners learn through play, with the teacher alternating between English and Spanish. Starting in kindergarten, children have different teachers in different classrooms for English and Spanish. Samara shares a building with two other schools. In its first years, it had room for children from outside the zone. (Mahalia Watson)

Brooklyn Schools

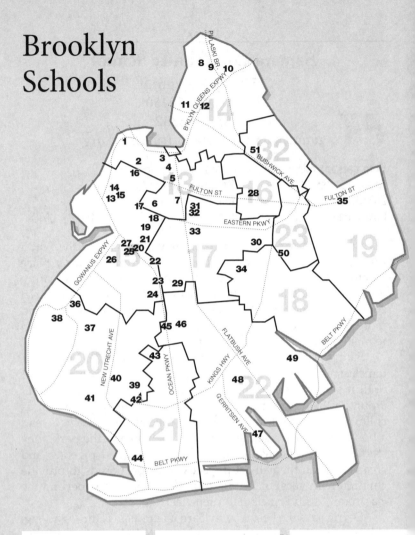

District 13
1 PS 8
2 Brooklyn Prospect Charter Elementary School
3 Community Roots Charter Elementary School
4 Academy of Arts & Letters
5 PS 11
6 PS/MS 282
7 PS 9

District 14
8 PS 31
9 PS 34
10 PS 110
11 PS 84
12 Brooklyn Arbor School, PS 414

District 15
13 Brooklyn New School
14 PS 29
15 PS 58
16 PS 261
17 The Children's School
18 PS 321

19 PS 39
20 PS 10
21 PS 107
22 PS 154
23 PS 130
24 PS 230
25 PS 295
26 PS 172
27 Hellenic Classical Charter School

District 16
28 PS 21

District 17
29 PS 249
30 PS 770, The New American Academy
31 PS 705
32 PS 316
33 PS 241

District 18
34 PS 235

District 19
35 PS/IS 89

District 20
36 PS 503
37 PS 69
38 PS 102
39 PS 247
40 PS 186
41 PS 748, Brooklyn School for Global Scholars
42 Brooklyn School of Inquiry

District 21
43 PS 121
44 PS 212

District 22
45 PS 134
46 PS 217
47 PS 277, Gerritsen Beach School
48 PS 222
49 PS 312

District 23
50 Riverdale Avenue Community School, PS 44

District 32
51 PS 376

BROOKLYN

From the elegant 19th-century brownstones of Brooklyn Heights to the public housing towers of Coney Island, the city's most populous borough has an extraordinary variety of places, people—and schools. Old-timers have long known about the borough's charms, but in recent years Brooklyn has become a destination for the young and the hip worldwide.

Gentrification has hit Brooklyn even harder than Manhattan—indeed, Brooklyn housing prices are sometimes even higher than Manhattan's. The arrival of newcomers has caused some friction as artists, musicians, lawyers, and journalists—including many whites—displace longtime working-class residents, including many African Americans. At the same time, the proliferation of charter schools has drawn the most motivated parents, particularly African Americans, away from the traditional public schools, leaving many of those schools with declining enrollments, shrinking budgets, and an increasingly high proportion of children with special needs.

The good news is that a pent-up demand for high-quality options is spurring parents of all races and ethnicities to work together to improve their neighborhood schools. Most promising is the work by an interracial group of Bedford-Stuyvesant parents who have decided they would rather support their zoned schools than enter a lottery to send their children halfway across the borough to a better-established alternative. This group, called the Bed-Stuy Parents Committee, has an active Facebook page and organizes regular get-togethers where parents can swap stories about what's going on and ideas about what to do about it. If you live in District 16, their blog is practically required reading; if you live outside the district, it may inspire you to start your own parents' group.

Like the schools in Manhattan and the Bronx, Brooklyn's schools vary a lot depending on their location. Two of Brooklyn's 12 school districts have consistently strong elementary and middle schools: District 15, which includes Park Slope, Carroll Gardens, Sunset Park, Red Hook, and Windsor Terrace, and District 20, which includes Bay Ridge, Bensonhurst, and Dyker Heights. School enrollments have increased dramatically in these two districts in the past decade, and many schools are overcrowded.

Other options include gifted programs, dual-language programs (with instruction in two languages), unzoned schools (which admit children from a whole district or even several districts), and charter schools. Children who score in the 97th percentile on the gifted and talented exam administered to 4-year-olds in January or February may be considered at Brooklyn School of Inquiry in Gravesend or NEST+m, a citywide gifted program on Manhattan's Lower East Side. Each district has its own gifted programs as well, with somewhat lower cutoffs.

Charter schools offer an alternative to traditional zoned neighborhood schools. We offer profiles of our favorite "mom-and-pop" charters here. In addition, charter networks, including KippNYC, Success Academy, Uncommon Schools, Achievement First, and Ascend, have opened dozens of schools in Brooklyn. For information about KippNYC and Success Academy, see the introduction to this book.

Uncommon Schools (www.uncommonschools.org) operates 22 schools in Brooklyn, mostly in Bedford-Stuyvesant and Brownsville. The network, which serves children in kindergarten through grade 12, includes an all-boys school and an all-girls school. These intense, academically demanding schools have high expectations and a traditional approach to academics, with an extra-long school day and school year. Children have no recess and little downtime; the strict discipline codes and rules and routines, such as a tightly structured lunch period, may not work for all students. The schools' test scores are well above average for the city. Admission is by lottery.

Achievement First (www.achievementfirst.org) operates 17 schools in Brooklyn, mostly in Crown Heights, Brownsville, and East New York. Some parents appreciate the sense of order and back-to-basics curriculum, but others complain that the network's "no excuses" discipline is too strict. Teaching techniques are very traditional.

Ascend Charter Schools (www.ascendlearning.org), launched in 2008, operates nine schools in Brooklyn. It originally used a "no excuses" approach, but teachers discovered that strict discipline and scripted lessons did not prepare children well for the independent work required in college. The network now strives to teach "empathy, collaborative problem-solving, and self-control," Ascend CEO Steven F. Wilson wrote in the *Hechinger Report*. "We don't counsel out challenging students, we fill all vacated seats through grade 9, and we proudly serve students with special needs and limited English proficiency."

As an example of the curriculum, Wilson wrote: "Fifth-graders study the timeless myth of Icarus and Daedalus, examine in the school's gallery Brueghel's exquisite painting of Icarus's fall into the sea, and undertake a close reading of Auden's famous 1938 poem, 'Musée des Beaux Arts,' which was inspired by Brueghel's painting." Admission is by lottery.

District 13: Fort Greene and Downtown Brooklyn

District 13 includes the stately homes of Brooklyn Heights; the newly constructed high-rises of DUMBO; and a mix of pleasant brownstones and housing projects in Bedford-Stuyvesant, Fort Greene, and Clinton Hill. The traditional neighborhood schools are of uneven quality, but there are bright spots. The district is also home to several progressive, racially integrated charter schools, two of which, Community Roots and Brooklyn Prospect, are profiled here.

The district has been embroiled in debates over race and class. With a few noteworthy exceptions, the zoned neighborhood schools are low-performing and serve predominantly black and Latino children, most of whom are from poor or working-class families. Middle-class children, many of them white or Asian, are clustered in a handful of more successful schools of choice, including unzoned schools and the progressive charters. As the district gentrifies, enrollment at most of the traditional neighborhood schools shrinks. The District 13 Community Education Council, charged with drawing up zoning lines, has taken some steps to counter this trend by changing the attendance zones and applying for magnet grants so under-enrolled schools can attract children from outside the zone. A few schools that serve predominantly middle-class students have set aside seats for low-income families as a way to foster economic integration. At three schools, in particular, these efforts may soon bear fruit—and the schools are good options for prekindergarten: PS 54, PS 133, and PS 307.

Anthony Pirro, a dynamic science specialist who became principal in 2015, is bringing fresh ideas to **PS 54**, 195 Sandford Street, in Bedford-Stuyvesant, (718) 834-6752. The school, serving grades Pre-K to 5, has a magnet grant with the theme of environmental science, technology, and community wellness. Children make water filters, observe fish and turtles in tanks in their classroom, and plant trees near the school. They go on trips with the Hudson River Sloop *Clearwater* and to the Alley Pond Environmental Center and Brooklyn Botanic Garden, where they learn to compost. Another plus: a Spanish-English dual-language program.

The population the school draws from has been shrinking as Orthodox Jewish families, many of whom choose to send their children to private yeshivas, move into the borough. Pirro taught in nearby District 16, then was assistant principal for 8 years at PS 503 in District 20. His goal is to bring to PS 54 some of the same diversity and vibrant arts that are a hallmark in that school.

When its new $66 million building opened at 610 Baltic Street in Park Slope in 2013, **PS 133**, (718) 398-5320, www.ps133brooklyn. org, adopted an updated admissions policy designed to foster socioeconomic and ethnic integration, including dual-language programs in French and Spanish.

Instead of drawing students from its old District 13 zone, in 2013 the school began accepting Pre-K and kindergarten students from across Districts 13 and 15. One-third of seats are earmarked for students from District 13 and two-thirds for District 15. Thirty-five percent of all kindergarten seats are reserved for English language learners and children who qualify for free or reduced-price lunch.

The expansion and move to the new building brought in families from different neighborhoods and increased parental involvement. PTA meetings are packed and there are many committees, the parent coordinator said. Fundraising has increased substantially. For example, parents pay for Studio in a School, enabling PS 133 to offer art instruction to all grades.

PS 307, 209 York Street, in Vinegar Hill, (718) 834-4748, www. ps307.org, provides hands-on activities in science and math in grades Pre-K to 5, thanks to a $1.8 million magnet grant. In 2016, the Community Education Council (CEC) voted to expand the PS 307 zone to ease overcrowding at PS 8. After the rezoning, 56 students within the zone enrolled in the school's kindergarten, up from just 18 the year before.

The rezoning was controversial: Some PS 307 parents worried that a community institution that has long nurtured black and Latino families would be "taken over" by outsiders from the gentrifying neighborhood of DUMBO. For their part, some DUMBO families worried that the school's low test scores meant their children might not be challenged. But Principal Stephanie Carroll said the increase in enrollment means the school will now be able to properly fund some of its specialized programs. The small school boasts two well-stocked music classrooms. Each has keyboards where all students learn some keyboarding, and 5th-graders learn guitar. The school has a rock band and a jazz group, which are part of an after-school program.

Another possibility for Pre-K, in downtown Brooklyn: **Hanover Place**, 15 Hanover Place, Brooklyn, NY 11201, (347) 916-0333, www.hanoverplacechildcare.com. It's an early childhood center with an excellent reputation for attracting a wide variety of families, said a parent who spoke highly of its caring staff. Full-day, year-round care is available.

Also recommended: **Helen Owen Carey Child Development Center**, 71 Lincoln Place, Brooklyn, NY 11217, (718) 638-4100, www.psnparents.org. Across the street from PS 282 in Park Slope, this child care center offers year-round full-day child care for younger children as well as prekindergarten for 4-year-olds.

A **Pre-K center** with 72 seats opened in 2016 in the 19 Dock Street building.

The district office is 335 Park Place, Room 116, Brooklyn, NY 11238, (718) 636-3284.

District 14: Williamsburg and Greenpoint

Just over the Williamsburg Bridge from Manhattan, District 14 serves the neighborhoods of Greenpoint and Williamsburg. Polish-American Greenpoint still has a small-town, Old World feel to it, with butchers and pastry shops, a church with a steeple, row houses, and neighbors who know one another. Some parts of Williamsburg, with large Hispanic and Orthodox Jewish populations, have the feel of villages from another time and place.

Both Greenpoint and Williamburg have trendy boutiques and restaurants catering to artsy types who were priced out of Manhattan. Both neighborhoods have large manufacturing zones, and artists have built lofts in old industrial buildings. Most of the schools offer prekindergarten. A few to watch:

PS 319, 360 Keap Street, (718) 388-1588, www.ps319williamsburg.org, is an oddity in the city's public school system, serving only prekindergarten through 1st-grade children. This tiny Williamsburg school has a Spanish and English dual-language program in addition to regular classes.

Staff members stay for years, even decades, which may account for the relaxed, close-knit atmosphere. "It's a small environment," said a parent. "I like the friendliness, the teachers." Teachers do not shy away from hugging a child if they feel it's beneficial. We watched a veteran teacher comfort a child who'd had a very rough start in September. "He responds to caring," she said, patting him on the back as he relaxed into her embrace.

PS 17, 208 N. 5th Street, (718) 387-2929, launched the city's first German-English dual-language program in 2016.

PS 147, Isaac Remsen School, 325 Bushwick Avenue, (718) 497-0326, www.ps147.org, received a federal grant to create the first Japanese-English dual-language program in New York City in September 2015. The school, serving grades Pre-K to 5, has dynamic leadership, strong community partnerships, and some of the most spacious, beautiful Pre-K classrooms that we have seen in this district. There are double-sized classrooms with a sand table, water table, block and dramatic play areas, and even a quiet area where kids can listen to music on headphones. Test scores are strong, and parents and teachers are thrilled to be a part of this safe and growing community where kids take many fieldtrips a year, eat healthy food, and learn to play guitar.

Black, white, Latino, and Asian parents arrive at **PS 132, The Conselyea School,** 320 Manhattan Avenue, (718) 599-7301, www.ps132ny.com, by bus, on foot, and via bike, greeting staff in English or Spanish. Solid wooden doors, neat-as-a-pin classrooms, and separate boy and girl lines in the hallway speak to the past, while a purple cafeteria, classroom libraries, bright murals, and live Komodo dragons reflect the school's progressive bent— and are a draw for the neighborhood's artsy newcomers. This classic red-brick school building hugs a large playground, designed with student input that includes a running track, climbing equipment, basketball hoops, and an "art zone."

The neighborhood includes Polish, Puerto Rican, Dominican, South Asian, and North African populations. The school serves children in grades Pre-K to 5 and has a gifted program as well as special education services.

Also consider **PS 196**, 207 Bushwick Avenue, Brooklyn, NY 11206, (718) 497-0139, www.ps196k.org, a warm and friendly school where children get lots of individual attention. It's a tiny school with fewer than 350 children in grades Pre-K to 5. Teachers and parents give high marks to Principal Janine Santaromita-Colon, a Williamsburg native.

The school has a Spanish-English dual-language program; it is adopting the Teachers College writing program; teachers weave in group work and social–emotional skills development into lessons. There are swim lessons for 2nd-graders, health and wellness instruction, early morning literacy and enrichment activities such as robotics, sports, and games, and free after-school and summer activities. The school received a large grant to convert a classroom into a technology and media center. The school offers Pre-K, including a rare 2-year program that serves qualifying 3- and 4-year-olds with special needs.

The district office is at 215 Heyward St., Brooklyn, NY 11206, (718) 302-7600.

District 15:
Park Slope, Carroll Gardens, and Sunset Park

District 15, a large district that includes the beautifully restored turn-of-the-twentieth-century brownstones of Park Slope and the run-down housing projects of Red Hook, has some of the best and most creative schools in Brooklyn. Nearly every school is a gem, and what's more, the middle schools are mostly high-quality as well. Enrollments at District 15 schools have boomed in recent years, and some schools have wait lists during the spring enrollment season, even for children who live in their attendance zone. (Luckily, these wait lists mostly clear by September—if you can stand the uncertainty.)

Because of the popularity of schools in District 15, most do not have room for prekindergarten. Nonetheless, we found a number of good bets.

PS 118, the Maurice Sendak Community School, 211 Eighth Street, (718) 840-5660, www.mauricesendakcommunityschool.org, is a new, small school designed to ease overcrowding in nearby PS 321 and PS 107. Principal Elizabeth Garraway has adopted many of the successful practices of PS 321, her previous school; PS 321 Principal Liz Phillips serves as Garraway's mentor. Spanish is infused into academics and play, and children hear it spoken throughout the day—not just in twice-weekly Spanish periods. At least one of the two teachers in every classroom is bilingual. The school, opened in 2013, is adding a grade every year until it serves Pre-K to 5. (Another option is the Pre-K center inside PS 118, Maurice Sendak Community School, called The Little Brooklyn Pre-K Center.)

In Red Hook, **PS 15, The Patrick F. Daly School,** 71 Sullivan Street, (718) 330-9280, has a Spanish-English dual-language program that begins in Pre-K, a rarity for this age group, a dedicated after-school for Pre-K and kindergarten, and a program for accelerated students. All three were initiated after feedback from parents, according to Principal Peggy Wyns-Madison. The school, which serves grades Pre-K to 5, has two inviting playgrounds, collegial and stable staff, and a welcoming attitude to all students. It has particularly vibrant math and special education programs.

In Windsor Terrace, our reviewers loved the progressive, discovery-based Pre-K **K-280 School of Journeys** at the Bishop Ford Complex, 500 19th Street, Brooklyn, NY 11215, (718) 369-4450, www.ps10.org/k-280. Opened in 2014 and overseen by Laura Scott, the well-regarded principal of nearby PS 10, Bishop Ford has the capacity to serve 500 children. Every day, 4-year-olds don their outerwear, pick up their journals, and venture into the world. On these "journeys," as their daily walks and fieldtrips are called, they make snow angels, examine icicles, observe seasonal changes in trees, or ponder construction signs that say "danger." The school draws inspiration from the Reggio Emilia Approach (named after a region in Italy), which encourages kids to ask questions, explore, and express themselves through art, drama, music, writing, and in other ways.

The center's staff developer, Marlene Ross, has an infectious, persuasive passion for this approach, which calls upon teachers to listen carefully to children's questions, tap into their curiosities, and then follow up with questions and activities that will deepen and extend learning. A few downsides: The sturdy old building has old gray high-school lockers and no in-class bathrooms for young children, who have to walk a long way with an adult to use them.

The Pre-K program at **PS 38**, 450 Pacific Street, (718) 330-9305, www.pacificschool.org, is in a spacious building with large, airy classrooms and entire rooms for blocks and LEGO play. PS 38, which serves grades Pre-K to 5 and also has a gifted program, is one of the few schools in District 15 that sometimes have room for children outside the zone and even outside the district. Parents give mixed reviews of the principal, Yolanda Ramirez, but say the school has many talented teachers.

PS 32, Samuel Mills Sprole, 317 Hoyt Street, (718) 222-6400, www.ps32.org, has long been known for its excellent special education services, particularly its ASD Nest program for children on the autism spectrum. It serves grades Pre-K to 5 and has a gifted program. Denise Watson-Adin, former assistant principal at popular PS 10, became principal in 2015. Enrollment at PS 32 has grown by more than 150 students in the past decade, a sign of the school's popularity in both the neighborhood and the district as a whole. A possible downside: The school has gifted classes and team-taught classes that mix children with special needs and general education pupils, but no general education classes.

Also recommended: **Hanson Place Child Development Center,** at 55 Hanson Place, Brooklyn, NY 11217, (718) 237 4303, www.

hansonplaceinc.com, offers year-round, full-day care for younger children as well as prekindergarten for 4-year-olds.

The District 15 office is at 131 Livingstone St., Brooklyn, NY 11201, (718) 935-4317.

District 16: Bedford-Stuyvesant

District 16, in Bedford-Stuyvesant, is a small district with shrinking enrollments. Most of the zoned schools are low-performing, but parent activism by the Bed-Stuy Parents Committee and the leadership of an energetic and optimistic superintendent, Rahesha Amon-Harris, offer rays of hope. If you live in the district, we strongly recommend you join the parents' Facebook group.

The Bed-Stuy parents have picked **PS 309,** 794 Monroe Street, Brooklyn, NY 11221, (718) 574-2381, www.ps309brooklyn.org, as a promising place to send their children and to work together to improve. Our reviewers liked the large prekindergarten classrooms, which have their own bathrooms and open out to a small, inviting play yard for Pre-K and kindergarten only. Prekindergarten has lots of space for dress-up and make-believe. We saw children play at a water table and at a sand table. Some staff members send their own children here, and some graduates of the school have come back to teach. With active parents, a friendly tone, and a forward-looking administration, PS 309 is a school to watch.

PS 628, Brooklyn Brownstone School, 272 MacDonough Street, (718) 573-2307, www.brooklynbrownstoneschool.com, with grades Pre-K to 5, has high test scores, strict rules of conduct, and a no-nonsense atmosphere. Some parents rave about the high expectations and serious and supportive atmosphere; others say the homework (one 1st-grader spent 2 hours a night on it) is oppressive and the school's narrow focus on test results is unhealthy.

Worth watching: **Brighter Choice Community School** at 280 Hart Street, (718) 574-2378, is merging with another school in the same building, Young Scholars Academy. Spanish music and movement classes start in Pre-K, and a Spanish-English dual-language immersion program has been launched. "I think this is the school that is going to set the pace for other schools," PTA President Victor Iroh told the DNAinfo website.

The district office is at 1010 Lafayette Ave., Brooklyn, NY 11221, (718) 574-2834.

District 17: Crown Heights and East Flatbush

District 17, which encompasses Crown Heights and East Flatbush, is a rapidly changing area of Brooklyn with new bars, coffee shops, and restaurants. It has a mix of large houses on tree-lined streets and more modest apartment buildings. As housing prices rise, longtime residents, including African American and Caribbean families, are moving out, and newcomers, including more white families, are moving in. Many Orthodox Jews in the neighborhood send their children to private yeshivas.

The schools, too, are in a state of flux. Superintendent Clarence Ellis gets high marks from principals, and the district's future seems promising.

For prekindergarten, consider **PS 375**, 46 McKeever Place, Brooklyn, NY 11225 (718) 693-6655. Schwanna Ellman, principal since 2014, is invigorating a school that has suffered from low academic achievement and declining enrollment. Ellman was an intern principal at high-performing PS 69 in the Bronx, and she hopes to adopt some of that school's teaching techniques, such as the Reggio Emilia Approach to early childhood education that encourages exploration and discovery. Prekindergartners may take part in a dual-language class in which they study in Spanish one day and English the next.

Also for prekindergarten, consider **New Bridges Elementary School**, 1025 Eastern Parkway, (718) 363-8200, www.ps532newbridges.org, opened in 2013. Founding Principal Kevyn Bowles, who studied theater as an undergraduate at Georgetown University and has a master's degree from Columbia University's Teachers College, says he wants to develop "the whole child" by engaging families, integrating arts in the curriculum, and developing children's social and emotional skills. The school offers music, drama, dance, and visual arts along with regular academic classes.

The school combines a joyful atmosphere with the structure, routines, and high expectations for which good charter schools are known. On our visit, we saw children who were happy to be there and a mother who called the school "amazing" and "a breath of fresh air in the community."

Also of note: A long-standing community institution and source of neighborhood pride, **PS 189,** 1100 East New York Avenue, (718) 756-0210, www.189bilc.org, is a successful dual-language school with a culture of discipline, tradition, and warmth. Instruction in Spanish and Creole attracts many students born overseas. The school serves grades K to 8. The school has high expectations and an open relationship with parents, according to the city's Quality Review. Longtime Principal Berthe Faustin describes her philosophy as "structured but not rigid." Mostly traditional classrooms feature desks in tidy rows and instructors up front.

The district office is at 1224 Park Place, Brooklyn, NY 11213, (718) 221-4372.

District 18: Canarsie and Flatbush

We haven't had much luck gathering information about schools in District 18: neither the district superintendent nor the school principals have responded to our repeated requests. PS 235 has a good reputation, and we offer a profile here based on telephone interviews with parents and staff.

For pre-K, we recommend **PS 208**, 4801 Avenue D, Brooklyn, NY 11203, (718) 629-1670, an old-fashioned school with a forward-looking principal, Nakoley Renville. It serves a mostly Caribbean-American community. The district office is at 1106 E. 95th St., Room 109, Brooklyn, NY 11236, (718) 566-6008.

District 19: East New York and Cypress Hills

A small district with mostly low-performing schools, District 19 serves East New York and Cypress Hills, neighborhoods with a mix of African Americans and new immigrants from the Dominican Republic, Guyana, Bangladesh, Ecuador, and Trinidad and Tobago.

One of the most respected Head Start programs in Brooklyn, **Cypress Hills Child Care Center**, 108 Pine St., Brooklyn, NY 11208, (718) 647-5005, has a joyful environment and teachers who love their work and stay for years. The school is accredited by the National Association for the Education of Young Children—a sign of high quality. On our visit, we saw happy children building with blocks, splashing at a water table, or singing and dancing as their teachers encouraged them to talk about their projects. In this way, children build their vocabulary and develop a curiosity about the world around them. Low-income families have preference in admission; there is a long waiting list.

The district office is at 557 Pennsylvania Ave., Room 205, (718) 240-2700.

District 20: Bay Ridge and Borough Park

You can't go wrong in District 20, in the southwest corner of Brooklyn near the Verrazano Bridge. People move to this well-run district just so they can enroll their children in the local schools; as a result the schools are seriously overcrowded. See www.inside-schools.org for schools not included here.

The district includes the pleasant residential neighborhoods of Bensonhurst, Borough Park, Bay Ridge, and parts of Sunset Park. Single-family houses with small yards are popular, and there are two- and three-family houses and apartment buildings as well. The area once had large Italian and Norwegian populations, and now includes many immigrants from the Middle East, Asia, the former Soviet Union, China, and Central America. There is a large Chinatown on 8th Avenue in Sunset Park. Former PS 176 parent Stanley Ng said that the success is in part the result of private test-prep among Asian immigrants or, as he calls it, "'the secret sauce' we have here in D20."

The district superintendent, Karina Costantino, wins praise from parents and principals. "Her door is open to every parent, every teacher, every child, every paraprofessional," said Cornelia Sichenze, principal of PS 102 in Bay Ridge. Costantino encourages schools to take a close look at special education if they want to improve schoolwide: "Whatever helps kids with special needs and kids learning English helps all kids," Sichenze says.

The district has a number of dual-language programs, including a Russian-English program at **PS 200,** 1940 Benson Avenue, (718) 236-5466, www.ps200.org, in Bath Beach, and an Arabic-English program at **PS 30, the Mary White Ovington School,** at 7002 Fourth Avenue, (718) 491-8440, www.psis30pta.org in Bay Ridge.

A new Italian-English dual-language program begins in pre-kindergarten at **PS 112** at 7115 15th Avenue, (718) 232-0685, in Bensonhurst.

District 20 has the largest Pre-K program in the city, with nine Pre-K centers serving hundreds of children. Call the office of Early Childhood Education at 718-759-3908 for information.

Also recommended for Pre-K: **Happy Dragon of New York, Inc.,** 5805 Seventh Avenue, Brooklyn, NY 11220, (718) 439-8816. The center, which serves mostly children who speak Cantonese or Mandarin, does a "good job of hiring teachers" and teaches children to be independent, schools chancellor Carmen Fariña said after visiting. For example, children serve themselves lunch instead of having teachers serve them.

The district office is at 415 89th St., Brooklyn, NY 11209, (718) 759-4908.

District 21: Sheepshead Bay and Coney Island

District 21 encompasses a stretch of southern Brooklyn from Bensonhurst and Midwood to Coney Island and Sheepshead Bay. A long sandy beach, the New York Aquarium, a boardwalk stretching from Coney Island to Brighton Beach, and, of course, the amusement park at Coney Island make these Brooklyn neighborhoods popular tourist destinations.

Bensonhurst, once largely Italian-American, now has a sizable Asian population. Midwood is increasingly an Orthodox Jewish community. Coney Island is predominantly African American, and Sheepshead Bay has many new immigrant communities, particularly families from Russia. A number of schools serve children in kindergarten through 8th grade—an attraction to parents who want their children to avoid the city's sometimes-chaotic middle schools. The district elementary schools are generally well run.

One prekindergarten pick in southern Brooklyn's District 21 is diverse, safe PS 212, which sometimes has extra space. Also recommended:

PS 216, Arturo Toscanini School, 350 Avenue X, (718) 645-2862, which serves kids from Coney Island, Gravesend, and Brighton Beach, houses the first "Edible School Yard" in Brooklyn, featuring an outdoor garden, a greenhouse, and a kitchen classroom outfitted with tables, sink, stovetop, and an oven, where harvested goods are made into fresh edibles.

PS 95, 345 Van Sicklen Street, in Gravesend, (718) 449-5050, www.ps95bk.org, has been "transformed" under an able principal, Janet Ndzibah, according to district superintendent Isabel DiMola.

PS 199, 1100 Elm Avenue in Midwood, (718) 339-1422, received the city's highest rating of "well developed" on all five sections of its Quality Review. It has an ASD Nest program for children on the autism spectrum.

The district office is at 1401 Emmons Avenue, Brooklyn, NY 11236, (718) 648-0209.

District 22: Ditmas Park and Mill Basin

District 22 is a huge district that stretches from Ditmas Park, with its grand Victorian houses, in central Brooklyn, to the suburban-feeling Mill Basin, where 10-year-olds may walk safely by themselves to the bowling alley, to the sleepy seaside community of Bergen Beach on Jamaica Bay, far from the end of the subway lines. There is some reasonably priced housing in the district and some of the schools are nicely integrated, with a good mix of children of different races and ethnic groups. The district office is at 5619 Flatlands Ave., Brooklyn, NY 11234, (718) 968-6115.

Schools vary greatly from one end of the district to another in District 22. The northernmost schools tend to fill with zoned students. Several schools have expanded in the southern areas and you can try getting on a wait list. Most of the zoned neighborhood schools have prekindergarten.

A high-performing school in an out-of-the-way location, **PS 195, Manhattan Beach School**, 131 Irwin Street, Brooklyn, NY 11235, (718) 648-9102, serves 450 children in grades Pre-K to 5, including a district G&T class. Housed in a charming building topped by a cupola in a well-to-do neighborhood overlooking Sheepshead Bay, PS 195 feels like a school in a small town. The city's Quality Review called the school "well developed," the highest rating.

District 23: Ocean Hill and Brownsville

One of the smallest in the city, District 23 serves Ocean Hill, Brownsville, and parts of East New York, and includes some of the city's poorest neighborhoods. Single-family homes are interspersed with old brownstones, apartment buildings, large public housing projects, and homeless shelters.

The District 23 Community Education Council voted in 2013 to do away with zoned schools, allowing parents to apply to any school in the district. However, parents complained that there were few viable choices. Riverdale Avenue Community School, profiled here, shows promise.

There is a lovely Pre-K program at **FirstStep NYC** (www.sco.org/firststepnyc), housed in the PS 41 building at 411 Thatford Avenue, (929) 234-6870. It is the site of the city's first education program for babies and toddlers, serving children as young as 6 weeks. Teachers are unusually attentive and the classrooms are well supplied with books and toys. FirstStep is a model for early childhood education citywide.

The district office is at 1655 St. Marks Ave, Room 125, Brooklyn, NY 11233, (718) 240-3677.

District 32: Bushwick

Serving Bushwick and the northern tip of Bedford-Stuyvesant, District 32 has long been one of the lowest-performing districts in the city. The neighborhood long suffered from a poor reputation as a crime-ridden and neglected area. In recent years, artists priced out of neighboring Williamsburg have moved into Bushwick, pushing real estate prices up, and longtime residents out.

Best bet for Pre-K: **Bushwick United Head Start,** (718) 443-0134, www.bushwickunited.org, has a number of locations. Its website is filled with photos of children poring over subway maps, out on fieldtrips, singing to guitar music, and building with blocks and Lincoln Logs, among other hands-on activities. This program has accreditation from the National Association for the Education of Young Children (NAEYC), a worldwide organization that works toward ensuring high standards in early childhood education programs.

The district office is at 797 Bushwick Ave., Brooklyn, NY 11221, (718) 574-1100.

PS 8

37 Hicks Street
Brooklyn, NY 11201
(718) 834-6740
www.ps8brooklyn.org

Who gets in: kids in zone
Grade levels: K–8   **Reading scores:** * * * * *
Enrollment: 924   **Math scores:** * * * * *
Low-income: 14%   **Ethnicity:** 61%W 14%B 12%H 6%A 7%O

Tucked away in a quiet corner of Brooklyn Heights, PS/IS 8 is an increasingly popular school with an imaginative curriculum, a focus on social studies, and a parent body that raises nearly $800,000 a year. It hums along like a well-oiled machine.

The school's enrollment ballooned from 369 pupils in 2006 to 924 in 2016, partly as a result of the explosion of new high-rise buildings along the Brooklyn waterfront near the Brooklyn Bridge, partly because it added grades 6–8.

After several years of having a long wait list for zoned kindergartners, there was a contentious rezoning battle in the 2015–2016 school year, and a chunk of the PS 8 zone in DUMBO and Vinegar Hill is now zoned for PS 307.

That change means that PS 8 may be able to take back some classroom space for music and dance rooms, although longtime Principal Seth Phillips thinks the reprieve from overcrowding may be brief, with so much new construction continuing in the area. "They keep putting up big buildings," he said.

Thematic social studies units are at the heart of the curriculum. Second-graders create a "Box City" of restaurants, banks, a hotel, and even an Irish pub from cardboard boxes—and learn about community, business, and architecture in the process. Each "citizen" is given $100 per day to "live" in the city and must figure out how to pay taxes.

Fifth-graders learn to argue for a cause they believe in as part of Project Citizen, a program designed to encourage participation in government. One group was avidly seeking more physical education time—PS 8 students get only one gym period per week—citing research that shows too many children are obese.

Disappointed by the city math curriculum, the PTA purchased the "Bridges in Mathematics" curriculum, the first—and maybe the only—public school in the city to adopt it. Adopting it "is one of the best things we've done," the principal said.

"Kids can speak about math," said Phillips. "Test scores are steadily increasing. The kids are remembering what they learn from year to year."

In addition to the math curriculum, the PTA pays for teaching assistants and enrichment programs such as a long-standing collaboration with the Guggenheim Museum to bring teaching artists into the school and to take 3rd- and 4th-graders to the museum, where they learn to become docents.

Classrooms are clean and clearly laid out, with well-defined centers. This lends a calm atmosphere; even in the art room, soft music was playing. Missing is the clutter of hanging paper charts—the use of SMART boards in each classroom means that teachers can display charts on them, teachers said.

Parents are encouraged to bring their children right to the classroom. There is no homework in kindergarten and only a little in 1st grade—a bone of contention for some parents. "It's a no-win—there are some parents who really want it and some who don't. We try to find a happy middle ground," said Phillips.

Children with special needs are integrated with children in general education, and there is at least one Integrated Co-Teaching (ICT) or team-taught class in every grade. "We're still strong believers in the ICT model," Phillips said. PS 8 enrolls some severely disabled children, including some who are nonverbal. Some have one-on-one assistants.

In 2012, PS 8 added middle school grades in a nearby high school, George Westinghouse, and became PS/MS 8. Some students are put off by its location and the fact that kids must go through a metal detector to enter the building, but many parents are grateful to have a good middle school option without the stress of applying to a new school.

Graduates get into some very competitive high schools: In 2016, two students were accepted into Stuyvesant High School, four into Brooklyn Tech, two into Brooklyn Latin, and 10–12 into Millennium Brooklyn. Midwood and Murrow high schools are other popular choices. (Pamela Wheaton)

Brooklyn Prospect Charter Elementary School

**80 Willoughby Street
Brooklyn, NY 11201
(718) 722-7634**
www.brooklynprospect.org

Who gets in: lottery, with District 13 preference
Grade levels: K–12   **Reading scores:** ***
Enrollment: 929   **Math scores:** ****
Low-income: 42%   **Ethnicity:** 37%W 15%B 34%H 6%A 8%O

Opened in 2013, Brooklyn Prospect Elementary Charter School has quickly become a sought-after place, with a multiracial student body and staff (including a number of male teachers), a curriculum that is based on the International Baccalaureate (IB) program, and a principal whose excitement about learning is infectious.

At the time of our visit, children were studying India as part of a "virtual trip" around the world: Kindergartners created tissue-paper marigolds, "a very popular flower in India," a 5-year-old proclaimed; 2nd-graders learned about the life of Mahatma Gandhi, colored an intricate Indian design, and watched an iPad video about cinnamon and other spices grown in India. Parents contribute to the virtual trip as well: Indian families taught the school audience a song at a schoolwide celebration, said Principal Jumaane Saunders, a Brownsville native.

"The great thing is we have a diverse population. At each stop family members come in," said Saunders, mentioning that a Nigerian family brought in food and clothes to help children learn about Nigeria on that stop of the virtual tour.

The IB curriculum is an internationally recognized course of study that emphasizes independent work and demanding projects. It calls for 2nd-graders to study "rules, rights and responsibilities," so children at Brooklyn Prospect selected airports as a place where there are lots of rules and responsibilities. They created a pretend airport with a helicopter, security gate, and metal detector, and parents and teachers dressed up like security guards. To get them "jazzed about math," students push a make-believe fuel tank around the school every morning collecting math problems from everyone, Saunders said.

Math seems particularly strong. Hundreds—maybe thousands—of math problems covered the bulletin boards at the time of our visit, and students were in the midst of a "Math Olympics" leading up to the 2016 Olympic games in Brazil and connected to the virtual world tour. "The attitude 'I'm not good at math'—we're going to counter that," said Saunders, a former high school chemistry teacher.

There are two teachers in every class, and the school is flexible about how children do their work. A child with ADHD may choose to sit on a bouncy chair or take time in the hallway to bounce a heavy ball to get his wiggles out. Some children kneel on cushions to work at a low table or stand at a higher one. There are cool-down corners in each classroom where children may choose to chill out or may be sent there by the teacher.

Students don't necessarily stay in their own rooms, but may switch off depending on the day's lessons and group configurations. They may be placed in a group with learners at a like level, or be interspersed with others—kids who qualify for G&T programs may be sitting next to a child with special needs.

Housed on the 8th, 9th and 10th floors of a Roman Catholic girls' high school, Brooklyn Prospect has no playground, so children play at MetroTech across the street for daily recess and go by bus to Fort Greene Park to play once or twice a week. For gym class, students use the Park Slope Armory and the high school's gym. Children eat in their classrooms, rather than the cafeteria.

Everyone gets immersion lessons in Spanish—from day one in kindergarten. "I don't think the children know that the teacher speaks English," said the principal. The teacher has a theatrical background and kindergartners excitedly participated in a game called "Que sera" (What is it?). As one student pretended to be a horse, her classmates had to guess what she was. In that way, the youngest children learn Spanish vocabulary.

Saunders, the father of three young children, welcomes parents, who read aloud to children, help out at recess, go on fieldtrips, and run after-school clubs.

The school day is longer than the typical public school schedule, ending at 3:45 p.m. in 1st grade and up. There is an active after-school program that begins at 2:45 for kindergartners, 3:45 for other grades (except on Wednesdays, when the school day ends early, at 1:30 p.m.).

Priority in the lottery goes to children in District 13 and siblings of Brooklyn Prospect students (including those in middle school in District 15). Forty-five percent of the seats are set aside for students who qualify for free or reduced-price lunch. In 2016, there were more than 857 applicants for 55 seats. (Pamela Wheaton)

Community Roots Charter Elementary School

51 Saint Edwards Street, Third Floor
Brooklyn, NY 11205
(718) 858-1629
www.communityroots.org

Who gets in: lottery, with District 13 preference
Grade levels: K–8   **Reading scores:** ****
Enrollment: 458   **Math scores:** ****
Low-income: 25%   **Ethnicity:** 39%W 33%B 16%H 4%A 8%O

Lots of people think of charter schools as places of strict, even punitive discipline and very traditional academics. Not Community Roots Charter School, where children sprawl out on rugs during reading periods and call teachers by their first names. Teachers refer to students as "friends," and students demonstrate that they have mastered a topic with projects and presentations rather than tests. Like many other charters, however, Community Roots has a school day that's longer than the typical public school's. Children may arrive at 7:30 a.m. for breakfast, and classes run from 8:15 until 3:45.

Co-directors Sara Stone and Allison Keil, who founded the school in 2006, remain committed to their vision of educating children to be socially active, to treat one another kindly, and to fight injustice. The school has almost equal numbers of black and white children with a smattering of Asians and Latino—an unusual mix in a city where many schools are racially segregated. Administrators are committed to increasing the number of low-income children who attend and, as result, have set aside 40% of kindergarten seats for residents of three nearby public housing complexes.

Community Roots prides itself on its inclusive environment and enrolls students with various disabilities, ranging from dyslexia to autism spectrum disorders. Every class has two teachers, at least one of whom is trained in special education.

"Diversity is our biggest strength and our biggest challenge. We're very mission-driven," said Keil. "Our work has aligned more with our mission as we have grown."

Community Roots, which shares a building with PS 67, makes a big effort to build a sense of community with families who come from diverse backgrounds and different neighborhoods. Parents who bring their children to school may stay in the classroom to read to them. A variety of workshops for parents are held in a spacious family room. There are family cooking and sports programs that are held regularly, not just one-off events like a multicultural potluck favored by many schools.

"We're not a neighborhood school, [so] we have to make school our community," said Sahba Rohani, director of community development. "We run cooking programs until 8 at night and do heavy recruitment to get [parents] to come."

Social studies is at the core of the curriculum. Kindergartners study families, and every family comes in to share their stories.

On the day of our visit, a kindergartner, her older brother, and parents were in the spotlight. The father, a chef of Korean heritage, taught the class how to make (and eat) gimbap—rice wrapped in dried seaweed. The class watched a slideshow of family photos and did spin art—painting on a spinning platform—one of their classmate's favorite activities.

Most classes—including science and art—have two teachers, one of whom is trained in special education. Teachers employ different strategies for children who fidget or struggle to stay still. "Let's take a walk," one teacher said to a child; another sat close to a child throughout a lesson. A late-arriving kindergartner sat at a small table eating breakfast while the rest of the class was gathered on the rug. A 5th-grader took a break to do jumping jacks.

In a 3rd-grade classroom, children were in reading groups with others of a like level and broke up into groups for math, doing different math worksheets. Some were paired with a partner. "I'm not very good at telling time," one girl told us. "She already knows so she's helping me."

Children are prompted to be nice to one another. "I want to remind you to use kind words to your partners," a teacher said. "Say it in a kinder way. Keep in mind that you have a shared purpose."

Most children go on to Community Roots Middle School at 50 Navy Street in downtown Brooklyn.

Admission is by lottery, with priority to District 13 and siblings of current students. There are far more applicants than seats available, but Community Roots maintains a wait list and accepts students in every grade as openings arise. A handful of seats open up in middle school, which begins in 6th grade. (Pamela Wheaton)

PS 492: Academy of Arts & Letters
225 Adelphi Street
Brooklyn, NY 11205
(718) 222-1605
www.artsandlettersbklyn.org

Who gets in: District 13 lottery; priority for low-income kids
Grade levels: K–8   **Reading scores:** * * * * *
Enrollment: 515   **Math scores:** * * * *
Low-income: 29%   **Ethnicity:** 31%W 39%B 17%H 7%A 6%O

The Academy of Arts & Letters, open to children from across District 13, infuses the arts into its curriculum and fosters personal responsibility and caring for others.

Each school day begins with a meeting: the entire middle school in the gym, and the lower-school students in their classrooms.

Parents, community members, and educators are invited to attend twice-annual presentations of work from students in grades 3–8—called Roundtables—and ask probing questions and give feedback. Arts & Letters was chosen by the Department of Education to share with other schools its strategies for fostering student voice, independence, and "thinking and wondering," Principal John O'Reilly said.

There is an emphasis on small-group work and discussion in classes, rather than test prep or worksheets. To build connections to the city, students take frequent fieldtrips. "They encourage them to go deeper with their ideas, even at kindergarten," a parent said, citing trips to Fort Greene Park for lessons encompassing science, social studies, and art. Kindergartners spend 4 hours outside every Wednesday to encourage play, teamwork, and problem solving.

Sixth-graders took a walking tour of neighborhood brownstones and made clay sculptures of what they saw.

Opened as a middle school in 2006, Arts & Letters was set up to serve grades 6–12, but in 2011 it changed course and began admitting kindergarten and 1st-graders as the first step to becoming a full K–8 school. With the wide age range in the school, kindergartners eat lunch in their classrooms because the cafeteria can be overwhelming for them.

The school shares a building with PS 20, a more traditional neighborhood school that serves more black and Latino children and more who qualify for free or reduced lunch than Arts & Letters.

"I'm struggling with diversity, both economic and racial," said O'Reilly. In 2015, Schools Chancellor Carmen Fariña agreed to his request to set aside 40% of seats for children who qualify for free or reduced lunch.

Active families are a hallmark of the school. Parents of kindergartners may spend the first 15 minutes of the day reading in their children's classrooms—and many do, especially at the beginning of the year.

Learning is project-based, and students do long "units of study." Third-graders have studied birds, each choosing a particular bird to focus on, and then presenting their findings at a Roundtable. Second-graders have studied folktales and created shadow puppets. Baking bread was a lesson in both science and math. There is a wide range of abilities, especially in the middle school. All 8th-grade students take the Algebra Regents exam.

Every middle school student has an adviser who meets with parents and students on parent-teacher conference night, as opposed to the speed-dating approach typical of most middle-school conferences. Middle school teachers lead advisories of 16 students. An online system, Jupiter, allows parents to see student assignments.

Middle school test scores are among the highest in the district, but they lag behind scores of top schools in neighboring districts. In recent years, most families have chosen to opt out of state standardized testing, primarily in protest over teacher evaluations being tied to test results, the principal said.

There is an active after-school chorus for both middle and elementary students, as well as LEGO robotics, chess, and Brooklyn Grange farming, where 40 middle school students spend two days a week at a rooftop farm in the Brooklyn Navy Yard. The elementary grades share some after-school programs with PS 20, which is in the same building. The schools work together on various projects, the principal said, including a renovation of the schools' playground.

Popular high school choices are Bedford Academy, Millennium Brooklyn, Midwood, Murrow, and Beacon, as well as arts-focused schools such as Art and Design, Brooklyn High School of the Arts, and LaGuardia. A handful of students go to specialized schools, including Brooklyn Tech and Brooklyn Latin. (Pamela Wheaton)

PS 11

**419 Waverly Avenue
Brooklyn, NY 11238
(718) 638-2661**
www.ps11brooklyn.org

PK

Who gets in: kids in zone, plus out-of-zone kids
Grade levels: PK–5   **Reading scores:** * * * * *
Enrollment: 831   **Math scores:** * * * * *
Low-income: 44%   **Ethnicity:** 12%W 68%B 11%H 4%A 6%O

Enrollment in PS 11 has increased dramatically in recent years, a sign of its growing popularity in the rapidly gentrifying neighborhood of Clinton Hill. At the same time, the school still has room for children outside its attendance zone, offering a good option to parents who are unsatisfied with their neighborhood schools elsewhere. PS 11 has a large prekindergarten program.

"I love the diversity," one mother said. "Not just the racial diversity, but every kind of diversity. We have homeless kids and kids who live in public housing, and the kids of doctors, lawyers, artists, and designers." The school doesn't have a gifted program, and perhaps for that reason it doesn't have the feeling of haves-and-have-nots that some schools have.

The school has an active, multiracial PTA that offers tours for prospective parents; organizes family movie nights, dances and workshops; and raises money for enrichment activities such as violin lessons and recess coaches on the playground.

The building, while clean, well-lit, and well-kept, has undistinguished 1950s-era architecture with drab gray and green tiled walls. The lunchroom can get noisy, and the library is a bit bare. But there are signs of life throughout, from the science room, where kids raise trout from eggs (and release them on a fieldtrip to Harriman State Park in the spring), to the auditorium, where kids can practice their dance steps in classes taught by Mark Morris dancers or learn to play instruments as part of a program with the New York Philharmonic.

The approach to academics is traditional. Test scores are among the highest in the district, and teachers make sure that the curriculum closely follows the Common Core State Standards on which the state's standardized tests are based. Children answer sophisticated questions about literary devices. For example, all 2nd-graders read *Justin and the Best Biscuits in the World*, Mildred Pitts Walter's story about a black cowboy and his grandson in the American West, and answer the same question: "Would you agree that Justin was influenced by Grandpa to behave or feel in a certain way? Use text details to support your argument."

While the writing samples posted on bulletin boards tend to be one-size-fits-all, it's clear that children are exposed to demanding and engaging books.

It's a happy place. Kids love PS 11 so much that they beg their parents to let them come to PTA meetings, one mother says. (Although other parents point out that the reason might be they get a pass on homework if they go to PTA meetings.) Another mother says she was thrilled to hear girls chatting about "math strategies" on their way home from school. And still another says the principal not only knows every child by name, she also knows what books they are reading.

Abidemi Hope became acting principal in 2015, when Alonta Wrighton took an administrative job in the Department of Education. Hope was previously assistant principal, and parents say the transition has been smooth. Wrighton remains the "Master Ambassador Principal."

In past years, some parents withdrew their children after a few years in school, in part because they feared the district's middle school options were inadequate. Those fears may be eased somewhat by the opening of a new district middle school, called Dock Street, in 2016.

The school offers self-contained and team-teaching classes for children with disabilities. While the test scores of special-needs children are in line with citywide averages, a goal of the school is to improve those scores, according to the school's yearly plan.

PS 11 sometimes admits children from outside the school attendance zone as well as outside the district. About one-third of children enrolled live outside the district. (Clara Hemphill)

PS 282

180 6th Avenue
Brooklyn, NY 11217
(718) 622-1626

PK

www.282parkslope.com

Who gets in: kids in zone, kids who pass gifted exam, plus out-of-zone kids

Grade levels: PK–8	**Reading scores:** * * * *
Enrollment: 892	**Math scores:** * * *
Low-income: 61%	**Ethnicity:** 9%W 59%B 25%H 3%A 4%O

PS 282 has long been a traditional school that welcomes children from across Brooklyn. Now a new administration is training teachers in progressive techniques that have been adopted by popular schools nearby such as PS 154 and PS 321.

Rashan Hoke, named principal in 2014, said he would like the school to be more "child-centered" and less "teacher-centered," with more time for children to explore their own interests and speak in class and less time spent listening to teachers.

PS 282 is in the heart of one of Brooklyn's toniest neighborhoods, but many students come from outside the zone. In recent years, parents who live in the zone—primarily white and upper-middle-class—have sent their children to PS 282 for early grades, but transferred them out by 2nd grade, opting for private schools or other public schools nearby. That may change with the arrival of a dynamic new principal and the expansion of the prekindergarten program, local parents say.

Teachers and some parents clashed with the school's previous principal, Magalie Alexis, who retired in 2014. While some parents defended her no-nonsense style, others said the discipline was too strict.

Hoke has worked to improve relations with parents while offering teachers the opportunity to perfect their craft. Teachers are invited to observe lessons at PS 154 and PS 321 and receive training in the Teachers College Reading and Writing Project. Prekindergarten teachers collaborate with colleagues from the well-regarded Helen Owen Carey preschool across the street.

"The school is changing, and it's changing fast," said parent Cheryl Cook. "It feels warm. It feels friendly. What's amazing about Mr. Hoke, if parents have an idea, he will back you 100 percent."

For example, when parents complained that school aides were unnecessarily harsh with children on the playground, Hoke welcomed parents' plan to hire a group called Kids Orbit to organize games at recess and after school.

Hoke, whose ancestry is Puerto Rican and Pakistani, has helped bridge the divide between white and black parents, parents say. When we visited, the PTO had two co-presidents, one black and one white.

Some of the school's longtime strengths include a champion chess team, a tag rugby team, a drama program, and a software engineering program that teaches computer coding to 3rd- through 5th-graders. On our visit, we saw lively prekindergarten classes, with children building with blocks and splashing in a water table. Some of the classrooms for older children were well equipped with plenty of fun-to-read books, but others had somewhat tattered textbooks. In some classes, children were happily engaged in their work, but in one, a teacher yelled to maintain order. Hoke acknowledges the school is a work-in-progress and that it will take time to carry out his vision.

The school has a gifted program open to children from across District 13. The general education classes have children from as far away as Sheepshead Bay and Bay Ridge.

The middle school, launched in 2008, has struggled to find its academic footing. Because of quirks in zoning, children who are zoned for PS 282, part of District 13, are eligible to attend District 15 middle schools, and many take advantage of that option. (Clara Hemphill)

PS 9

80 Underhill Avenue
Brooklyn, NY 11238

PK

(718) 638-3260
www.ps9brooklyn.org

Who gets in: kids in zone, kids who pass gifted exam, some out-of-zone kids

Grade levels: PK–5   **Reading scores:** ★★★★
Enrollment: 838   **Math scores:** ★★★★
Low-income: 44%   **Ethnicity:** 28%W 45%B 14%H 7%A 6%O

PS 9 has popular music and dance performances, a promising partnership with Park Slope's fabled PS 321, and steadily increasing enrollment—a sign of the community's growing confidence in the school.

The school has a mix of children of different racial and ethnic groups, which parents say is a great strength. "In the lunchroom, on the playground, in the halls, PS 9 has a Sesame Street level of mixture," one parent said. "In addition to black and white, PS 9 has a bunch of mixed-race kids and a number of South Asian kids. It's a warm, tolerant, and diverse place." Both the office staff and Principal Sandra D'Avilar are welcoming to parents.

The school has a Spanish-English dual-language program and gifted and talented classes that attract children from across the district. The dance and art teachers collaborate on the musical productions that include 200 children and have specially made scenery and sets.

Teachers use the city's Engage NY math curriculum, and supplement it with resources from the challenging Singapore Math and Math Exemplar curricula.

The Reading and Writing Project at Columbia University's Teachers College trains the staff to develop children's writing skills, teaching them to write with a voice and to revise multiple drafts.

Some teachers are excellent, engaging their pupils in imaginative projects that involve significant research. For example, children in a 5th-grade gifted class wrote polished essays on topics such as Buffalo Soldiers (African American soldiers in the American West), The Trail of Tears (Native Americans' forced migration to Oklahoma), and the Transcontinental Railroad. Unfortunately, the quality of teaching is inconsistent: The school's 2015

Quality Review said there should be less teacher talking, more class discussions, and a higher level of student engagement.

On the positive side, PS 9 has joined what's called the Learning Partners Program, in which teachers and administrators visit one another's schools to share best practices. PS 9 is paired with PS 321, widely considered one of the best schools in the city, and teachers visit one another's classes at least four times a year. D'Avila says her teachers have focused on improving reading instruction in small groups; three have been named "model teachers" and are beginning to share what they've learned with their colleagues. (Two of the model teachers are in the gifted program, and one teaches special education.) PS 321 Principal Liz Phillips says she has seen the "real impact" of the program.

The Spanish-English dual-language program, started in 2011, has grown steadily and now serves 12 classes of children. These classes, which mix children who speak Spanish at home with those who speak English, are designed to make children fluent speakers, readers, and writers in both languages.

PS 9 shares a building with Brooklyn East Collegiate Charter School.

For children with special needs, the school offers team teaching as well as self-contained special education classes. One of the school's "model teachers" is in the self-contained class. Teachers trained in a special program called Reading Recovery assist children with reading difficulties.

Children from outside the zone are admitted to the G&T class based on an exam given by the Department of Education. There is also sometimes space for students outside the zone who apply to the dual-language class. (Clara Hemphill)

PS 31

75 Meserole Avenue
Brooklyn, NY 11222

PK

(718) 383-8998
www.ps31brooklyn.com

Who gets in: kids in zone, plus out-of-zone kids
Grade levels: PK–5   **Reading scores:** *****
Enrollment: 611   **Math scores:** *****
Low-income: 72%   **Ethnicity:** 42%W 5%B 43%H 8%A 1%O

At PS 31, parents take pride in their school's long-standing reputation for solid academics and old-fashioned values. The school is an orderly place where children are primed to follow the rules, but the environment is pleasant and teachers have shifted their lessons to emphasize group work and class discussions.

"We used to be very traditional, with children sitting in rows facing the teacher," said longtime principal Mary Scarlato. "Now they share ideas and critique each other's work."

There's plenty of traditional learning going on, too. We saw 5th-graders working in pairs to solve math problems in a textbook. Second-graders learn cursive writing and must use it exclusively starting in 3rd grade. A few parents we spoke with said they appreciated that the teachers were "strict" with their students.

Located in the Greenpoint section of Brooklyn, PS 31's student body is changing, but not as dramatically as in rapidly gentrifying areas such as nearby Williamsburg. The school attracts middle-class families new to the area, but continues to serve working-class families, including many who speak Spanish or Polish at home.

Prekindergarten classes are vibrant spaces. During math time in one class, teachers worked one-on-one with students as their classmates played with stackable counting blocks or threaded string through labeled cardboard shapes such as a rhombus, rectangle, and oval. Next door a very experienced Pre-K teacher was at ease among the hubbub of center time, where children were enjoying their activity of choice: sand table, painting, playing with cars and trucks, building with blocks, or playing a computer math game.

Children go outside for recess and nature walks; they have phys ed once or twice a week with their classroom teacher in a basement space (because the gymnasium isn't functional). PS 31 typically has room for students outside its zone. (Laura Zingmond)

PS 34

131 Norman Avenue
Brooklyn, NY 11222
(718) 389-5842
www.ps34.org

PK

Who gets in: kids in zone, plus some out-of-zone kids
Grade levels: PK–5 **Reading scores:** * * * * *
Enrollment: 481 **Math scores:** * * * *
Low-income: NA **Ethnicity:** 73%W 4%B 19%H 4%A 1%O

PS 34 is a close-knit neighborhood school with good attendance, high test scores, and a warm sense of community. The neighborhood has long been home to working-class Polish and Spanish-speaking immigrants. Increasingly, Greenpoint has gentrified, and PS 34 has successfully integrated the old-timers and newcomers, parents say. In 2015, PS 34 became the first school in New York City to offer a Polish-English dual-language program.

Patriotism is prized: Children begin the day with the Pledge of Allegiance. The school celebrates Flag Day in June with dances, songs, and readings with members of the community. Children also mark Veterans Day in November, inviting veterans to speak.

"We still have a traditional heart," says Carmen Asselta, principal since 2012. "This is a true community school. No child is lost. We make every effort to welcome our parents."

One of the oldest schools in Brooklyn, PS 34 was used as a hospital in the Civil War. There are few hallways in the building—one must walk through one classroom to get to another, ducking under student artwork hanging from clotheslines in the makeshift corridors. Surprisingly, the arrangement works: Classes are orderly and teachers keep kids focused despite the distractions. "Everyone gets to see what everyone else is doing, so it's actually very nice."

"The principal knows every child by name," said a parent volunteer in the lunchroom the day of our visit. "I feel like I just walked into a family."

Reading instruction begins with the highly structured Core Knowledge approach, which emphasizes phonics instruction and lessons in history and science. For example, 2nd-graders study Greek mythology, Westward Expansion, and the human body. Starting in 3rd grade, children use the Expeditionary Learning reading curriculum, which emphasizes interdisciplinary projects. Every grade has STEM enrichment classes. (Clara Hemphill)

PS 110

124 Monitor Street
Brooklyn, NY 11222
(718) 383-7600
www.ps110k.org

PK

Who gets in: kids in zone, plus out-of-zone Pre-K, French speakers
Grade levels: PK–5   **Reading scores:** * * * *
Enrollment: 447   **Math scores:** * * *
Low-income: 35%   **Ethnicity:** 64%W 6%B 23%H 5%A 3%O

PS 110, housed in a stately brick building constructed in 1895, has a rich arts curriculum and a popular French-English dual-language program. Enrollment has steadily increased as this formerly Polish working-class neighborhood has become home to young professionals with school-aged children.

The number of native French speakers has been growing each year in the French-English dual-language program. In 2016, nearly half were native speakers. In these classes, half the instruction is in French, half in English.

Depending on the grade, children study dance, musical theater, visual arts, and Shakespeare. All children have lessons in Italian, computers, music, and art. There are engaging science projects: 4th- and 5th-graders cultivate a hydroponic garden and raise trout that they eventually release in the Hudson River.

Children may choose topics such as Minecraft, World Wars I and II, geology, gardening, and endangered species to study in 8- to 10-week cycles as part of a program called Schoolwide Enrichment Model. "Enrichment clusters allow for real engagement, and the more engaged kids are the more invested they are in their learning," said Principal Anna Cano Amato.

Cano Amato and Assistant Principal Dana Raciunas, who both specialize in literacy, have worked at the school for more than 20 years.

Fourth- and 5th-grade classes are divided into separate departments; the arrangement gives kids a smoother transition to middle school, where they have different teachers for different subjects.

The school has five prekindergarten classes equipped with blocks, dress-up corners, and lots of books. These classes usually have room for children from outside the attendance zone. (Mahalia Watson)

PS 84

**250 Berry Street
Brooklyn, NY 11249
(718) 384-8063**
www.ps84k.org

PK

Who gets in: kids in zone, plus some out-of-zone kids for Pre-K
Grade levels: PK–8   **Reading scores:** * *
Enrollment: 749   **Math scores:** * *
Low-income: NA   **Ethnicity:** 27%W 3%B 62%H 3%A 5%O

Once a struggling school with low enrollment, PS 84 has become a popular neighborhood option thanks to strong leadership, a sought-after Spanish-English dual-language program, lots of parent involvement, and a rich curriculum.

The tone throughout the large building is sweet and cheery. Children walk calmly in the hallways and are well behaved in class. We saw lots of writing, group work, and creative projects across all subjects.

Principal Sereida Rodriguez-Guerra took the helm in the middle of the 2009–2010 school year. A public-school parent herself, Rodriguez-Guerra grew up in the area and proved adept at building consensus among the longtime working-class Latino residents and the more affluent, mostly white newcomers to the school's Williamsburg neighborhood. For instance, during Hispanic Heritage Month, which occurs at the beginning of the school year, students learn about important contributions from the Hispanic community, but also work on projects about their own cultural heritage and share them with their classmates.

"In the beginning, I sat in on every school committee to make sure everyone felt welcomed," said Rodriguez-Guerra. "That's changed. We have very active parents from all backgrounds, and there are lots of ways to be involved." Parents fundraise to support enrichment activities, but they also help out with school tours and in the library; they happily show up for class and schoolwide events such as the annual Halloween parade.

The school adopted the Teachers College Reading and Writing Program, which encourages students to read books of their choosing and to write and revise multiple drafts of work on a variety of topics. Teachers also draw from other reading programs to weave in explicit instruction in phonics, spelling, and vocabulary.

There are two dual-language classes per grade in the elementary school, which allows for the Department of Education's preferred method of side-by-side classrooms with separate teachers for English and Spanish. Students spend a whole day immersed in one language in one room and then switch the next day. All other elementary school classes have Spanish instruction once or twice a week.

In some schools, the dual-language programs attract the most resources, but at PS 84 we didn't observe any difference in the quality or pace of instruction between dual-language and other classes.

There are separate science rooms for grades Pre-K–2, 3–5, and the middle school. The school has a rooftop greenhouse featuring state-of-the-art hydroponics equipment. Staffed by a full-time teacher, the greenhouse functions as an additional science classroom. The youngest children grow fruits and vegetables in their dedicated science room.

The school has extensive special education services. Every class that is not dual-language follows the team-teaching model with two teachers (one certified in special education) serving a mix of general education and special-needs students. There is also an ASD Nest program for children with autism spectrum disorders (ASDs). ASD children are team-taught in classes that are smaller than typical classes and that serve a mix of general education and ASD Nest students.

The school typically has spots open for out-of-zone Pre-K students, and there are usually a few seats for students from outside the zone in grades 1–5. (Laura Zingmond)

PS 414: Brooklyn Arbor School

325 South 3rd Street
Brooklyn, NY 11211
(718) 963-0393
www.brooklynarbor.org

PK

Who gets in: kids in zone
Grade levels: PK–5
Enrollment: 583
Low-income: 68%

Reading scores: ***
Math scores: ****
Ethnicity: 26%W 3%B 67%H 2%A 2%O

Founded in 2012, the Brooklyn Arbor School serves both longtime neighborhood residents and artsy newcomers. The school strikes a pleasant middle ground between "traditional" and "progressive," incorporating lots of creative playtime while keeping kids on target with appropriate grade-level skills.

Beginning at 8 a.m., the principal, assistant principal, and parent coordinator welcome families outdoors. The "dropoff" scene reflects the changing neighborhood: Hipster dads on bikes, moms in yoga pants, and Spanish-speaking grandmothers. The hand-picked young staff as well as the parents say founding principal Eva Irizarry is a "visionary." "Children's well-being is [the] top priority," one parent told us. A grandmother said every day is her grandson's "best, greatest day!"

The tone is orderly and calm, much like Irizarry, a native of the Netherlands. Some student work is on display in classrooms, but not enough to overload students. "Everything should have a purpose and should be used," said Irizarry. There should be "natural light, shades up, not too much visual distraction, and clean, organized, labeled bins. It should be easy for kids to navigate."

A playroom is dedicated to unstructured play and visited daily by Pre-K and kindergarten students and by appointment by other grades. "We feel it is important for kids to use imaginative play," said Irizarry. Students go out every day in the spacious schoolyard.

Dual-language classes (one in each grade) are equally mixed with the mostly Dominican native–Spanish-speakers and English-speakers—an enviable ratio that many schools can't achieve. Students are instructed in Spanish one day, English the next.

Tours begin in November and continue on the first Friday of every month at 9 a.m. (Pamela Wheaton)

PS 146: Brooklyn New School

610 Henry Street
Brooklyn, NY 11231
(718) 923-4750
www.bns146.org

Who gets in: lottery (set aside for low-income kids)
Grade levels: PK–5   **Reading scores:** ****
Enrollment: 652   **Math scores:** ***
Low-income: 24%   **Ethnicity:** 44%W 20%B 22%H 5%A 9%O

Brooklyn New School, founded by parents and teachers in 1987 as a progressive alternative to traditional education, has become one of the most sought-after schools in the city. Strong leadership, seasoned teachers, active parents, and an imaginative curriculum combine to make the school an engaging, happy place.

In recent years, BNS has become the center of a rebellion against standardized testing, with some 95% of children opting out or boycotting the state reading and math tests in 2015 and 2016. Instead of tests, children complete projects; in lieu of grades on report cards, teachers write a narrative report for each child that outlines progress in each subject area and sets goals for the future.

In the early spring, while other schools are drilling students in test prep, students in grades 3–5 at BNS show off their knowledge by hosting "museums." For example, 4th-graders make a Native American "museum" with real deer hide they have scraped and tanned themselves.

Longtime principal Anna Allanbrook, who taught as a substitute teacher in the school's first years, encourages children to advocate for themselves, to express their opinions, and to speak up in class. On our visit, we were impressed by how well even kindergartners could explain their work.

Parents are encouraged to take part in the life of the school. Once a week they are invited for a PTA meeting or an activity such as a workshop to explain the math curriculum.

Interdisciplinary studies combine science and social studies. Prekindergartners may go to the nature playground in Prospect Park to learn about birds and their nests, and kindergartners learn about where water comes from. First-graders cook vegetables they grow themselves in the school garden. Second-graders visit and build bridges, 3rd-graders study China and Africa, and 4th-graders delve into Old New York by writing long historical fiction books. The 5th-grade curriculum is framed around the question

"What are you willing to stand up for?" It might include study of topics such as the Holocaust, the civil rights movement, or the Vietnam War.

The school has an eclectic approach to math, drawing on the state's Engage NY curriculum as well as Math in the City and the progressive Investigations program, which focuses on conceptual understanding. As for literacy, most teachers use fun-to-read books and teach some phonics, spelling, and cursive.

Asphalt play yards, a large grassy field, a small playground, and climbing equipment surround the school. Children go out every day unless it's below 20 degrees or raining hard. On bad-weather days, students may choose to stay in.

BNS shares a building with Brooklyn Secondary School for Collaborative Studies, and there is a nice relationship between the kids in the two schools. On one of our visits, high school students listened to children read and supervised their woodworking projects; 11th-grade physics students observed the little kids at play before designing mock playgrounds for a class project of their own.

The school has always been proud of the fact that it serves children from different races and income levels. In recent years, the proportion of white children has grown and the proportion of children receiving free lunch has declined. At the request of the BNS administration, the Department of Education agreed to give priority in admissions to children who receive free or reduced lunch as a way to ensure a mix of children of different income levels in the school.

A possible downside: The progressive approach may not work for everyone, and some parents say children who need more explicit instruction may be left behind. There is very little homework in the early grades, which for parents of struggling students can be frustrating, because they don't get a feel for how to reinforce what's happening in class.

Transitions between activities can be slow, and it can take children a while to settle down in some classes. But if students are a little chattier and more active at BNS than at other schools, it doesn't seem to faze teachers or administrators, who believe that movement and talk are an integral part of learning.

Priority in admissions goes to children who live in districts 13, 14, 15, and 16 and then to other Brooklyn residents. BNS gives priority in kindergarten admissions to children who qualify for free or reduced lunch. Siblings of current students get first priority. There are about 10 tours for prospective parents each year. (Mahalia Watson)

PS 29

425 Henry Street
Brooklyn, NY 11201

PK

(718) 330-9277
www.ps29brooklyn.org

Who gets in: kids in zone
Grade levels: PK–5   **Reading scores:** *****
Enrollment: 895   **Math scores:** *****
Low-income: 9%   **Ethnicity:** 74%W 4%B 11%H 5%A 6%O

Parents from across the world email the principal of PS 29 as they seek to move to its historic, tree-lined Cobble Hill neighborhood. This cohesive school rivals any area private school, rave current parents. Every effort is made to connect studies with children's lives and to include them in decisions. Parents help run an after-school program, a journalism club, and a lunchtime running club. They raise money to pay for assistants in kindergarten.

Like the best progressive schools, everything is fodder for learning here, from the basement plumbing that prekindergartners examine to see how water gets inside the building, to the school garden. Children take up causes, like banning household products containing microbeads, a water pollutant. There are two science teachers who fuel children's curiosities. "We take it a step further to make the connection with real life," said one, "then kids take the lead."

Writing is at the heart of the school and many parents are writers themselves. A parent volunteer (and writer at *The Nation*) handed us the latest edition of the *PS 29 Post*. It is written by 4th- and 5th-graders and funded by parent advertisements. Writing often takes practical form: Students are required to submit an essay to be considered a "green team" monitor, for example. Monitors take photos, gather data, and do audits that include an examination of the waste bin in the principal's office.

Classrooms are alive with movement and talk. Kindergartners take part in dress-up, block-building, and other "choice time" activities. We saw a high level of achievement throughout the building, but efforts are made to reach kids who may lack skills, too. Teaching assistants have training to help struggling readers, and children receive phonics and other foundation skills lessons. Math performance is above average and improving, as teachers deepen their practice with a math coach. Second-grade teacher Kim Van Duzer cofounded NYC Math Lab, a collective of teachers working together to enhance their math practice.

The school has grown by about 250 children since Principal Rebecca Fagin arrived in 2011. She taught at the flagship Mott Hall in Harlem and was an assistant principal at Mott Hall II for 4 years. She wants kids to "take the reins" at PS 29 so they "internalize the learning." Therefore, it is the children who create posters for the annual "Eat Pie & Shop," and take up collections for City Harvest, a coat drive, and Toys for Tots.

Because PS 29 lacks a full gymnasium, a resourceful teacher makes the most of a double-wide classroom outfitted with gymnastics equipment. Children visit the spacious playground even in cold weather.

A downside is the school's popularity. The three Pre-K classes fill with siblings, and the staff anticipates wait lists for kindergarten in the future.

Team-taught classes, with two teachers, mix special-needs kids and children receiving special education services. These are "100% integrated," said Fagin, meaning low-, middle-, and high-achievers are mixed in every class. However, not everyone is satisfied with the special ed. services. One mother said that the school was slow to provide help to her child with dyslexia.

There is one open house for prospective families in December. About 15 students from out of district were admitted in the upper grades in 2015 through the Public School Choice program, which provides families of children attending failing schools with other options. (Lydie Raschka)

PS 58

330 Smith Street
Brooklyn, NY 11231
(718) 330-9322
www.ps58.org

PK

Who gets in: kids in zone, occasional wait lists
Grade levels: PK–5   **Reading scores:** * * * * *
Enrollment: 994   **Math scores:** * * * * *
Low-income: 11%   **Ethnicity:** 72%W 3%B 12%H 4%A 9%O

A solid neighborhood school in brownstone Carroll Gardens, PS 58 is best known for its French-English dual-language program, which draws French-speaking children from France and Canada.

The school's enrollment has tripled in the past decade, a trend administrators view with pride and a little concern. Specialists use every nook and cranny in the sprawling building, even converting half of a large hallway into a semipartitioned space. Nonetheless, the school still has space for a large art room, library, and science lab. From 2016, two of the three prekindergarten classes were relocated to an offsite annex.

We saw a few classes where kids seemed bored as they silently filled out workbooks. We also saw some imaginative projects: 5th-graders created a wall display of hand-drawn book covers and essays on topics such as the Trail of Tears, the forced relocation of Native Americans. In a nearby room, a 4th-grade French-English dual-language class was hard at work on essays about life in colonial Canada.

The school puts a premium on high-quality, bilingual educators to staff the dual-language program. In kindergarten and 1st grade, students spend half the day in French and half in English with one bilingual teacher, while 2nd-graders alternate a full day in French with a full day in English, also with a single teacher. In 3rd–5th grade, students alternate between side-by-side classrooms, one with a teacher fluent in French, the other in English.

Families come to school on a regular basis to watch 5th-grade musical productions of, for example, *Shrek*, or to see a performance of the student string orchestra. The school has full-time music and art teachers. PS 58 offers ballroom dancing and chess, and has artists-in-residence from the New York City Ballet and the Metropolitan Opera. Only children who live in the attendance zone are admitted. (Aimee Sabo)

PS 261

314 Pacific Street
Brooklyn, NY 11201
(718) 330-9275
www.ps261brooklyn.org

PK

Who gets in: kids in zone, plus out-of-zone kids
Grade levels: PK–5   **Reading scores:** ****
Enrollment: 797   **Math scores:** ****
Low-income: 40%   **Ethnicity:** 39%W 29%B 22%H 5%A 5%O

PS 261 has an active parent body that includes lawyers, hair-dressers, writers, and maintenance workers. This frank-talking community embraces the friction ethnic and economic diversity can sometimes bring, believing that kids coming together from different backgrounds creates a better world.

The school welcomes children of different racial and ethnic groups, and multiracial families often seek it out because no one group dominates.

Unique to the school is a partnership with the Qatar Foundation, providing an explicit welcome to Brooklyn's Arab community, with its hub near the school. The foundation pays for a second science teacher, who weaves Arabic words into science lessons, an art/Arabic language teacher, and a partnership with the Metropolitan Museum of Art that focuses on the collection of Islamic art.

PS 261 encourages students to think critically about social issues. Students made pinwheels to help Syrian children affected by the refugee crisis in a dollar-matching program. Every year they reenact Dr. Martin Luther King, Jr.'s March on Washington.

The arts have long been a hallmark of PS 261, and there's something for everyone. Kindergartners act out stories such as The Gingerbread Boy, 3rd-graders take on folktales, and 4th-graders study Greek myths in a theater arts class. Third-graders study the guitar with Harlem School of the Arts.

Some concern about discipline and order shows up on school surveys. We saw at least one overly long lesson, during which kids got restless, but most instruction seemed focused. "We definitely have kids coming from really troubled situations," said a parent. "Some are not easy to deal with in the classroom." A guidance counselor, school psychologist, and social worker meet with struggling kids, and the school is adopting Responsive Classroom methods to improve the school climate.

Parents pay for a part-time librarian and substitute teachers. They run a fee-based after-school program and offer scholarships. We saw some parents prepare cardboard Google glasses for a science lesson, while others taught a group of kids in the garden. "It's a culture that celebrates that kind of collective work and volunteerism," said parent Rachel Porter.

PS 261 attracts a large number of children with special needs and has several offerings, including self-contained classes, which take students from outside the zone, and team-taught classes.

The school was on the forefront of the "opt-out-of-testing" movement in 2015, when approximately 60% of students did not sit for state exams. Even so, teachers follow data closely to spot gaps and trends in learning. After a slump in test results during the Common Core State Standards rollout in 2013, scores for those children who did take the state exams are now above the citywide average and rising. An administrator said that she hoped it was a reflection of improved instruction due to increased coaching with experts in reading, writing, and math. The school's current approach to math, which includes lessons from Engage NY, is challenging and several girls and boys we spoke to on our visit said math was their favorite subject.

Jackie Allen Joseph, formerly assistant principal, replaced Zipporiah Mills in 2016. Joseph has a master's degree in early childhood from Bank Street College. She has taught grades K–5 and worked as a literacy coach. Her two children graduated from PS 261.

PS 261 has a small zone and often has space for students from outside the zone, amounting to roughly one-eighth of the total student body. Pre-K typically fills with zoned students and siblings. There is rarely room for new students in the upper grades. (Lydie Raschka)

PS 372: The Children's School
512 Carroll Street
Brooklyn, NY 11215

PK
(718) 624-5271
www.inclusions.org

Who gets in: District 15 lottery (set aside for low-income kids)
Grade levels: PK–5   **Reading scores:** *****
Enrollment: 479   **Math scores:** ****
Low-income: 42%   **Ethnicity:** 64%W 7%B 18%H 8%A 3%O

One of the most sought-after schools in Brooklyn, The Children's School is a pioneer in educating special-needs children alongside their typically developing peers. Skillful teachers manage to challenge strong students while giving struggling students individual attention and extra help.

Some children have mild learning problems, while others have severe emotional or academic difficulties. Some have high intelligence and unconventional behavior. But children are used to one another's idiosyncrasies. Classroom outbursts are dealt with quietly and quickly, with assistant teachers quickly removing a troubled child or bringing one onto a lap.

Every classroom has at least two teachers—often more. "There are lots of grown-ups," said veteran 2nd-grade teacher Steve Quester. "I can't tell you how much time I spent in the hallway yesterday with one of the top readers. It's all about careful groupings."

Children might not stay with one teacher for the whole day, but move into different groups depending on the activity and their skills. For a math lesson, for example, the school's 5th-grade teachers—three general ed and two special ed—each took a group of children.

Later, children were divided into different groups by reading ability. Each chose a book with a social theme and spoke about how the theme was reflected in his or her own life. One boy who read a book about disabilities said that his brother had a disability; his partner said he "couldn't really hear that well" when he was younger, which caused a speech problem. His classmates could relate.

We heard teachers use confident, warm, and supportive voices and saw engaged kids in all classes. Kindergartners confidently shared their short "essays" about which character traits they shared with Max or Ruby in a children's story, *Bunny Cakes*.

"I am like Max because I am determined," one little girl read. "Because I do the monkey bars."

"Raise the roof for this girl," the teacher said. After all sat quietly cheering on the readers—hands in the air—the teacher put on a lively dance video and children joyfully sang and danced to "Five Little Monkeys."

Academics are firmly in place in kindergarten, but movement is built into the day, as is time for dramatic play, block-building, and art. By the end of kindergarten, many children choose to read or write at center time, she said.

"A teacher has to know how to incorporate both [academics and play] to make learning fun," she said.

The PTA has a corner of the cafeteria and does fundraising for programs like Learning by Design, a music program, and one with Mark Morris Dance Group, where children learn to choreograph their own dances, some even performing with Mark Morris dancers. Together with the science teacher, students were responsible for starting a school garden just outside the gymnasium.

Students grow and harvest basil to eat on Pizza Fridays. Since the school is open year-round for special-needs kids with a year-round Individualized Education Program (IEP), produce is harvested all summer.

Founded in 1992, the school hums along steadily even after changes in leadership. In January 2016, longtime Assistant Principal Rosa Amato (Ms. Rosa) took over when Artie Mattia (Mr. Artie) left. Despite a few hiccups along the way (some members of the PTA complained in 2016 when an early-morning dropoff program was changed for security reasons), most staff and parents said the transition has gone smoothly.

A downside: The school is awkwardly housed in two locations separated by a play yard. A satellite site is a mile away at MS 113.

District 75, the district for children with disabilities, determines assignment for the 40% of seats set aside for children with disabilities. The general education children, who make up 60% of the seats, are selected by lottery open to residents of District 15. Siblings get priority. Half of the general education seats in Pre-K and kindergarten go to children from the northeastern half of the district (Park Slope, Windsor Terrace, Greenwood Heights, and Cobble Hill); half go to children from the southwestern half (Red Hook and Sunset Park). In 2016 the school began to set aside one-third of the open kindergarten seats for students who are learning to speak English or who qualify for free and reduced lunch. In 2016 there were approximately 600 applications for just a handful of kindergarten spots. Nearly all the prekindergarten seats went to siblings of current students. (Pamela Wheaton)

PS 321

180 7th Avenue
Brooklyn, NY 11215
(718) 499-2412
www.ps321.org

Who gets in: kids in zone
Grade levels: K–5   **Reading scores:** *****
Enrollment: 1,459   **Math scores:** *****
Low-income: 8%   **Ethnicity:** 75%W 4%B 8%H 7%A 6%O

PS 321 has a well-deserved reputation as one of the best schools in the city. Children learn to think deeply, to work independently, and to take responsibility for their own education. Teachers work together as a team and think seriously about how they can continuously refine their techniques. Both children and adults are excited about learning.

Longtime principal Liz Phillips, whose own children attended the school, has created an atmosphere that's both demanding and fun. "To be successful, kids have to love school," says Phillips. She serves as a mentor for a number of principals in Brooklyn; some of the best principals in the city have trained under her and served as assistant principals at PS 321.

While each classroom has its own personality, there is a consistency to the instruction from class to class and from grade to grade—a remarkable feat considering there are nearly 90 teachers in the school. The school does a good job challenging top students while giving children who need extra help the support they need.

The biggest problem is overcrowding. For more than 3 decades, some classes have been held in the "mini-school," which covers part of the playground. In the main building, teachers meet with children in small groups sitting on the floor of the corridor. In one classroom, children made room for a dance lesson by pushing their desks to the side. Students in kindergarten to grade 2 have art in a studio, but the art teacher comes into regular classrooms in the upper grades. There is no room for prekindergarten, and on-site after-school programs are limited.

Despite the overcrowding, PS 321 has managed to keep class size reasonable, with 25 or 26 students in the lower grades and 29 in the 5th grade.

In every class we visited, there was a happy hum of activity as kids worked thoughtfully and purposefully. In kindergarten and 1st grade, children build towers and other structures from wooden blocks, writing labels to identify them, such as a "bank."

They interview adults in the school, such as the custodian or the security guard, to learn about their jobs. They walk to Prospect Park as part of a "tree study." They make mobiles to learn about balance and motion.

The school has been working with the Teachers College Reading and Writing Project for more than 30 years, and writing is one of the school's strengths. Teachers balance traditional skills like spelling and cursive writing with imaginative assignments.

In 3rd grade, as part of their study of China, children wrote essays with topics as varied as "traditional medicine," "pandas," and "the first emperor." By the time children are in 5th grade their projects are quite sophisticated. One essay, part of a study of the Civil War and Reconstruction, gave "reasons why you would not want your leg amputated."

The school has an eclectic approach to math. Teachers take pride in their ability to create math games that build children's skills in fun ways. They created a math website, www.ps321math.com, to share their games with one another and with parents.

Firmly in the progressive camp, PS 321 has been part of the rebellion against standardized testing. More than one-third of children "opted out," or refused to take state tests for reading and math in 2015.

Parents are welcome in the school and are invited to see their children's classrooms once a month, on "Family Friday." The school will often have over 1,000 parents attend on these days.

A hyperactive PTA raises about $1 million a year. At the same time, the school takes steps to ensure that fundraising efforts don't alienate parents who might not have much money. "Even if only 10% of children qualify for free lunch, that's still 140 children," says Phillips. While the annual auction is expensive ($125 per person), the school has free events such as a potluck supper and family arts nights designed to include everyone.

The proportion of black and Hispanic children enrolled at the school has declined in recent years, and whites now make up 75% of the population. For more than a decade a multiethnic group of parents and staff have organized a "diversity committee" to ensure that all feel welcome.

The school integrates children with significant special needs in regular classrooms with extra supports. For example, a child with significant emotional problems may have a full-time aide assigned to help her manage her behavior. A mentor teacher with significant special education experience is available to give classroom teachers guidance and support.

In 2015 and 2016, the school had room for all the children in its attendance zone. (Clara Hemphill)

PS 39

417 6th Avenue
Brooklyn, NY 11215
(718) 330-9310
www.ps39.org

PK

Who gets in: kids in zone, wait list
Grade levels: PK–5   **Reading scores:** * * * * *
Enrollment: 422   **Math scores:** * * * * *
Low-income: 15%   **Ethnicity:** 76%W 6%B 9%H 7%A 2%O

Housed in a 19th-century building with a brick exterior and an elegant mansard roof, PS 39 has a peculiar interior that resembles a railroad flat. Tiny classrooms are connected to one another without any hallways. Tall teachers need to duck to get into some classrooms, and bathrooms for upper grades are in the basement. It's a bit awkward, but the unusual layout adds to the sense of community and intimacy at this small school.

"I love this school. You get to know everybody," a 5th-grade girl told us. "Teachers are very understanding. None are very strict or mean."

To make the most of the small, connected kindergarten classrooms, one is dedicated to reading and writing, its walls lined with books; another to math, where puzzles and small blocks called manipulatives abound; and a third to "center time" and social studies, where children happily learn through play at different stations throughout the room. Pre-K and kindergarten students use bathrooms on the first floor.

Anita de Paz, principal since 2005 and a 1st-grade teacher for many years before that, has deep roots at PS 39: As a child she would tag along with her mother, a teaching assistant at the school.

Even the smallest children are encouraged to follow their own interests. Prekindergartners visited a hair salon to interview the owner—and had an animated discussion about the difference between barbershops and hair salons. Children spoke to a chef at a neighborhood restaurant, then set up their own restaurant in the classroom's play kitchen.

Second-graders were designing their own communities and made town maps with keys for the local businesses "so people will know which places are there," a student explained.

For their end-of-the-year social studies projects, 5th-graders chose to research a current event or a topic from history. One group made a board game about Aztec life; another researched whether rock climbers should be permitted to climb cliffs without ropes. An articulate bunch, they happily discussed their projects and had plenty of praise for PS 39.

The gym is located across the street at Camp Friendship. There is an art studio and a science lab in the building, complete with egg-laying crayfish. Students were making twirly birds out of paper. First they made one according to a set model, and tried modifications to see what would happen. The principal stepped in to show one girl that her twirly bird actually would work when it was dropped from the principal's much taller height.

The largest room in the 1877 building is dedicated to music. PS 39 students work with musicians from the New York Philharmonic, learning to compose and play their original music, which they performed to a standing-room-only audience of families at Camp Friendship.

"We get to listen to the orchestra and learn with teachers who play in the orchestra," a 5th-grader said. "It lets us express ourselves in meaningful ways."

In bad weather, the ground-floor music space is used for indoor recess.

As the neighborhood's population has changed, so has the school: 10 years ago nearly 70% of the students qualified for free lunch; in 2016 only 15% did. Parents actively fund-raise to pay for arts partnerships, assistant teachers, staff training, and recess coaches. On the day of our visit, a group of parents sat at a table outside the building selling remaining items from a recent auction.

The school works to maintain its diversity; in 2012 in the midst of a rezoning of neighborhood schools, PS 39 fought to keep the westernmost blocks going down to 4th Avenue.

In recent years there has not been enough space for all kindergartners in the zone, some of whom were assigned to PS 124. (They have the right to return in 1st grade, space permitting.) There are occasionally a handful of seats in the upper grades for students from outside the zone as families grow and move out of the increasingly expensive neighborhood, the principal said. (Pamela Wheaton)

PS 10

511 7th Avenue
Brooklyn, NY 11215
(718) 965-1190
www.ps10.org

Who gets in: kids in zone
Grade levels: K–5   **Reading scores:** *****
Enrollment: 942   **Math scores:** *****
Low-income: NA   **Ethnicity:** 49%W 8%B 31%H 7%A 6%O

PS 10 is located in a rapidly changing area of Brooklyn on a block where the neighborhoods of Windsor Terrace, Greenwood Heights, and South Slope converge. Once a school serving mostly working-class Spanish- or Arabic-speaking families, PS 10 now also includes the children of professors and professionals and a mix of different races and ethnicities.

The enrollment has increased by more than 60% in the past decade, a sign of the school's growing popularity (as well as an expanded attendance zone). In fact, PS 10 has become a destination school: While it may not yet have the cachet of PS 321, some parents move into the neighborhood just so they can send their children here.

"The culture is extraordinary," Anita Skop, superintendent of District 15, wrote in her assessment of the school, called a Quality Review. "Students are comfortable explaining their projects with other students or with adults. They see themselves as part of a community and are expected to contribute to that community."

Principal Laura Scott runs a tight ship, but the administration has been strained since opening up a preschool facility at a nearby location. This is perhaps one reason why nearly one-third of teachers complained about her management style in the annual school surveys. But parents almost unanimously recommend the school, and Scott gets high marks on the city's principal assessments.

"Most of the teachers are very good, and there are a number of true master teachers who mentor the others," one father said. "There are a few teachers who have been there for a long time whose methods are a bit outdated. On the bright side, the school gets many, many applicants for any teacher opening, and so any new hires are always great."

While the school is large, kids don't get lost—the assistant principal and principal seem to know every child's name. The size brings advantages in terms of the physical plant—the gym, science labs, and cafeteria—that smaller schools nearby don't have.

PS 10 has a strong commitment to serving children with disabilities as well as new immigrants learning English. The building is mostly wheelchair-accessible, and children with limited mobility are not only made to feel welcome, they are an integral part of the school.

One kindergarten class launched a "wheelchair study" after they discovered a classmate couldn't go down the subway stairs because he used a wheelchair. They learned how their classmate used a lift to ride the school bus, researched which parts of the school were wheelchair-accessible, and even built toy wheelchairs out of blocks. (The wheelchair study was described in a book edited by Julie Diamond called *Teaching Kindergarten: Learning-Centered Classrooms for the 21st Century.*)

The school offers workshops for parents who are learning English, both to make them feel a part of the community and to offer strategies to help their children study at home. There are also General Education Development (GED) classes for parents.

Teachers have time to plan lessons together and perfect their craft. They work together to develop a curriculum that works for children of different abilities.

Kids have a chance to meet luminaries: Henry Louis Gates visited the school to shoot an episode of his PBS series, and the entire 5th grade went to Washington, DC, for a personal audience with U.S. Supreme Court Justice Sonia Sotomayor one year.

Scott is particularly proud of the school's relationship with the Metropolitan Opera Guild, Brooklyn Conservatory of Music, Carnegie Hall, and Lincoln Center; children across all grade levels learn everything from music and lyrics to set design and building. Kindergartners also learn keyboarding with Music and the Brain. There is an after-school program run by the PTA, and the YMCA runs a free after-school pickup. Scott said children need "more than just math and reading; we have to give them something to look forward to every day."

There is no room for prekindergarten in the PS 10 building, but in 2014, a large "Pre-K center" opened nearby that is administered by Scott. As mentioned, this has added a bit to the school's growing pains, but it also appears successful and set to expand. (Clara Hemphill)

PS 107

1301 8th Avenue
Brooklyn, NY 11215
(718) 499-2054
www.ps107.org

Who gets in: kids in zone
Grade levels: K–5   **Reading scores:** * * * * *
Enrollment: 572   **Math scores:** * * * * *
Low-income: 8%   **Ethnicity:** 77%W 4%B 10%H 7%A 2%O

Housed in a quirky, historic building with a plum location on leafy Eighth Avenue, PS 107 has a well-developed writing program; a winning track team; and an active parent body that raises money for programs in dance and music, and a much-vaunted after-school. The school's enrollment has increased along with its popularity in recent years.

Eve Litwack, who became principal of PS 107 in 2011 after serving as assistant principal of PS 321, has adopted some of the practices of her former school, encouraging children "to take charge of their work." For math and social studies, classes are set up in stations and children rotate from one activity to the next, working at their own pace. Some children use a computer program for math, getting feedback as they master a level. Writing is a huge focus: Beginning in kindergarten, children learn the basics of story structure, then write, edit, and publish their own stories.

Litwack wants to give children a voice: One year, the student council learned about the City Council's "participatory budgeting" process, which gives community groups a say in how city money is spent. The children then applied the principles to their own school, and, with a $1,000 contribution from the PTA, bought balls and jump ropes for the play yard and more equipment for the science lab.

Fifth-graders have separate teachers for reading, math, and writing/social studies. Students have planners and carry backpacks from class to class. "It really prepares them for what they'll encounter in middle school," said the principal.

Test scores are among the highest in the district, and—unlike some nearby schools—not many families opt their children out of taking state exams. Under Litwack, the emphasis has shifted away from test prep. After hearing stories from parents about the amount of test-related homework their children were getting, in 2016 she asked teachers to limit it to just one period per day for 3 weeks before the tests and to give test-prep homework only twice a week. "As a school we want our kids to do well," she said. "But the best test prep is good teaching."

Although the school has no gymnasium, it has a winning track team. All children in grades 1–5 have physical education twice a week in the Armory track across the street. Kindergartners run laps on the school playground because the cavernous Armory was daunting for them, the principal said. Once a week, families meet at 7 a.m. for "fun runs" the length of Prospect Park, followed by breakfast with the gym teacher.

The 19th-century building has a cramped, awkward layout; some classrooms are accessible only by going through other classes. A large, sunny space on the top floor is used for a library. In 2016, an arts studio was reclaimed as a classroom space to accommodate increased enrollment. The art teacher now teaches from a cart.

On the first Friday of the month, the school is open for families to visit their child's classroom. The PTA pays for authors such as R. L. Stine to visit the school. It also funds programs with the Brooklyn Museum of Art, Alvin Ailey Dance Company, Martha Graham Dance Company, Together in Dance, and ballroom dancing.

Popular middle school choices include MS 51, MS 839, and Mark Twain.

PS 107 has long been known for its many after-school offerings. "People used to come for after-school but kind of stayed for the day. I'd like it to be that they come for the quality of the school and the after-school is a bonus," said Litwack. Offerings include puppet-making, instruction in Mandarin, and fencing. About two-thirds of the students attend the after-school program.

The school hosts many school tours. (Pamela Wheaton)

PS 154

1625 11th Avenue
Brooklyn, NY 11215
(718) 768-0057
www.ps154.org

Who gets in: kids in zone, some wait lists
Grade levels: K–5   **Reading scores:** *****
Enrollment: 534   **Math scores:** *****
Low-income: 17%   **Ethnicity:** 64%W 3%B 20%H 6%A 7%O

Nestled in quiet, family-friendly Windsor Terrace, among stately brick and limestone houses, PS 154 is a just-right neighborhood school, according to local families. Not too big, not too small, this close-knit school community boasts strong academics, lots of fieldtrips, and constructive parent input. The downside is limited space and a budding wait list for kindergarten.

Literacy is the bedrock here, supported not only in school but also at home. High-quality writing covers the walls in the form of "mini-books," reports, persuasive essays, and poetry. Even the youngest use "voice" in their writing, just as they speak up boldly in class to offer their opinions. Well-thumbed books are stacked on children's tables and fill baskets on classroom shelves. When children read, it's an active process, as they mark passages related to a book's theme, or jot unknown words on sticky notes. Classroom libraries are filled with more advanced novels and nonfiction than we usually see on school visits.

Parents are very involved, volunteering in classrooms and raising money for special programs. "There's such a feeling of community through the school—it feels like a small town," said parent coordinator Debby Wattenbarger. Parent opinions matter; for instance, teachers scaled back 2nd-grade homework based on responses to a survey sent to students' homes.

Each grade participates in at least one special program, such as chess, capoeira (a dance-like martial art), hip-hop, and ballroom dance, all of which are PTA-funded. Fourth-graders raise trout in the science lab and release them in Carmel, New York, a project started by Principal Erik Havlik when he was assistant principal. He learned about the program through his fly-fishing hobby, he said. Many students work above grade level, and these special activities help keep them engaged.

The parent coordinator said the school has gotten savvier about integrating enrichment activities into classroom studies.

For example, when 3rd-graders study world cultures, they also explore dance in world cultures. Trips are integrated into social studies units; when 2nd-graders study New York City they may study and walk across the Brooklyn Bridge; when kindergartners study communities, they visit a firehouse. Fourth-graders travel to Philadelphia to see historic sites of the American Revolution. "I liked the Benjamin Franklin Museum and the printing shop best," a child said.

Fifth-graders move from class to class for math, reading, and a combined social studies/writing class, as students do in middle school. This is to help them get used to middle-school structures (many go on to the much larger MS 51), and so teachers can focus on one subject in depth. "At first I was upset but I got used to it," said a 5th-grade girl who said she is most comfortable in her homeroom, where children gather for silent reading and to eat a snack. The writing teacher said she sometimes misses having her own class, and yet, "The writing seems stronger this way," she said.

There is no gymnasium, but the gym teacher takes kids outside as often as possible, and they use the cafeteria. At least once a month, 2nd- through 5th-graders go to the Brooklyn Armory for physical activity. During the spring, lower grades also go to the Armory.

Class sizes have grown steadily as the school and neighborhood have gained popularity. Five kindergarten classes were whittled to four, and there is a wait list. "Our building can't sustain that growth," said Havlik. "I want to keep our science lab," he said. "I'd love to have a gym." (Lydie Raschka)

PS 130

70 Ocean Parkway
Brooklyn, NY 11218
PK
(718) 686-1940
www.ps130brooklyn.com

Who gets in: kids in zone
Grade levels: PK–5   **Reading scores:** ★★★★
Enrollment: 770   **Math scores:** ★★★
Low-income: NA   **Ethnicity:** 40%W 7%B 27%H 20%A 6%O

As Brooklyn has gentrified, many schools' enrollments have shifted from mostly working-class children of color to mostly white children of professionals. PS 130 is home to an experiment designed to preserve the racial balance for which the school is proud.

When the city proposed building a new school on the other side of Fort Hamilton Parkway, PS 130 parents were concerned that their community would be divided: One side of the parkway is mostly professional families, while the other side is mostly working-class. If the PS 130 attendance zone were cut in two, all the children from one group would go to one school; all the children from the other would go to the other.

So, with the help of their local city councilman and the Community Education Council, they came up with a plan: PS 130 would continue to serve all the children in the zone from Pre-K to 2nd grade. And, then when the new MS 839 building at 713 Caton Avenue opened in September 2015, grades 3–5 of PS 130 moved there.

"The grades and classes will remain diverse, all kids will benefit from the new facilities, and the school community will remain united," said city councilman Brad Lander, who backed the plan.

Many speak a language other than English at home, including Spanish, Cantonese, Haitian Creole, Urdu, and Bengali. The administration has long worked hard to teach children of different groups to resolve conflicts peacefully.

As part of a program called the Morningside Center for Teaching Social Responsibility, children volunteer to be "mediators" who work with their peers to help them get along better. (Clara Hemphill)

PS 230

1 Albemarle Road
Brooklyn, NY 11218
(718) 437-6135
www.ps230.org

PK

Who gets in: kids in zone, plus kids who pass gifted exam
Grade levels: PK–5   **Reading scores:** * * * *
Enrollment: 1,210   **Math scores:** * * * *
Low-income: NA   **Ethnicity:** 18%W 2%B 32%H 47%A 1%O

At PS 230 in Kensington, girls in headscarves play happily in the block corner with new immigrants from Mexico, while their mothers may be attending an English class elsewhere in the building. The school is a welcoming gathering place for neighborhood residents.

Some 80% of students speak another language at home—mostly Bengali, Spanish, or Chinese—said Principal Maria Della Ragione. Newcomers arrive regularly. On the day of our visit, a shy Puerto Rican girl was being shown around by several other Spanish-speaking girls.

Della Ragione, a longtime teacher of English as a second language (ESL), has thought carefully about how to integrate children who are still learning English as well as those with special needs. Instead of pulling kids out, ESL and special education teachers often work with children in their regular classrooms so they don't miss class time. Teachers use drawings and pictures to illustrate written lessons on the boards and walls. There are 13 ESL teachers.

Art projects give all children a way to express themselves. In a 3rd-grade lesson, children tell stories through collage; 4th-graders make comic books and storyboards; and 5th-graders produce stop-action claymation and animate it, presenting their 3-minute shorts in a film festival in May. "The arts connection provides a way for children to represent their thinking visually," said the principal.

Chinese dancers come in for the Lunar New Year. There's a feast for Bengali New Year, costumes for Dia de los Muertos, and even an American hoedown with square dancing. Parents turn out in high numbers on the weekends to participate in activities such as Science Saturday, where children make volcanoes or conduct other experiments. Parents may take English classes. PS 230 is a family-friendly place, and some teachers enroll their own children in the school.

Long-standing collaborations with arts organizations help enrich the curriculum. These include Mark Morris for dance, Brooklyn Children's Theater for musical theater, and music with Ms. Suzi, a former school parent. New York Cares is a huge presence: Volunteers lead robotics workshops, cooking groups, and tennis lessons on Saturday. They even take children on visits to the Metropolitan Museum of Art. The PTA and the school split the bill for many of the arts programs, and film companies that shoot in an empty subway station nearby use the school's cafeteria and facilities, and donate money to the school.

Children come by school bus or subway to the districtwide gifted and talented program. "We dig a little bit deeper into some of the ideas," the 1st-grade G&T teacher said. Children in G&T classrooms are together from kindergarten to 5th grade. "Families get very close, with playdates and even vacationing together," said the principal. All classrooms, including G&T, are bright and inviting, with students intent on learning.

Della Ragione was an assistant principal under the tutelage of Sharon Fiden, the well-respected principal she replaced in 2014. She is an energetic, hands-on leader. "My passion is to be in the classrooms. I am an educator and I am a coach and I am a mother," she said. "I'm going to jump in with you and we're going to do it together, if you're struggling."

PS 230 is housed in two buildings one block apart. The main building, a traditional-looking schoolhouse constructed in 1930, houses grades 2–5. The annex, for Pre-K to 1st grade, is brightly lit and clean, with each floor painted a different color. There is a tiny outdoor area with padded flooring that individual teachers use on occasion, but children play mainly in a large indoor gym for recess. "It's a challenge, absolutely," said the gym teacher. "They need the gross motor skills." They do take regular walks around the neighborhood, recording what they see.

Both buildings have elevators and are accessible for students with physical disabilities. There are four self-contained classrooms for children with disabilities only, including some on the autism spectrum. Parents started a support group for families with children on the spectrum. PS 230 uses flexible scheduling and integrates special-needs children into other classrooms when possible, the principal said. There are team-taught classes in every grade. (Pamela Wheaton)

PS 295

330 18th Street
Brooklyn, NY 11215
(718) 965-0390
www.ps295.org

PK

Who gets in: kids in zone
Grade levels: PK–5   **Reading scores:** ★★★★
Enrollment: 489   **Math scores:** ★★★★★
Low-income: NA   **Ethnicity:** 32%W 6%B 47%H 11%A 5%O

An arts-focused school with a strong sense of community, PS 295 has an involved staff and very active parents, with many working artists in the mix. There is a welcoming environment for all children, including those with special needs and those learning to speak English.

PS 295 shares a 100-year-old building in South Park Slope with New Voices School of Academic and Creative Arts middle school. There are small dance and drama studios and a stage, complete with sound and lighting systems. The interior is nicely painted and there is a welcoming shared library. The building lacks a full-size gym, and the noisy cafeteria, split in two different sections, is inconveniently located in the lobby.

Students go to the nearby Armory for phys ed, or do yoga classes in the dance studio. CBE Kids runs an after-school program, while parents run a fee-based program offering classes in yoga, circus arts, science, and tennis. Additional after-school programs are provided through a grant from Councilman Carlos Menchaca.

Linda Mazza, a longtime teacher and principal since 2013, is well known and liked by the community. She has monthly "Bagel Bits" morning meetings with parents, and parents are invited to visit classrooms afterward.

Math lessons occur first thing in the morning, and students get plenty of hands-on work. The school uses a combination of the Investigations curriculum, used in District 2, and more standard workbooks from the GO Math! curriculum, offered by the city. There is an emphasis on logic and applying math lessons to real life, the principal said. In a 5th-grade class, the teacher asked children to figure out what size turkey she should buy based on the number of guests she expected at the dinner and how much they were likely to eat. Students also had to come up with a plan for solving the problem and explaining their decision, writing up their thought process. "There's not a predetermined answer," said the principal. "It's about: 'What is your reasoning and is it logical?'"

Teachers follow the Readers and Writers Workshop model in which students choose books at their level and share information with a partner. Parents are invited to some publishing parties to celebrate books written by the children. About half of the reading time is devoted to reading nonfiction books, to better align with Common Core standards. The school spends little time on dedicated test prep for state exams. "Good instruction is test prep," said the principal.

In 5th grade, students have different teachers for different subject areas in order to prepare them for middle school.

The arts flourish here. Students write and perform their own plays; some are actors, others directors or stagehands. All grades get music instruction: singing, learning to play the recorder, or drumming. A band and chorus meet after school. Parent grant-writing helps fund many arts initiatives, and parent artists and writers frequently volunteer. An annual silent art auction features work by parents and their friends.

Fieldtrips tie into the curriculum. Second-graders studying New York take a trip to Rockefeller Center and the "Top of the Rock"; 3rd-graders studying China visit Chinatown. Hands-on projects abound both in and out of the art room. Second-graders studying the Lenape Indian tribe created typical shelters; 1st-graders made and shared a delicious sweet potato dish the week before Thanksgiving.

PS 295 was one of the first schools to offer at least one Integrated Co-Teaching (ICT) class in every grade and takes particular pride in its special education program, which serves nearly a quarter of the school population.

There is occasionally space for out-of-zone children. (Pamela Wheaton)

PS 172

825 4th Avenue
Brooklyn, NY 11232
(718) 965-4200
www.ps172.org

PK

Who gets in: kids in zone
Grade levels: PK–5   **Reading scores:** * * * * *
Enrollment: 587   **Math scores:** * * * * *
Low-income: 85%   **Ethnicity:** 13%W 4%B 77%H 6%A 0%O

PS 172 has long won recognition for its high test scores—a remarkable achievement considering that most of its children are poor enough to qualify for free lunch and many speak another language at home. Its math and science programs are particularly strong. The school also has a good record of integrating special-needs children in general education classes.

What are the secrets to its success? The school has strong, stable leadership and gives teachers lots of time to plan their lessons together. Rather than relying on textbooks, the staff has put together its own curriculum with a rich mix of carefully-thought-out units on topics such as poetry, the solar system, multiplication, or the history of Mexico. There is consistency from class to class and a logical progression from grade to grade. Every month the curriculum is revised based on the needs of the students. Each summer, the entire staff revises the curriculum after discussing what worked best and what needs improvement.

In math, the staff has mastered one of the trickiest tasks of teaching: how to challenge strong students while giving weaker students the help they need to be successful. We sat in on a 5th-grade math class in which the teacher managed to adapt the same complex problem for different children: If two teachers, shopping together, each buy a pair of shoes at a "buy-one, get-one-for-half-price" sale, what's the fairest way to divide the cost?

Some children worked on the problem independently or in pairs, others got little hints from the teacher, and still others got step-by-step instructions from the second teacher in the class, who is trained in special education. At the end of the class, all children sat on a rug and discussed how they arrived at the answer.

Science is an integral part of the curriculum. Children might make their own toothpaste in a simple chemistry experiment, connect electrical circuits, or dissect owl pellets. First-graders learn about the human body, not just the skeletal system and the digestive system, but even the parts of the brain. These lessons build their vocabulary—which helps them become better readers.

Jack Spatola, who has been principal since the mid-1980s, and Assistant Principal Erika Gundersen assigned the teachers so that their strengths complement one another. "There is at least one teacher in every grade who really loves math," said Spatola. "We try to have some in each grade who have a love of science, and a love of history." A number of teachers majored in math in college—unusual among elementary school teachers.

Starting in November, teachers identify children in grades 3–5 who are struggling and invite them to attend special classes from 9 a.m. to noon each Saturday. Parents are kept abreast of the situation and offered concrete suggestions of what they can do to help.

Despite this intense focus on academics, PS 172 has a warm, calm atmosphere. On one of our visits, parents dropped by to talk—in English and Spanish—to Spatola.

Even the kindergarten classes focus on academics, with no designated area for blocks or dramatic play. The school has no main library or real gym; one cafeteria doubles as a gym, a second as a dance studio. The auditorium has been partly sectioned off to create storage cubicles for resource teachers.

Most of the teachers are certified both in special education and in general education. Special-needs students are integrated into general education classes. Speech therapy and most other assistance take place in the classroom. This also puts extra adults in the classroom to help all students. The school offers team teaching in every grade. It has no self-contained classes.

The school occasionally admits out-of-zone students but may not know if it has space until September. Seats are awarded on a first-come, first-served basis with an eye toward maintaining diversity and not overburdening special ed services. (Clara Hemphill)

Hellenic Classical Charter School

646 5th Avenue
Brooklyn, NY 11215

PK

(718) 499-0957
www.hccs-nys.org

Who gets in: lottery, with District 15 preference
Grade levels: PK–8   **Reading scores:** * * * * *
Enrollment: 494   **Math scores:** * * * * *
Low-income: 54%   **Ethnicity:** 28%W 26%B 41%H 3%A 3%O

Hellenic Classical Charter is a winning, spirited school where kids are motivated to participate wholeheartedly. Children study the world through the rich lens of Greek language and culture, and take their expertise into a wider sphere through their participation in local and citywide Greek events. This dynamic school community is a source of pride among the city's Greek community but has benefits for all students.

Kindergartners study modern Greek through games, flash cards, skits, and songs. They also listen to *Aesop's Fables* and enjoy puppet shows, an important part of any Greek childhood. Greek instruction continues 5 days a week through middle school, where students add the study of Latin and ancient Greek, and read excerpts from Greek classics such as *The Iliad*, *The Odyssey*, and Plato's *Republic*.

The school embodies the Greek concept of "filoxenia," or hospitality. Children are taught to take ownership of their school by serving on the student government or as "ambassadors" in each classroom. At their open houses, students and staff receive visitors with smiles, snacks, and information. The middle school science teacher said kids love all this warmth and community. "At the end of the day we kind of have to kick kids out of the building," he said.

Founded in 2005, Hellenic Classical Charter grew out of the Soterios Ellenas School, a long-standing Greek-Orthodox parochial school that has educated Brooklynites of Greek heritage for decades. Soterious Ellenas was phased out of the building and closed in 2007. Demographic changes reduced the number of local families wanting Greek parochial education, and the idea was born to create a not-for-profit charter school based on Hellenic culture and drawing in a broader range of students.

The school population is ethnically and economically diverse, with rising numbers of Hispanic students; not even one-quarter are of Greek heritage. Still, at least one 45-minute period of each

8 a.m. to 4 p.m. school day is devoted to studying modern Greek with five native-speaking professional teachers. But other cultures are celebrated, too. Each classroom studies a different country in preparation for the school's multicultural fair; Cinco de Mayo and Martin Luther King, Jr. Day are important holidays.

What's particularly successful here is how subjects are knit together for greater meaning. We watched theater/dance teacher Petros Fourntios weave geography, history, and language instruction into one of his Hellenic dance classes. Using a map, a child located the origin of the sharper, percussive dances of the mountainous Pontus region, and made a comparison to the smoother-flowing island dances. Sixth-graders danced with a respectful, Zen-like focus without a trace of the rebelliousness typically attributed to this age.

Since her arrival in 2007, Principal Christina Tettonis has increased arts and literacy instruction. More than 20 1st-graders receive one-on-one help in reading, and teachers work with coaches from Teachers College Reading and Writing Project. "We put a lot of resources into the lower grades," Tettonis said.

The school also adopted the practice of Socratic Seminars, or "Paideia time," as it's called, as a way to debate topics. The result is a refreshing forthrightness in student discourse. Kids don't have to wait to be called on by the teacher, and in the older grades children serve as discussion leaders. A 3rd-grader explained Paideia seminars like this: "We all have different opinions. We agree. We disagree. You can speak more than once but not too much, so others can speak." She added, "We love it."

Classroom teachers in kindergarten to 5th grade are responsible for science, a subject that typically falls to a specialized teacher in a larger school, and we saw evidence of science lessons, although children said that hands-on experiments occur more frequently in the 4th grade, a testing grade. "Science is strong in the building and we're looking to make it even stronger," said school director of operations Joy Petrakos. Children grow seeds, dissect frogs, and study mechanical science, she said. In the middle school, science is taught by a specialist teacher.

Any student may take advantage of free Kaplan preparation for the specialized high school test. About 12% of graduates qualify, and others attend a wide range of public and private high schools. High school–level Regents classes are available in Greek, algebra, and Earth science.

There is no outdoor play space, so the younger children walk to a nearby playground, schedule and weather permitting.

Students are admitted by lottery, with priority to District 15. There is a long wait list. (Lydie Raschka)

PS 21

180 Chauncey Street
Brooklyn, NY 11233

PK

(718) 493-9681
http://www.crispusattucks.school/

Who gets in: kids in zone, plus out-of-district kids
Grade levels: PK–5   **Reading scores:** ***
Enrollment: 615   **Math scores:** ****
Low-income: NA   **Ethnicity:** 2%W 89%B 8%H 1%A 1%O

A community institution, PS 21 is a traditional school with consistently solid test scores, a stable teaching staff, and involved parents. The principal's high expectations translate into academic success for the school's pupils, despite the fact that most of their families are poor enough to qualify for free lunch.

Girls wear burgundy plaid jumpers. Boys wear gray trousers, white shirts, and burgundy plaid ties. Friday is the weekly test day, when desks are arranged in rows and students do fill-in-the-blanks quizzes and other tests. Even kindergartners take midterm exams. The tests allow teachers to better understand which children need extra help. Principal Leslie Frazier, who attended PS 21 as a child, taught in District 2's progressive PS 40 before returning as a teacher and assistant principal.

There are lots of hands-on science and math lessons, including a robotics program and a computer station that incorporates engineering programs. Students spread out on the floor and use little plastic blocks called manipulatives, games, and dice to learn math skills. A 1st-grade teacher used a puppet to introduce vocabulary to the children, who chanted different letters and word sounds including rhyming words and those that sound similar.

A hydroponics lab offers children the chance to grow vegetables and learn about energy using lessons from the Environmental Study Center in Brooklyn.

The school's enrollment has declined in recent years, a result of rising housing prices that have forced many families to move. School tours are held on the last Friday of each month. There is usually room for students from outside the zone and sometimes even outside the district. (Pamela Wheaton)

PS 249

18 Marlborough Road
Brooklyn, NY 11226
(718) 282-8828

PK

Who gets in: kids in zone, plus out-of-zone kids
Grade levels: PK–5   **Reading scores:** *****
Enrollment: 894   **Math scores:** *****
Low-income: NA   **Ethnicity:** 4%W 40%B 50%H 6%A 1%O

PS 249 is a happy, active place, where strong academics and enrichment activities give all children a chance to excel. "Grandparents," easily spotted in bright red Department of Aging jackets, help watch over little ones and provide extra hands in the classroom. Students may play intramural soccer, dance to the beat of African drums, or learn the violin during the school day. There is always a buzz of activity, even on Fridays, when children typically are distracted by thoughts of a school-free weekend.

That's mostly because of "Super Science Fridays," an entire school day each week devoted to science-related instruction. "Attendance on Fridays was kind of a challenge," says Principal Elisa Brown, so she had to come up with something special. Students may conduct experiments in class, build volcanoes with the science teacher, and devote themselves to nonfiction books during reading period. "When they leave on Fridays, they leave with a project, something they made, and in a calm, happy tone," Brown says.

Those in grades 3–5 stay until 5:30 p.m. 2 days a week and come in on Saturday mornings.

Artists from the Ifetayo Cultural Arts Academy teach African dance, drumming, drama, capoeira, and art. The Noel Pointer Foundation brings in musicians to teach students to play the violin. There's a drama teacher on staff.

Students also get the opportunity for travel: 3rd-graders spent a week on a farm in Vermont; 5th-graders visited historical sites in Philadelphia.

Students from countries such as Mexico, the Dominican Republic, Panama, Honduras, and El Salvador are in Spanish-English dual-language classes. Other new immigrants, such as those from Haiti or African nations, are taught in regular classrooms by teachers trained in English as a Second Language. (Pamela Wheaton)

PS 770: The New American Academy

60 East 94th Street
Brooklyn, NY 11212

PK

(718) 221-5837
www.ps770.org

Who gets in: District 17 lottery
Grade levels: PK–5   **Reading scores:** ***
Enrollment: 303   **Math scores:** **
Low-income: 60%   **Ethnicity:** 16%W 65%B 8%H 1%A 11%O

The New American Academy isn't a typical elementary school: Sixty-five children and up to four teachers share a large classroom, where they divide into small groups and work on projects. Teachers stay with the same children from grades K–2 and 3–5, and sometimes K–5. There is no homework. Children go out for recess in all kinds of weather.

New American Academy takes its inspiration from the open classrooms of the 1970s and from Waldorf education, based on the theories of Rudolf Steiner. Steiner was an Austrian philosopher who believed that children's moral and creative development is as important as their intellectual pursuits and that children learn best through play and practical activities. At New American Academy kids make solar ovens from pizza boxes and design structures for baby chicks. Lessons follow 5-week-long themes on topics like identity/communication, transportation, and energy.

Master teachers in each classroom earn the same six-figure salary the principal earns, a practice made possible because the school does not hire deans or assistant principals. The master teachers coordinate and mentor their own small teams of apprentice teachers. "That's kind of the strength and the vulnerability," said a parent, adding that her child's team is effective.

There are three staff members still in place here since the school's 2010 founding by Harvard-educated Shimon Waronker. A few left to teach at one of two additional New American Academy schools. Former kindergarten teacher Jessica Saratovsky became principal in 2013. A longtime 1st-grade teacher at PS 33 in Manhattan, she has recruited several former colleagues.

Teachers plan lessons during a 90-minute morning meeting while children eat breakfast and exercise in other parts of the building with support staff. Then around 65 children filter into one large room and divide up for lessons. "My one worry was the size of the class," said a father who works in TV sound production. "But it works so well. The kids help each other out."

The relaxed and positive atmosphere is a draw for parents. "What I see here is empathy," said a 4th-grade parent. "Everybody knows each other." One mother who moved her son to the school in 3rd grade has been particularly pleased with the school's emphasis on positive feedback to parents, while not neglecting a child's challenges. "He's happy to come to school now," she said.

The principal said teachers try to avoid dull workbook test prep in favor of solid instruction and hands-on projects. One change to help kids prepare has been to adjust the schedule to allow for additional small-group lessons and to ask kids to tackle shorter reading passages in 3rd grade. "My child is in a testing grade, so that's important to me," said a 4th-grade parent, who admitted she'd like to see stronger test scores.

Even-keeled Saratovsky leads a parent forum on Friday mornings with coffee, pastries, and food for thought. On the day of our visit, she showed a video in order to brainstorm ways PS 770 students might use technology in the classroom. This sparked a discussion on race, the school's "no homework" policy, and the fears children were expressing related to news of police aggression. Saratovsky, who is herself a mother of young children, was able to draw candid comments from a diverse group of Caribbean, African American, Asian, and Caucasian parents.

The makeup of the student body is changing as gentrification gains a foothold in Crown Heights. In the lowest grades blondes and brunettes are beginning to outnumber the larger schoolwide African American majority. The administration actively recruits children from the community to try to retain the school's racial and economic diversity, which members of the school community said they value.

Priority in enrollment goes to children who live in District 17. In recent years, there have been about 200 applications for 36 Pre-K spots, and 200 for 75 kindergarten seats (36 of which are reserved for Pre-K students). (Lydie Raschka)

PS 705

443 St. Marks Avenue
Brooklyn, NY 11238
(718) 230-0851
PK   *www.brooklynartselementary.org*

Who gets in: kids in zone
Grade levels: PK–5   **Reading scores:** *
Enrollment: 356   **Math scores:** * *
Low-income: 69%   **Ethnicity:** 14%W 49%B 29%H 6%A 2%O

PS 705, the Brooklyn Arts and Science Elementary School (BASES), is a cheerful and orderly school on the border of two gentrifying neighborhoods, Prospect Heights and Crown Heights. A popular dual-language program gives children the chance to become fluent readers and speakers of English and Spanish. The school offers classes in dance, music, art, and fencing.

Founding principal Sandra Beauvoir Soto works hard to balance the concerns of a range of parents—families who want a progressive approach to education and those who prefer traditional methods; homeless families who live in nearby shelters and upper-middle-class families who live in brownstones. The PTA has a "diversity committee" to make sure that all parents feel included; the leadership of the PTA includes people of different races. Soto's own family is multiracial—she is of Haitian ancestry and her husband is Puerto Rican—and she seems to have a good rapport with parents of different ethnic groups.

Most grades have two classes: a dual-language class (in which the language of instruction alternates between English and Spanish each day) and a team-teaching class (which mixes special needs and general education pupils, with two teachers). On our visit, we saw some traditional teaching methods—such as math drills on worksheets—as well as some progressive approaches—such as lessons on the life cycle of the trout, from eggs hatched in a classroom aquarium. Classes are small, and most have an assistant teacher or an aide in addition to the classroom teachers.

The building that houses PS 705 has seen a noteworthy transformation. Formerly known as PS 22, it was a chaotic, low-performing school with a declining enrollment and one of the lowest-rated principals in the city. Soto, who was a staff developer and literacy coach at the well-regarded PS 189, opened her new school in 2012 with grades K–3 and added a grade each year; Explore Exceed Charter School, a traditional school with high expectations and strict discipline, opened in the building the same year. The two schools shared the space amicably. (PS 22 took in no new students in 2012 and closed permanently in 2014.)

Starting a new school was easier than turning around an old school would have been, Soto said. "You get to set the tone. You get to choose your staff." Key to the school's success is the attention to children's social and emotional development. A full-time social worker and up to six social work interns staff the "feelings room," where they help children manage their frustrations before they become behavior problems.

While Soto's vision is clear, the school is a work in progress. In the school's first years, some parents withdrew their children after kindergarten or 1st grade to transfer to better-established schools. Attendance and test scores are below average. But parents who are willing to stay and work together to improve the school can count on the support of the administration and a cohesive staff.

"You have to be a pioneer, and you have to be willing to fight through the growing pains," Soto said.

Eager to keep the mix of different kinds of families as the neighborhood becomes more wealthy, Soto received permission from the Department of Education to give preference, when seats are available, to out-of-zone families who are learning English or who are in the child welfare system. Any child who lives in the zone is automatically admitted. (Clara Hemphill)

PS 316

750 Classon Avenue
Brooklyn, NY 11238
(718) 638-4043
www.ps316brooklyn.org

Who gets in: kids in zone, kids who pass gifted exam, some kids with autism

Grade levels: PK–5
Enrollment: 429
Low-income: 75%

Reading scores: * * *
Math scores: * * * *
Ethnicity: 6%W 72%B 20%H 1%A 2%O

Once a disorderly, low-performing school avoided by anyone with a choice, PS 316 now has a booming enrollment, strong instruction in math and science, and an exhaustive list of extras including piano, violin, dance, chess, computer coding, debate, yoga, and gardening. The school has made a remarkable turnaround under the strong leadership of Olga Maluf, principal since 2011.

PS 316 has an ambitious plan to join the International Baccalaureate program, an internationally recognized course of study that emphasizes independent work and demanding projects. The school has also received a grant to start a Spanish-English dual-language program in 2017. The school's gifted program attracts children from across the district.

In this gentrifying Prospect Heights neighborhood, PS 316 serves mostly longtime local families; the children are often the offspring of former students. Parents say they are happy their kids have a chance to shine in so many ways, with engaging classes in science, drama, art, and music.

In some ways PS 316 looks old-fashioned, with kids in uniforms walking in boy and girl lines, and banners proudly extolling the school's accomplishments. We saw workbooks open to the same page. But we also heard meaty conversations between teachers and kids, and saw teachers pause long enough to give kids time to formulate answers. Most teachers routinely defined big words.

The music and science programs are particularly strong. The lower-school science teacher surveys frogs in the wild in his spare time, bringing knowledge back to the kids. He has students conditioning their pet fish by shining a red light at feeding time. The science department has its own website.

The school has an ASD Nest program for kids with autism. (Lydie Raschka)

PS 241

**976 President Street
Brooklyn, NY 11225
(718) 636-4725**
www.ps241.org

PK

Who gets in: kids in zone, out-of-zone kids
Grade levels: PK–5   **Reading scores:** * * * *
Enrollment: 552   **Math scores:** * * * *
Low-income: 87%   **Ethnicity:** 2%W 86%B 10%H 0%A 1%O

An engaging curriculum, high expectations, creative lessons, and a group of teachers who work together as a team have earned PS 241 high marks on the city's Quality Review. The school takes advantage of its location to take children on frequent class trips to the nearby Brooklyn Museum, the Brooklyn Botanic Garden, and the Brooklyn Children's Museum.

The teachers are adept at sparking lively class discussions, and there are lots of hands-on projects and fun activities. Children are grouped by ability; the strongest students are placed in an "enrichment class."

Students seem eager to share their ideas, often in the grammatically correct complete sentences their teachers want. In a 2nd-grade class, the teacher asked what it means to fight for a cause and then asked children to identify causes and people who had fought for them. Kindergartners animatedly considered whether a character in a story was "mean" or "unhappy."

Teachers find unusual topics for students to write about. Third-graders in the enrichment class were assigned two countries and asked to write an essay on which one was more deserving of the free books a fictional librarian planned to distribute. Another class wrote about whether snakes or sharks posed a greater danger to other animals.

In addition to trips to local museums, children may visit the United Nations and a local farm. In addition, teaching artists come to PS 241 to offer a theater program and dance. All students also take computer science.

The school can pay for some special programs because of the largesse of Peter Malkin. He attended PS 241 in the 1940s and went on to graduate from Harvard and own the Empire State Building. Every year he returns as "principal for a day" and has helped the school purchase technology and rebuild a playground. (Gail Robinson)

PS 235

525 Lenox Road
Brooklyn, NY 11203
(718) 773-4869

Who gets in: kids in zone, plus out-of-zone kids
Grade levels: PK–8   **Reading scores:** * * * * *
Enrollment: 1,274   **Math scores:** * * * *
Low-income: 73%   **Ethnicity:** 2%W 93%B 2%H 2%A 2%O

PS 235 is a huge neighborhood school with a long history of high academic standards and a well-regarded dance program. Children from across Brooklyn apply to SOAR, as the school's enrichment program for academically gifted students is known, and to its selective middle school, Lenox Academy.

SOAR, which stands for Stimulating Outstanding Achievement through Reading, is no longer officially a gifted program since the Department of Education centralized admission to gifted-and-talented programs. However, out-of-zone children may take a test at the school between January and March to be admitted to the SOAR program, a school official said. Forty percent of the classes at PS 235 are designated as SOAR classes, according to the school website. PS 235 consistently posts high test scores.

The sprawling school occupies three buildings, each several miles from the others. The main building houses prekindergarten classes and grades 1–5. Kindergarten students attend classes at the Early Childhood Center at 5811 Ditmas Ave. at 58th Street, (718) 629-6875. The Lenox Academy serves about 300 students in grades 6–8 at 10001 Flatlands Avenue, (718) 927-5228, a building it shares with a small alternative high school. One principal, Laurence Lord, oversees all three buildings, as well as an annex called a "minischool."

Dancers and artists from National Dance Institute (NDI) offer dance instruction to all 4th-graders at the school. Some go on to dance in NDI's citywide children's dance troupe. PS 235 also has programs with Theatre for a New Audience and Symphony Space.

The school has consistently declined our request to visit. This information was based on telephone interviews with staff and Department of Education documents.

Out-of-district children may take an exam for the SOAR program; however, the vast majority of admitted students are from the district. (Clara Hemphill)

PS 89: Cypress Hills Community School

PK

265 Warwick Street
Brooklyn, NY 11208
(718) 964-1180
www.cypresshillscommunityschool.org

Who gets in: open to kids citywide, with District 19 preference
Grade levels: PK–8   **Reading scores:** ** **
Enrollment: 458   **Math scores:** *
Low-income: 95%   **Ethnicity:** 0%W 3%B 95%H 1%A 1%O

At PS/IS 89, children spend one week studying entirely in English, then the next week studying entirely in Spanish. Textbooks come in both English and Spanish, as do the many fun-to-read books in classrooms and in the well-stocked library. About half of the teachers have more than ten years' experience and almost all speak Spanish.

PS 89 accepts children from all five boroughs, beginning in prekindergarten. Almost all students stay through the 8th grade.

The school moved into a new building in 2010, which includes a greenhouse where students learn about hydroponics, aquaponics, and composting with worms.

The tone of the school is supportive, respectful, and caring, and we were impressed that both children and staffers laughed a lot, while staying focused on their work. Class sizes range from 20 to 25.

The students at PS 89 boast a terrific attendance record, perhaps because of the school's unusually high level of parent involvement. A group of activist parents founded the school in 1997 in collaboration with Cypress Hills Local Development Corp., a community housing program, and with the help of the Manhattan education group New Visions for Public Schools, which is led by a parent and an educator. Parents accompany children on trips to places like the Bronx Zoo.

Unfortunately, so far the school's reading and math scores have been disappointing. One contributing factor may be the school's primarily English language learner population. The few children whose first language is English seem to do fine here. We saw strong Spanish writing samples by a 3rd-grader who spoke only English when she entered in kindergarten. Students living outside the neighborhood must provide their own transportation. Unfortunately, rising rents have resulted in some families moving farther out to areas like Howard Beach. (Lydie Raschka)

PS 503

330 59th Street
Brooklyn, NY 11220
(718) 439-5962
www.ps503online.org

Who gets in: kids in zone
Grade levels: K–5   **Reading scores:** *
Enrollment: 1,110   **Math scores:** ***
Low-income: 97%   **Ethnicity:** 4%W 1%B 76%H 19%A 0%O

PS 503 is a vibrant, friendly place where new immigrants, children with special needs, and general education students learn side by side. Students move about their classrooms, asking questions and collaborating with one another on projects. The bulletin boards display the products of a rich curriculum and of students who are producing thoughtful and complex work at different levels.

One 5th-grade class studied the Syrian refugee crisis. After a student volunteered that she is a refugee from Central America, the class, which is predominantly Hispanic, began to study the refugee crises of 2012–2014, when many unaccompanied children crossed into the United States from Mexico.

On the day of our tour, more than 100 parents participated in a morning math workshop held in the auditorium. As an assistant principal spoke in English, three people translated the talk into Spanish, Mandarin, and Arabic. Throughout the school, even more parents were in classrooms that morning, joining their children for the monthly family day.

With almost 2,000 children in the building shared with PS 506, space and scheduling are very tight. Some students do not eat lunch until 1:20 p.m., near the end of the school day, and there is no library.

Most children speak another language at home, and some parents are not fully literate in their native tongue. To meet that challenge, each classroom has two teachers for at least half the day, one of whom is certified to teach English as a Second Language. The school has 25 ESL teachers, and many more staff members, including Principal Nina Demos, are bilingual.

The test scores are low, but Demos says they don't reflect the quality of instruction. One sign of success: Nearly all PS 503 graduates pass their classes in 6th grade, according to city statistics. (Elizabeth Daniel)

PS 69

**6302 9th Avenue
Brooklyn, NY 11220
(718) 630-3899**
www.ps69k.org

Who gets in: kids in zone, kindergarten wait lists
Grade levels: K–5   **Reading scores:** ★★★★
Enrollment: 845   **Math scores:** ★★★★★
Low-income: 98%   **Ethnicity:** 4%W 0%B 5%H 90%A 0%O

There's a lot to like at PS 69, a well-organized and joyful school on the border of Brooklyn's expanding Chinatown. Its approach to teaching all students—many of whom are Chinese-speaking—is through exploration of the arts. PS 69 was chosen as a showcase school of the arts in 2014, a school teachers from around the city visit to see how arts are infused into the curriculum.

Some youngsters learn to play the violin, beginning in 1st grade; there's a band, guitar instruction, and a chorus for older students, theater with TADA! Youth Theater, and dance lessons with American Ballroom Theater. Teachers recognize the connection between language and music.

"We pay special attention to music," said Jaynemarie Capetanakis, principal since 2006. "Music is that pathway for English."

Visual arts projects connect to the curriculum. Fifth-graders studying explorers of America in social studies learned about a different kind of exploration in art class: how farmers in China discovered the Terracotta warriors. The lesson was enriched by the art teacher's summer in China as a Fulbright fellow.

More than half of the students are not fluent English speakers (most of these speak Mandarin at home), yet the school's state standardized test scores are well above the city average. The principal credits the work of math and literacy coaches, who regularly meet with teachers to go over lesson plans, help adapt curriculum, and conduct regular teacher training. "Teachers need a peer to turn to who's an expert in their area," said Capetanakis.

There is consistent instruction throughout the classrooms. Much learning is done actively, with body movements mimicking text, and visual aids such as pictures to supplement verbal lessons.

Teachers have regular one-on-one meetings with children, and those who need extra help work in small groups with the reading intervention teacher.

The building is sparkling, with lots of nooks and crannies where parents, children, and teachers can congregate for meetings or small-group lessons. There is a full-size gymnasium and an auditorium that seats 275. The school, opened in 2002, quickly outgrew its space. The city made the zone smaller and built two new schools, PS 310 and PS 971, just a few blocks away. Still, the kindergarten has had a waiting list every year since 2005, and sometimes children from other grades are sent to an overflow school. The building enrolls some 845 students, instead of the 650 it was built to serve.

Class size is large—up to 32 in grades other than kindergarten, but the principal doesn't complain: "We make the most of what we have so every room is just right."

Her positive tone carries throughout the school. Children are reminded to be kind to one another at the end of each day's announcements. Acts of kindness are rewarded with a book and an invitation to breakfast with the principal for the child and his parents.

Classrooms are well stocked with books, manipulatives, and other learning materials. There is a block corner and puzzles in kindergarten but no time for free play other than recess. Art and music are integral to the school day and built into the lessons.

For reading instruction, PS 69 uses the city's ReadyGen materials. "We decide what skills and strategies to use and how to make it our own," said reading coach Dana Marinaro. "We T-C-ify it," she said referring to the school's longtime affiliation with the Teachers College Reading and Writing Project.

The Brooklyn Chinese American Association offers an on-site after-school program, and after-school academic enrichment begins in January. Twenty-two different groups come to pick up children for programs elsewhere.

There are two small classes for students with special needs only, but many of those children spend at least part of the day in other classrooms, the principal said. Unlike many schools that offer Integrated Co-Teaching (ICT) classrooms, PS 69 prefers that teachers work individually, or in small groups, with students with special needs, rather than in a larger classroom setting with two teachers. "What we find is that children blossom with one-on-one instruction," said the principal.

There is frequently a wait list for kindergarten, but all zoned children have the right to return in 1st grade, space allowing. (Pamela Wheaton)

PS 102

211 72nd Street
Brooklyn, NY 11209
(718) 748-7404
www.ps102.org

Who gets in: kids in zone; kids who pass gifted exam; plus program for visually impaired

Grade levels: K–5
Enrollment: 1,425
Low-income: 65%

Reading scores: * * * * *
Math scores: * * * *
Ethnicity: 56%W 1%B 26%H 15%A 2%O

On the far fringe of gentrification, in an area not yet hip enough for recent college graduates, PS 102 is one of Brooklyn's large melting-pot schools. Children pour into this massive building in the morning and receive a solid foundation in reading that bolsters both struggling and advanced students. The school has several academic tracks, including a districtwide gifted and talented program called "Delta," two AP (advanced placement) classes per grade, team-teaching classes that mix in children with special needs, and small classes for children with severe disabilities. It houses one of the few programs for children with visual impairments in the city.

Principal Cornelia Sichenze started her career at the school in 1984 and taught 3rd grade before becoming a Reading Recovery teacher. She believes every child benefits from consistent phonics, grammar, word study, and comprehension work. Almost all of her ten kindergarten teachers and many of her 1st-grade teachers have Reading Reform training, a structured, multisensory approach to reading. It is unusual for so many teachers to have the same training and coaching. In 2015, 48% of all tested students and 15% of students with disabilities scored at or above proficient on the state English language arts test, higher than the district- or citywide averages.

Children do hands-on project work even in the upper grades, a practice they call STEAM (science, technology, engineering, art, and math). In one such project, 5th-graders envisioned utopian societies with economic and education systems, food and culture, and geographical features. Younger kids studied the history of bridges, read about bridges in literature, and constructed bridges from cardboard and recycled materials. Teachers offer children choices in their projects, such as writing a diary entry, creating a diorama, or composing a song.

231

Like all District 20 schools, teachers take a close look at the work of students with disabilities to locate gaps in learning. "We try to find what's missing and how we can give those students what's missing," said Sichenze. It might be difficulty organizing an essay, so teachers will try using paper with boxes to check off, or a memory aid to help children recall writing steps. When something works, the idea is shared with all teachers. PS 102 operates on the belief that "What's good for children with special needs is good for all kids," said Sichenze. This practice has led to better scores on the English language arts exam, she said.

In addition to the Delta program, teachers test children for placement in one of two advanced classes in every grade (AP1 and AP2). "It's nice to have AP on top of Delta," said a parent. "It gives kids who didn't pass some standardized test a chance—say if they didn't pass by a point or two." Another parent said, "They move a little faster than the other classes. You have to keep up. They take you out if you don't keep up with grades, unlike G&T." The rest of the classes have an equal distribution of kids learning English, kids who struggle with behavior, and low-, middle-, and high-achievers.

To maintain a feeling of connectedness in such a large school, staffers greet parents at the door during drop-off time and mingle informally at events and performances. Every Friday, parents receive a robo call with the following week's events. Notes and newsletters go home the old-fashioned way, in backpacks, and are posted on the school website.

Parent coordinator Margaret Elliott invites parents to be involved in a variety of ways. "I like to throw out a lot of things—academics, art, gardening," she said. "When we put in the tree guards, parents I'd never seen before came." Perhaps as a result, fathers come out in good numbers, she said.

The principal said she'd love more space "for the million things we do," including a dance studio and room for the small-group instruction that now takes place in the library.

The school has a good variety of services for kids with special needs and provides them with a strong academic foundation. (Lydie Raschka)

PS 247

7000 21st Avenue
Brooklyn, NY 11204
(718) 236-4205
www.ps247.org

PK

Who gets in: kids in zone, kindergarten wait lists
Grade levels: PK–5   **Reading scores:** ****
Enrollment: 820   **Math scores:** *****
Low-income: NA   **Ethnicity:** 37%W 1%B 14%H 48%A 0%O

PS 247 is a welcoming, well-organized school that serves many immigrants from Eastern Europe, South Asia, China, and Central America. Students get plenty of instruction in small groups or one-on-one, and the personal attention pays off in high achievement.

Math instruction is particularly strong. Children spend at least 75 minutes on math each day, with extra work on solving word problems twice a week. There are lunchtime groups for tutoring, and it's not uncommon to see small groups of kids meeting with specialists in hallway corners.

There is an emphasis on reading nonfiction, which Principal Christopher Ogno says is particularly good for children with learning disabilities. "They feel more successful because they have photos and captions," he said.

Teachers meet three times a week to plan lessons. Preparation for state tests is limited mostly to the 4 weeks before the exams, during which there is a 3-hour Saturday Academy open to all students; about half attend.

As part of a college partnership program, children visited the Fashion Institute of Technology, where they sat in on a dressmaking class, or Columbia University, where they saw a robotics program. College students come into the school at least twice a year. "Most families are first-generation immigrants, and this is an opportunity to introduce them to college," said the principal.

The school is overcrowded: Hallways are used for teaching small groups of kids; science and art teachers travel with their carts. There's only a small outdoor yard, the cafeteria doubles as a gym, and an all-purpose room can fit only one grade at a time.

In a quirk of zoning, PS 247 students may apply to middle school in both District 20 and District 21. (Pamela Wheaton)

PS 186

7601 19th Avenue
Brooklyn, NY 11214
(718) 236-7071
www.ps186.com

PK

Who gets in: kids in zone
Grade levels: PK–5
Enrollment: 995
Low-income: NA

Reading scores: ****
Math scores: ****
Ethnicity: 33%W 0%B 27%H 39%A 1%O

American flags, Chinese restaurants, and statues of the Virgin Mary are common sights along the avenues of Bensonhurst, a traditionally Italian enclave also known as Brooklyn's second Chinatown. Once an old-fashioned school with desks in rows, PS 186 now serves many children of new immigrants with cutting-edge technology, in classrooms that hum with movement and chatter as kids work on learning tasks, projects, and games.

Academics start early. There is lots of variety, choice, and activity to hold a child's interest at every age. Teachers move energetically among tables to assist children like supportive coaches on a ball field.

Particularly successful here are the many different ways children cover a topic. During a science lesson on states of matter, some children watched a video, others read a picture book, and a few did an experiment with the teacher. Then the groups rotated. In one class, kids played geometry games with colorful shapes and iPads, using quick response (QR) codes to check their answers.

One-quarter of the students are new to speaking English, and there are many opportunities for them to practice their English.

Children are noticeably kind and helpful. Attendance is better than average, which means the teacher does not have to slow down to help kids who missed lessons catch up.

Independence is prized, so children try to find their own answers, rather than relying only on the teacher, whether it's finding the word "purple" posted on the wall, or checking a pocket guide on copyediting marks as they edit a classmate's work.

Parents flock to the school for the solid instruction as well as the free after-school program from 2:20 p.m. to 5:20 p.m. However, roughly 150 families choose not to put their children in extended day, opting for private tutoring instead, Principal Bayan Cadotte said. (Lydie Raschka)

PS 748: Brooklyn School for Global Scholars

1664 Benson Avenue
Brooklyn, NY 11214
(718) 382-3130
www.ps748scholars.com

Who gets in: kids in zone
Grade levels: K–5
Enrollment: 615
Low-income: 66%

Reading scores: *****
Math scores: *****
Ethnicity: 38%W 0%B 21%H 39%A 2%O

PS 748, also called the Brooklyn School for Global Scholars, is a vibrant and well-run school with strong leadership and a friendly vibe. A zoned neighborhood school, it serves a multicultural student body, including many English language learners, from within its zone.

From the time it opened in 2010, the school has been committed to project-based learning. "What you will not see here are worksheets or test prep," said the founding principal, Ursula Annio, who gets high marks from teachers and parents based on their responses to annual school surveys. Teachers develop their curriculum in-house, injecting a lot of creativity into lessons while doing a nice job of addressing learning fundamentals as well as doing more complex work. Math drills, phonics, and grammar lessons help shore up basic skills, but what drives instruction here is the emphasis on hands-on, in-depth, and inventive work.

A history lesson may be paired with writing and art assignments. When students study the history of New York State, they research early explorers of the region, and then each child composes an illustrated book and creates a doll in the likeness of the researched explorer. In math, students develop computational accuracy by completing calculation-dense projects such as designing a dream home with room-by-room specifications or plotting out a 60-kilometer bike trip complete with stops for food and rest.

In classes there's a nice balance of independent and collaborative work. Students select books from well-stocked classroom libraries to read and write on a range of topics; they critique one another's writings and present their polished pieces to the class. Instead of answering questions from a textbook, 5th-graders we observed were creating their own study guides to help them prepare for a math test.

Beginning in 3rd grade, classes are departmentalized—essentially a modified middle-school format. The idea is that students learn better when taught by a teacher who spends most or all of the day focusing on specific subjects. Students, including those in special education classes, have one teacher for English and social studies and another for math and science. Special needs students have the added assurance that they're getting the same quality of instruction as their peers in other classes because they share the same teachers. "Some of these students came to us nonverbal and now they can participate in Socratic Seminar," said Annio, referring to the practice where the teacher prompts a classwide discussion with an open-ended question and then students comment on and challenge each other's responses.

In addition to taking art, music, gym, and technology, students participate in weekly "enrichment" activities that vary by grades but include offerings such as music (recorder or keyboard), LEGO robotics, movement, and games. Teachers plan regular fieldtrips to museums and other cultural institutions, and students in all grades join in on community service projects.

Parent involvement is good, and the staff puts a lot of effort into parent communication. Teachers send home weekly newsletters and have students compile "goal booklets" to share with their parents. The staff invites parents to weekly talks that cover a range of academic and parenting topics. For their part, parents raise funds to support arts instruction and other programs and volunteer to help out during the school day.

The Federation of Italian-Americans runs a free after-school program on-site that is open to students in grades 1 through 5. (Laura Zingmond)

Brooklyn School of Inquiry

50 Avenue P, 4th floor
Brooklyn, NY 11204
(718) 621-5730
www.brooklynschoolofinquiry.org

Who gets in: kids who score in 99th percentile on city's gifted exam
Grade levels: K–8
Enrollment: 521
Low-income: 21%
Reading scores: * * * * *
Math scores: * * * * *
Ethnicity: 71%W 5%B 5%H 18%A 2%O

Opened in 2009, Brooklyn School of Inquiry (BSI) has quickly become a sought-after school, with a lovely building, a welcoming atmosphere, and some of the brightest kids in the city.

The school has resources other city schools can only dream of: traditional learning materials alongside abundant technology, a kid-scaled science lab, and entire classrooms dedicated to block-building, science, music, and studio art.

Principal Donna Taylor, formerly a vice president at Time Inc., is directing her creative drive into Brooklyn's first and only citywide gifted and talented school and building a beacon for rigorous, progressive education.

Children who qualify for seats in the elementary grades at BSI must score extremely high on the city's gifted and talented exam. (Most score in the 99th percentile, although siblings may be admitted with scores in the 97th percentile.) But Taylor's approach to education doesn't include drill work, memorization, and overly burdensome homework.

The teachers, hand-picked by Taylor, are all certified in G&T education and have a strong voice in shaping the school. Parents pitch in too. Thanks to fundraising efforts—over $500,000 per year—many classrooms have two teachers: one experienced teacher and an assistant. Student teachers abound.

Teaching balances hands-on experiences and projects with plenty of academic content. With the help of a professional architect, 5th-graders studying Marine Park's salt marshes and the Canarsie Indians who once lived there were building a modern-day dwelling that the Canarsie Indians might have imagined in their future, with the help of a professional architect.

The current science lab is well used and a new lab is being built on the roof to become a lab site for teachers from all over the city.

Beginning in 2nd grade, students have different teachers for math and humanities to capitalize on teachers' expertise in one area, Taylor said. They see a homeroom teacher every day, too.

The homework policy is humane. In kindergarten through 1st grade, homework is optional, assigned sometimes for targeted needs. "These kids need to play," said Taylor. "These are over-booked children."

Homework starts in earnest in 3rd grade 4 days a week, and "there is plenty of homework in middle school," the principal said.

Outside organizations bring in music, theater, and movement.

Class size is 25 in kindergarten, but goes up to 32 in 2nd through 5th grade. There are 30 students in middle-school classes.

Building a cohesive community is a challenge for a school that draws its students from many diverse neighborhoods, Taylor said. Students come from nearby neighborhoods such as Brighton Beach, Bath Beach, and Bensonhurst, but several dozen come from downtown and brownstone Brooklyn, and a few trek in from Staten Island, and the Rockaways in Queens.

Parent engagement is "formidable," Taylor said, with spill-over crowds at school information nights, full-force showings at parent-teacher conferences, and robust fundraising that pays for special enrichments.

While BSI easily shares its building with the Academy of Talented Scholars and a District 75 school, the tiny, shared schoolyard is too small, a drawback for young children. Middle school students are allowed to go out of the building for lunch and frequently congregate in the city playground across the street, watched over by an assistant teacher. The building is bright and airy, but there are no lockers, so backpacks tend to line the otherwise attractive hallways.

About 10 children have one-on-one paraprofessional aides for challenges such as ODD (oppositional defiance disorder) or ADHD. The school also has occupational therapy, physical therapy, speech therapy, a guidance counselor, and SETSS.

There are many more qualified applicants than seats. (Pamela Wheaton)

PS 121

5301 20th Avenue
Brooklyn, NY 11204
(718) 377-8845

PK

www.publicschool121.weebly.com

Who gets in: kids in zone, plus ASD kids
Grade levels: PK–8
Enrollment: 356
Low-income: NA

Reading scores: ★★★★
Math scores: ★★★★
Ethnicity: 35%W 3%B 42%H 18%A 1%O

With just two classes in most grades (one in the middle-school grades), PS 121 is a small, nurturing school where children from Uzbekistan, Mexico, and China happily work and play together.

Special needs kids are included to an unusual degree: Nearly every class has at least two adults and a mix of general education kids and kids with disabilities. Each elementary grade has an ASD Nest classroom with between 12 and 22 students, a handful of whom are on the autism spectrum. The speech therapist gives them pointers on how to play with their classmates and learn social norms.

The school has a stable staff and many sweet traditions—showcasing student work at parent-teacher night, annual dance performances, and Saturday events such as family portrait art day and bingo. Science is a focus, and the school plans to add a greenhouse. Preschoolers made little bird feeders to go into the garden, planted seeds, and watched a Magic School Bus video.

On our visit, students were engrossed in their work and seemed happy to be at school; some skipped through the hallways. Principal Anthony Mungioli brought stability when he arrived in 2013; before he came, PS 121 had three principals in 4 years.

"Mr. M is a great principal," a teacher told us. "He's approachable. The environment is calm. Everybody is working together."

The building, constructed in the 1930s, has roomy classrooms, but the gymnasium is small and there is no auditorium. Performances are held in the cafeteria. A small garden in front gives children an opportunity to get their hands dirty planting flowers and vegetables. The school is in an Orthodox Jewish community where most families send their children to private yeshivas. (Pamela Wheaton)

PS 212

87 Bay 49th Street
Brooklyn, NY 11214
(718) 266-4841
www.ps212brooklyn.org

Who gets in: kids in zone, plus out-of-zone kids
Grade levels: PK–5   **Reading scores:** ***
Enrollment: 689   **Math scores:** ***
Low-income: 87%   **Ethnicity:** 18%W 15%B 33%H 34%A 1%O

Just off the Belt Parkway, PS 212 is a school to watch. Rina Horne, principal since 2015, has "uncovered hidden talents of the teachers" and brought "new life" to the school, District 21 Superintendent Isabel Dimola told us.

In her first year, Horne hired 23 new staffers, including an attendance teacher, brought on to lead the school's long struggle with high absenteeism, and a gym teacher, who serves as a kind of coach for sports and social skills. The gym teacher supervises the playground at recess, encouraging active play. He is also active in the basketball clinic—one of the popular after-school clubs, which include dance, leadership, drama, tech, chorus, cheerleading, and arts.

The brightly decorated classes in the younger grades are mostly vibrant and engaged. All three of the full-time Pre-K classes were studying water on the day of our tour. Each room had vivid water-related displays; in one, a shimmery waterfall of paper strips cascaded at the entrance. In another Pre-K class, two girls happily mixed water and sandy soil at a "mud station."

In a kindergarten class, one student read aloud a simple cookie recipe as the teachers and classmates, who were gathered on a rug, helped with sounding out the words. In another, kindergartners clustered around centers—a rainbow-coloring project, computer time, and a game building new words. In the upper grades, however, some of the classrooms were drab, and a number of the students appeared disengaged and restless.

Some children live in temporary housing or nearby housing projects. At least 13 languages are spoken at the school, including Spanish, Chinese, and Uzbek. Parents are invited for "Family Fun Fridays" at the school. About 200 children attend classes on Saturday. (Elizabeth Daniel)

PS 134

4001 18th Avenue
Brooklyn, NY 11218
(718) 436-7200
sites.google.com/site/brooklynps134/

PK

Who gets in: kids in zone
Grade levels: PK–5
Enrollment: 549
Low-income: NA

Reading scores: *****
Math scores: *****
Ethnicity: 36%W 9%B 13%H 41%A 1%O

In the heart of Brooklyn, the neighborhood of Kensington draws new immigrants from Pakistan, Uzbekistan, Haiti, Mexico, the Dominican Republic, the Darfur region of Sudan, Poland, Russia, and many other places. PS 134 welcomes them all. Teachers are experienced and tend to stay at the school for many years.

Children who are learning English make up more than one-quarter of the population, and some older children have never been in school before, said principal Debra Ramsaran. Yet the school has above-average test scores and the city called it "well developed" in all areas, the highest rating a school can receive.

The school has a calm tone. Many classrooms have a homey atmosphere, with curtains, plants, rugs, and books. Children wear uniforms and are noticeably courteous to one another. Classrooms we visited were generally quiet and orderly, and we sometimes had trouble picking out the teacher because he or she was sitting alongside students at tables or on the rug.

In addition to help from a literacy coach and staff developer, all teachers receive support from Teachers College, Columbia University, for reading and writing instruction. Children study phonics, grammar, and word study, and they meet in small reading groups with a teacher.

Each grade has one "Eagle" class for high achievers. Admission is based on students' classwork. At a glance, we couldn't tell the difference between Eagle and general classes, which are both ethnically diverse.

The school works with the Brooklyn Botanic Garden on its science curriculum. Children learn how to dance, and they take trips to Covenant Ballet. They study the American Revolution and visit historic Fraunces Tavern Museum. (Lydie Raschka)

PS 217

1100 Newkirk Avenue
Brooklyn, NY 11230
PK   **(718) 434-6960**
www.ps217brooklyn.org

Who gets in: kids in zone, some out-of-zone kids
Grade levels: PK–5   **Reading scores:** ****
Enrollment: 1,214   **Math scores:** ****
Low-income: NA   **Ethnicity:** 19%W 11%B 19%H 49%A 2%O

Once called "mini-Pakistan," this part of Brooklyn's Flatbush neighborhood is now a kaleidoscope of ethnicities and incomes, the happy outcome of a wide range of housing options in very close proximity. PS 217 sits at a jaunty angle like a beloved landmark in a small town square, amidst gracious Victorian homes, plain brick co-ops, and double-wide duplexes. Hair salons, laundromats, grocery stores, and upscale eateries serve a polyglot community that works the entire spectrum of jobs and professions.

The school is large, peaceful, and offers an array of arts that allows kids to shine in many ways, whether it's singing the lead in the school musical, playing guitar, or sewing a drawstring bag. The school is led by Principal Franca Conti, who keeps a close eye on academic progress and prefers her staffers to dress "in a professional manner," but, in practice, graciously accepts the jeans-wearers, too. Classes are large—we counted up to 29 in one of the upper grades—yet orderly and buzzing with cheerful and curious children.

The arts program is one of the school's finest features and culminates in dance and music festivals, a poetry slam, an art fair, and theater performances. Although it is a school that serves many low-income families, it also attracts the children of business professionals who contribute money for the arts. Parents contribute talents by leading clubs on Friday afternoons such as filmmaking, graphic design, or Arabic. Kids meet in weekly arts clubs in grades 4 and 5, and several clubs collaborate on two yearly theatrical productions, such as an adaptation of *The Odyssey* or a production of *The Little Mermaid* in full costume.

The school was a pioneer in mixing children who are learning English into general classrooms, with two teachers. There is a program for high achievers, which is not an official city G&T (gifted and talented) program, but one that allows the school more flexibility, the principal said. A child may move into the gifted class as late as 5th grade, for example, which is not a practice in the city's G&T programs.

"We're always kid-watching," said magnet coordinator Judy Brandwein. "We want to celebrate every child." This includes dental and eye screening, birthday celebrations, and close attention to kids who are struggling academically. "We look really closely at data, especially the bottom third [on state test scores]," and children learning English, said the principal.

In an effort to include more non-native-English-speaking parents in classroom activities, the school has tapped parent leaders from each of the largest parent language groups, such as Russian, Arabic, Bengali, and Spanish, to serve as translators. These leaders are available one morning a week for translation and to lead craft or learning activities.

The parent who coordinates the program has found that little changes make a big difference in parent involvement. For example, some parents were deterred by a "no strollers inside the building" rule, because they had to wake up their babies to go inside, so the school set out to change the rule. When a Pakistani translator invited parents in on Friday mornings, she learned that Pakistani nail salon workers would miss out on their busiest day of the week, so she switched the day.

At the end of the 2014–2015 school year, about a dozen teachers left for various classic reasons teachers leave, including retirement, illness, and moving closer to home, but also, in some cases, because they weren't up to the principal's standards. "I'm demanding," Conti said matter-of-factly. "Teachers here work very hard." However, she said that she makes a special effort to listen to teachers. Teachers adopted the GO Math! curriculum (with adaptations), for example, even though the principal at first preferred the Envision curriculum.

Every grade has at least one team-teaching class that incorporates children with disabilities. There are two small mixed-age classes for children who need additional help. G&T classroom placement is based on observations, assessments, and classroom work.

Prekindergarten classes are well equipped for learning through play, with blocks and sand tables. Older children plant and compost in the school garden. They study guitar, ukulele, and xylophone, and sing and dance.

There are sometimes places for children from outside the zone, but in 2015 the school admitted only zoned students. (Lydie Raschka)

PS 277: Gerritsen Beach School

2529 Gerritsen Avenue
Brooklyn, NY 11229

PK

(718) 743-6689

Who gets in: kids in zone
Grade levels: PK–5   **Reading scores:** * * * * *
Enrollment: 442   **Math scores:** * * * * *
Low-income: 46%   **Ethnicity:** 77%W 3%B 11%H 9%A 1%O

Tucked on a peninsula between Marine Park's salt marshes and Shell Bank Creek, PS 277 serves the children of firefighters, police officers, teachers, nurses, electricians, and other public service workers. Bungalows with fences and flags line quiet side streets ideal for learning how to ride a bike.

The school has long had a marine biology program. Children walk to the saltwater creek to observe sea plants and animal life. Local fishermen drop off sea bass and puffer fish for the impressive 1,000-gallon saltwater tank in the school's science room.

Fourth- and 5th-graders use nets to catch small fish and crabs, which they bring to the tanks for further study. Once or twice a year they walk to the Salt Marsh Nature Center near the school. At school, children have jobs keeping track of weather statistics.

"It piques their interest," said Principal Jeanne Fish, adding that at least one former student became a marine biologist. She is particularly proud that the school has sparked an interest in science among girls.

At PS 277 children receive a solid education, and the school earns above-average test scores. Classroom instruction has an ordered, timeless quality: We saw desks in rows, teachers talking, and children working in textbooks.

Students from other schools visit PS 277's marine biology lab to participate in water filtration experiments and to make Japanese fish prints using paper and ink.

The outdoor space is wonderful. Curiously, on a mild 55-degree day children were inside watching a video. The principal said it's uncommon for kids to stay in when the weather is above 40 degrees, but it sometimes happens if they are understaffed that day. (Lydie Raschka)

PS 222

3301 Quentin Road
Brooklyn, NY 11234
(718) 998-4298

PK

Who gets in: kids in zone
Grade levels: PK–5
Enrollment: 883
Low-income: 51%

Reading scores: * * * * *
Math scores: * * * * *
Ethnicity: 45%W 15%B 20%H 19%A 3%O

A large school in quiet Marine Park, PS 222 serves its diverse population well. In a wheelchair-accessible building, the school welcomes children with special needs and does a good job of tailoring programs for each child. Bright and orderly classrooms, a spacious playground, and two separate gyms—one outfitted with adaptive equipment—create a cheerful environment where all students can thrive.

Children who scored above the 90th percentile on the city's gifted and talented tests are placed in an "enrichment class." Those classes delve more deeply into subjects and proceed at an accelerated pace, administrators said. In a 4th-grade class, one student was reading *Moby-Dick*.

In most classrooms students are separated into small groups, each led by an adult who customizes lessons to their abilities. In a special education 5th-grade classroom, a few students were doing simple subtraction problems, another group was doing division, and a third was learning how to use multiplication facts to help solve a division problem.

We saw a lot of innovative instruction and teacher collaboration. In an ASD Nest class, which included three autistic boys, two teachers practiced "reciprocal teaching," demonstrating how to work together and learn from one another. They took turns asking and answering one another's questions about the exploration of North America. Speaking to her co-teacher, one said, "Okay, so he was looking for a route to Asia and instead he ended up in Canada. Why did he do that? They didn't have the technology we have—there was no GPS." The teachers began reciprocal teaching because they found it distracting to hold two separate groups in a classroom, they said. "We want children to question themselves and each other." Russian, Spanish, Urdu Arabic, and Cantonese are among the languages spoken by students. (Pamela Wheaton)

PS 312

7103 Avenue T
Brooklyn, NY 11234
(718) 763-4015

PK

Who gets in: kids in zone; out-of-zone kids may attend for Pre-K
Grade levels: PK–5   **Reading scores:** *****
Enrollment: 862   **Math scores:** ****
Low-income: 52%   **Ethnicity:** 44%W 39%B 11%H 4%A 2%O

On a spring day, you can smell the ocean outside PS 312, a large school with a suburban feel in a remote corner of southeast Brooklyn. It's a lively, sometimes noisy place where the students have interesting projects and debates.

In recent years, PS 312 has seen an influx of children from Russia, Haiti, China, Pakistan, and Korea. Children of different races and ethnic groups seem to mix easily and get along well. "Kids in the playground really, truly embrace one another," says Sungmin Yoo, who became principal in 2014. "They care for one another."

PS 312 in Bergen Beach is close to Jamaica Bay and the Kings Plaza shopping mall. The Department of Education's environmental study center is next door. Classes visit the center often, and in some parts of PS 312, children can hear the sound of gobbling turkeys.

While the school has fairly strong test scores, what is most apparent to a visitor is the energy and enthusiasm of this diverse group of children. A 3rd-grade class for high-performing students was loud as children discussed how various groups fared during the Civil War, but the sometimes boisterous conversation kept to the issue at hand. Opinions came hot and heavy before the teacher said they had to move on to another topic. "I really love the way you guys are challenging each other," she said.

Instead of a packaged curriculum with textbooks, the school teaches reading using children's literature, trade books, and articles. Students do not get lots of homework, but are expected to read books at home that they choose with guidance from their teachers.

The school has a large prekindergarten program open to children outside the zone. Unfortunately, not all can remain for kindergarten. (Gail Robinson)

PS 446: Riverdale Avenue Community School

76 Riverdale Avenue
Brooklyn, NY 11212
PK **(718) 485-1679**
www.riverdaleavenuebrooklyn.org

Who gets in: kids who live in District 23
Grade levels: PK–5   **Reading scores:** ***
Enrollment: 370   **Math scores:** **
Low-income: 95%   **Ethnicity:** 1%W 81%B 14%H 2%A 2%O

A sweet place in a tough neighborhood, Riverdale Avenue Community School has strong leadership and a strong sense of camaraderie among the staff. Children have the same teacher for two years—a practice called "looping"—which allows them to get to know one another well. Teachers form strong bonds with the children and their parents.

Principal Meghan Dunn, a graduate of Bank Street College of Education, encourages children to play with blocks. "I think play is important," Dunn said in a telephone interview. "I want my 1st-graders to learn to read and to learn to play well together, because those are the skills they will need for the rest of their lives."

There are full-time art, music, and dance teachers. Students in 4th and 5th grades participate in Studio in a School, a program that brings teaching artists to the school. All students have dance, gym, music, and art twice a week. Second- and 3rd-graders may join chess club, art club, the step team, and Girl Scouts and Boy Scouts, and all students have the opportunity to engage in the after-school program. Science and computer science are offered to students in 3rd–5th grade.

Children play outside even on cold days; on extremely cold days they may play indoors with a coach who organizes games.

As a whole, District 23 schools have seen declining enrollment, partly as a result of competition from charter schools. At the time of our visit, PS 446 had three Pre-K classes that were fully enrolled, impressive for this district. Dunn attributed her success to word-of-mouth and talking directly to day cares in the area.

The school, opened in 2012, faces many challenges. The neighborhood suffers from crime. Many children have difficult home lives. Attendance is poor, and test scores are disappointing. Yet the school has a climate where safety and responsibility are valued. (Clara Hemphill)

PS 376

194 Harman Street
Brooklyn, NY 11237
(718) 573-0781
www.ps376.com

Who gets in: kids in zone, plus kids who pass gifted exam
Grade levels: K–5   **Reading scores:** ****
Enrollment: 564   **Math scores:** ****
Low-income: 93%   **Ethnicity:** 2%W 7%B 90%H 1%A 1%O

Walk into just about any class at PS 376 and you'll see kids who are happily engaged in their work. Children studying about Japan make pretend sushi from clay and chopsticks from pipe cleaners, while their classmates program a doll-like "robot" to teach the alphabet to younger children.

Children grow hydroponic vegetables in an environmental lab, or discuss a book in a "Socratic seminar," in which they sit in a circle and answer open-ended questions from their teacher. In one class, children dance the hokey-pokey. In another, 5th-graders learn to fox-trot.

Rarely do you see a teacher talking to the whole class here. Instead, children talk quietly among themselves as they work in groups or individually on their laptops. "My kids are very talkative," Principal Maria Vera-Drucker said proudly as she took us on a tour.

PS 376 uses technology to an unusual degree. Even small children write their essays on computers, and children use computers to learn to match letters and sounds. Some use earphones to listen to books read aloud.

The technology curriculum includes the NAO Humanoid Robot Coding Program and LEGO robotics. In classes ranging from special education to G&T (gifted and talented), kids use laptops for math drills and coding. Kindergartners learn to type; by 5th grade, children are using Keynote (Apple's answer to Power-Point) and iMovie.

PS 376 houses the only G&T program in District 32. It draws children not only from District 32 but also from other nearby districts that have no gifted programs. The gifted classes are demanding—kids learned words like "metacognitive" in one— but there doesn't seem to be a division between G&T and other classrooms as there is in some schools. The quality of teaching in all classes seemed high.

Drucker, a graduate of New York Institute of Technology, was assistant principal at PS 112 in Queens before becoming principal here in 2010 and encourages collaboration among the staff. Decisions about curriculum are made jointly.

Parents are welcome, and the day of our visit one group of mothers was chatting in the parent room, while others learned how to use computers in the computer lab. Families hail from Central and South America and the Caribbean, with a handful of children from England and China.

Teachers shy away from the scripted reading programs used in many city schools; children learn to read from fun-to-read picture books rather than textbooks. The school uses the I-STEAM curriculum, which encourages project-based learning through technology. The school has embraced the progressive Investigations math program, which encourages children to learn different ways to solve problems. Assistant Principal Angel Ortiz says the program teaches math, not merely arithmetic. "I teach you how to add, that's arithmetic. I teach you 'why,' that's mathematics," he says.

There are no blocks or dress-up corners in kindergarten, but there is a kitchen where children may prepare real snacks like fruit salad or peanut-butter-and-jelly sandwiches. There is no prekindergarten. The playground is small.

Students take fieldtrips related to science. They visit a recycling plant, Green Meadow Farm, the Prospect Park Zoo, and the New York City Watershed. Teaching artists from Studio in a School provide art instruction.

The school offers ICT, or team-teaching, classes that include both children with special needs and general education students. It also offers self-contained special ed classes.

There is a citywide test for the districtwide gifted and talented program. In addition, the general education classes sometimes have room for children outside the school attendance zone. (Clara Hemphill)

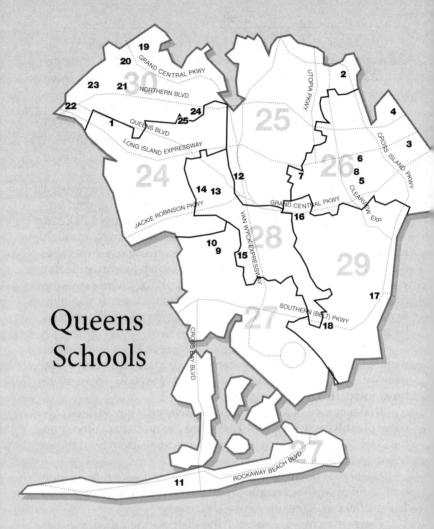

Queens Schools

QUEENS

Queens was once a place of scattered villages set amid farmland. Today the farmland is gone, but the identity of the old villages remains. Ask people where they live, and they're likely to say Richmond Hill or Woodside or Douglaston rather than Queens.

Much of Queens was rural until World War II, and the eastern part of the borough still has many suburban neighborhoods with single-family homes and large lawns. The population boomed in the 1980s and 1990s, with newcomers from all over the world, particularly from Asia.

Nearly half the population of Queens is foreign-born, and with some 138 languages spoken, it's one of the most diverse places on Earth. You may hear Greek spoken on the busy streets of Astoria, where the music from bouzoukis fills the air late into the night. In Little India in Jackson Heights, you'll see women dressed in saris and smell curry spices wafting through the streets. Bayside is home to Korean, Chinese, and Japanese immigrants; southeast Queens is home to African Americans and immigrants from the Caribbean.

The western part of the borough, closest to Manhattan, is more urban, with multistory apartment buildings, an enormous number of restaurants, and good subway connections. District 30 serves Jackson Heights, Sunnyside, Astoria, and Long Island City, which hug the East River. District 24, a giant and overcrowded district, serves Elmhurst, Middle Village, Maspeth, Corona, and Glendale

The eastern and southern parts of the borough are more suburban, with a mix of apartment buildings and single-family houses. Some communities are well served by the subway, but commuters in northeast and southeast Queens are likely to rely on cars or the Long Island Railroad. District 26, serving Bayside and northeast Queens, has long had the top-scoring schools in the city, and many parents move there for that reason. Because of the distances involved, children tend to go to their zoned neighborhood schools. There is less shopping around for schools than in Manhattan or Brooklyn.

District 24: Corona and Sunnyside

The neighborhoods of District 24 historically have had large numbers of Irish and Italian Americans. In recent years, they have become home to increasing numbers of new immigrants from Latin America and Central Europe. School construction fell far short of what was needed to accommodate new immigrants, and the district remains one of the most overcrowded in the city.

Most children attend their zoned neighborhood schools, which generally offer a solid, traditional education. Because of overcrowding, not all have room for prekindergarten. Profiled here is the Children's Lab School, a new school that's off to a terrific start and has two prekindergarten classes. The city opened six stand-alone prekindergarten centers to provide extra seats. See InsideSchools.org for addresses and telephone numbers.

The district office is at 98-50 50th Ave., Queens, NY 11368, (718) 592-3357.

District 25: Flushing and Whitestone

District 25 includes neighborhoods in north-central Queens, from Flushing's bustling Chinatown to Whitestone's quiet residential streets. Many immigrants from Korea, India, and China have moved to the district. The southern part of the district feels very much a part of the city, with busy commercial streets and apartment buildings and a fast connection to Manhattan via the number 7 train. The northern part has a suburban feel, with big trees and single-family houses and stops on the Long Island Railroad. Schools tend to be smaller and less crowded in the northern end of the district. Many parents are satisfied with their neighborhood schools; in fact, many people move to the district to take advantage of its schools.

One unusual option: **PS 32, The State Street School,** 171-11 35th Avenue, in Flushing, (718) 463-3747, offers classes in English for most children but also has a Korean dual-language program designed for children who speak Korean at home; the program offers instruction in both English and Korean.

Prekindergarten options are limited. Three schools serve grades PK–3 and accept applicants from across the district: **PS 130,** 200-01 42nd Avenue, in Bayside, (718) 819-2230; **PS 242,** 29-66 137th Street, Flushing, (718) 445-2902; and **Active Learning Elementary School,** 137-20 Franklin Avenue, (718) 445-5730, also in Flushing. All three get rave reviews from parents and have top test scores. The only drawback: Parents hate to have their children leave after 3rd grade.

PS 201, at 65-11 155th Street, Flushing, NY 11367, (718) 359-0620, which got high marks on its Quality Review by the Department of Education, is another possibility, with four Pre-K classrooms and a magnet program in inquiry and research.

The **International Nursery School**, 171-39 Northern Blvd., Flushing, NY 11358, (718) 353-0932, founded in 1948 by a group of United Nations families, is a good choice for Pre-K. Educational Director Patricia Augugliaro said children "learn through experiences and by celebrating cultures."

One block from the Queens Botanical Garden, **Rainbow Child Development Center**, 133-20 Avery Avenue, Flushing, NY 11355, (718) 321-1610, offers a well-rounded Pre-K program with quality teachers and many opportunities for kids to learn how to be independent and to try out new words and ideas. Chancellor Carmen Fariña praised the creative artwork, learning centers, and clear routines. "I am finding it difficult to express in words how much I enjoyed visiting the Rainbow Child Development Center," she wrote in a letter after her visit. The school is located near two public elementary schools, PS 20 and PS 120.

The District 25 office is at 30-48 Linden Place, Flushing, NY 11354, (718) 271-7605.

District 26: Bayside and Fresh Meadows

District 26 consistently has the top test scores in the city, and many parents move to the district just so they can send their children to its schools. The District 26 schools are well equipped and beautifully maintained. They have incorporated the latest teaching techniques while maintaining a traditional tone, with rituals such as reciting The Pledge of Allegiance. The district also has well-regarded zoned middle schools and—rare in New York City—well-regarded zoned high schools.

We've listed some nice ones, but, honestly, you can't go wrong in the district. Every single school in District 26 has test scores that are well above the citywide average in both reading and math. The schools are mostly cheerful, with experienced teachers, effective principals, and parents who help out in any way they can. Parents here take their children's education seriously, and many sign their children up for after-school enrichment and test prep at an early age in the hope that they'll gain admission to super-selective schools such as Hunter College High School or Stuyvesant High School in Manhattan.

One of the great benefits of District 26 schools is their small size. Elsewhere in Queens, you'll find gigantic schools with 1,000 or even 1,500 children, but many District 26 schools have 300 or 400 children, and few are larger than 800.

The neighborhoods that make up District 26 have a suburban feel, with single-family houses, large yards, and big shade trees, particularly in the areas closest to the Nassau County border. But, unlike Nassau just over the city line, this section of Queens hasn't succumbed totally to car culture and shopping malls. The old villages of Bayside, Little Neck, and Douglaston retain their pre-automobile charm, and it's possible to get a quart of milk without getting into a car. Many families own only one car, and the adults commute to Manhattan on the Long Island Railroad. Many immigrants from Korea, China, and Japan have moved to the district in recent years, attracted by the reputations of the schools.

Enrollment for prekindergarten is tight. Most of the public schools limit Pre-K admission to children living in their attendance zone. Exceptions: **PS 205**, **PS 266** (profiled below), **PS 178,** 189-10 Radnor Road, Fresh Meadows, NY 11423, (718) 464-5763, and **PS 213,** 231-02 67th Avenue, Bayside, sometimes have room for children outside their zones. Also consider: **The Lutheran School** of Flushing and Bayside, 3601 Bell Blvd., Bayside, NY 11361, (718) 225-5502, http://lsfb.org/, voted "Best of the Boro" by the *Queens Courier* in 2015; and the **Chabad Early Learning Center**, 21212 26th Avenue, Bayside, NY 11360, (718) 279-1457, http://www.chabadnequeens.com/, which has a progressive approach, with wooden unit blocks, plants, well-lit classrooms, and creatively engaged kids.

PS 186: Castlewood, 252-12 72nd Avenue in Bellerose, does a good job with all its children, but it's known for what it offers students with disabilities, particularly autism-related disorders. PS 186 was the first school in Queens to have an ASD Nest program for children with autism spectrum disorders (ASDs). In a neighborhood of garden apartments and the Queens County Farm Museum, PS 186 feels like a suburban school. The school's small size—fewer than 400 in a building that once had more than 1,000—means it has room to spare. It serves grades Pre-K to 5.

Also in Bellerose, **PS 266,** 74-10 Commonwealth Blvd., (718) 479-3920, is a welcoming Pre-K-through-8 school open to all children in District 26. It is located in a bright, airy facility on the Frank Padavan campus in eastern Queens. Students, selected by lottery, come from far-flung neighborhoods—Fresh Meadows to Bellerose. On the plus side, that creates a diverse school; a downside is that almost all students must take buses or cars to get there and may live far from one another. School-sponsored clubs and special programs give the children the sense of community they might have in a neighborhood school.

The district office is 61-15 Oceania St., Bayside, NY 11364, (718) 631-6943.

District 27: Richmond Hill and the Rockaways

District 27 in southern Queens includes the neighborhoods around JFK International Airport and the Rockaway Peninsula. It includes the island community of Broad Channel, where children ride their bikes to school and seagulls drop clams on the roof of the high-performing **PS 47,** 9 Power Road, (718) 634-7167; the summer bungalows, single-family homes, and high-rise housing projects near the beach; and the new immigrant neighborhoods of Richmond Hill, where children hail from Ecuador, Mexico, the Dominican Republic, Yemen, Guyana, and the Philippines.

Overcrowding, limited choice at the elementary- and middle-school level, and the district's expansive territory make it difficult for most students to attend anything but their zoned school.

Goldie Maple Academy, 3-65 Beach 56 Street, (718) 945-3300, is a promising Pre-K to 8 school in Arverne on the Rockaway Peninsula. Students have a longer school day and, starting in Pre-K, change classes for select subjects. The school is a model site for Core Knowledge instruction and hosts visitors from schools across the state. Based on the work of Dr. E. D. Hirsch, author of *Cultural Literacy: What Every American Needs to Know*, Core Knowledge is designed to expose students to a broad range of historical, scientific, and cultural topics from an early age. For instance, all students, including Pre-K, study Shakespeare, with teachers using age-appropriate adaptations for the lower grades.

The district office is at 82-01 Rockaway Blvd., Ozone Park, NY 11416, (718) 642-5800.

District 28: Forest Hills and Jamaica

District 28 stretches from the posh houses and quiet, tree-lined streets of Forest Hills to the modest bungalows of south Jamaica. It includes the planned garden community of Kew Gardens, the bustling immigrant neighborhood of Rego Park, and parts of Richmond Hill. The district as a whole is overcrowded, and parents are encouraged to send their children to their neighborhood school. Prekindergarten seats are at a premium.

PS 303, The Academy for Excellence Through the Arts, 108-55 69th Avenue, (718) 459-1358, serves grades Pre-K to 3 and is open to children in District 28 by lottery. The school integrates drama, music, and visual arts into its curriculum and gives its students the chance to participate in artistic activities. Its test scores are so high they are off the charts. The school is just a few blocks from the super-popular PS 196 in Forest Hills, where most kids go for 4th grade.

The district office is at 90-27 Sutphin Blvd., Queens, NY 11435, (718) 557-2618.

District 29: Southeast Queens

District 29 includes the middle-class, mostly African American communities of St. Albans, Hollis, and Springfield Gardens and the ethnically mixed neighborhoods of Holliswood and Queens Village. Two nice Pre-K programs are at PS 251 and PS 176.

Worth watching: **PS 95,** 179-01 90th Avenue in Jamaica, (718) 739-0007, is a big, arts-rich K–5 school that welcomes students from all over the world, particularly Bangladesh and Latin America. The school is undergoing a change in the instruction: Teachers are talking less and kids are talking more. On our visit, children seemed to relish this approach—they readily discussed books, math problems, and their writing. In a 5th-grade class we heard a meaty debate on aspects of colonization by Christopher Columbus, as children took notes on paper divided into sections to help them stay organized. Practice speaking is particularly important for children learning English. Teachers make a point of stocking books that reflect all cultures, and notifications go home in several languages. Teachers also read aloud daily, with expressive voices, providing another way for children to hear spoken English. Parents are happy, and principal Kim Hill sets a very positive tone. The school started a Spanish-English dual-language program in 2016.

The district office is at 222-14 Jamaica Ave., Queens Village, NY 11428, (718) 264-3146.

District 30:
Astoria, Long Island City, and Jackson Heights

Refugees from Manhattan's sky-high real estate prices have moved to western Queens, attracted by fabulous views of the

East River and the Manhattan skyline, good subway connections, and a huge variety of restaurants. The district includes new high-rise luxury apartments in Long Island City; the longtime Greek American community of Astoria; and polyglot Jackson Heights, with its Indian and Latin American communities.

Most children attend their neighborhood schools, but there are a number of charters, gifted programs, and dual-language programs that accept children from across the district.

Worth watching: **Our World Neighborhood Charter School**, a K–8 school at 36-12 35th Avenue in Astoria, (718) 392-3405. As the name suggests, children speak many different languages and come from different ethnic groups and the staff works hard to make everyone feel welcome and valued. Teachers balance a structured curriculum and traditional academics with the arts and hands-on projects.

The elementary and middle schools are housed in two different buildings a few blocks apart. The elementary school building is directly across the street from the Museum of the Moving Image, a popular fieldtrip destination, and the Kaufman Astoria Studios.

Like neighboring District 24, zoned schools in District 30 are mostly crowded. For prekindergarten, consider **PS 85,** 23-70 31st Street, (718) 278-3630, in Astoria, with 72 Pre-K slots. PS 85 has an abundance of outdoor play space. There's enough room to separate older and younger kids during recess and dismissal time, and enough for a garden, a greenhouse, and a small climbing wall. The one thing that mars the setting is the elevated tracks of the N and Q train lines, which run directly along the front of the building at classroom-window height.

PS 150 in Sunnyside has a large annex that houses Pre-K and kindergarten at 41-12 44th Street. The school has high expectations for its students, and even prekindergarten and kindergarten students are assigned homework. Despite its large size—nearly 1,200 children in Pre-K to 5—PS 150 has a sweet and welcoming tone. It has a dual-language program for English and Spanish speakers as well as a districtwide gifted and talented program. The telephone number for the main building is (718) 784-2252 and its address is 40-01 43rd Avenue, Sunnyside, NY 10014.

The district office is at 28-11 Queens Plaza North, Long Island City, NY 11101, (718) 391-8323.

PS 343: Children's Lab School

45-45 42nd Street
Queens, NY 11104
(718) 361-3300
www.ps343.org

PK

Who gets in: kids in zone
Grade levels: PK–5   **Reading scores:** NA
Enrollment: 215   **Math scores:** NA
Low-income: 78%   **Ethnicity:** 12%W 1%B 58%H 28%A 1%O

The Children's Lab School, which serves a largely immigrant community of Spanish-, Bengali-, and Nepali-speaking children, is a warm but serious place that hums with a sense of expectation.

Opened in 2014 to relieve overcrowding at nearby PS 199, Children's Lab is off to a good start. Principal Brooke Barr gets high marks from teachers on the annual survey, parents are enthusiastic, and District Superintendent Madelene Chan praised the school's leadership and high expectations in her annual Quality Review.

Classrooms are large and bright, with spaces set aside for creative play, block areas, and reading nooks with small sofas and chairs. Teachers use every moment to demonstrate proper English using a formality and structure designed to help children, particularly new immigrants, learn both conversational and academic language. To start the day, children in one kindergarten class greeted one another in an activity called "hello neighbor." They listened carefully to their teacher, then cheerfully tried to use proper English as they asked questions about a museum object.

In a creative social studies project to learn about food, all 1st-graders visited a farm, interviewed employees at a local grocery store, and wrote a recipe—including measurements, ingredients, and steps—for a dish they made. They wrote a menu and invited other 1st-graders to sample their dish.

Children are engaged and self-directed. Some 1st-graders read relatively complex books independently and others worked in small groups on a class book; some read to one another, some read with a teacher in a guided reading activity, and others wrote about what they were reading.

The new building has plenty of space for play. There is a beautiful, full-size gym (that also doubles as an auditorium). Pre-K has access to a dedicated play yard, while the other students have a rooftop play area with stunning views. (Elizabeth Daniel)

PS 169

18-25 212nd Street
Queens, NY 11360
(718) 428-6160

PK

Who gets in: kids in zone
Grade levels: PK–5
Enrollment: 423
Low-income: 32%

Reading scores: ＊＊＊＊
Math scores: ＊＊＊＊
Ethnicity: 40%W 5%B 20%H 34%A 2%O

Located at the northeast tip of Queens, PS 169 is a warm, well-run community school with high parent involvement and a record of strong academic performance. While the school takes academics and testing seriously, Principal Vanessa Chambers also wants to ensure that her students are well-rounded and have fun. Lessons give children a refreshing amount of choice and autonomy. Children select their own books (at a range of levels) and even choose what type of paper is best for them.

In 4th and 5th grade, students have one teacher for math, science, and social studies and another for language arts. Chambers said this lets teachers go deeper into their subjects and "makes the kids feel very grown-up and gives them less anxiety about changing classes."

About 90% of graduates go to Bell Academy, a middle school in the same building, strengthening the sense of community. The schools share a full-size gym. The bright, inviting cafeteria has an unusually appetizing salad bar. Children go out for recess even in cold weather.

Arts play a role in the school. First-graders produce work in the style of Swiss artist Paul Klee to help them learn about shapes. Children have a weekly enrichment class, such as fashion, scrapbooking, or baseball, culminating in a community service activity, such as a visit to a local senior center for the scrapbookers.

Fifth-graders may use the iPads to watch a video on ecosystems. They then choose an area of interest and, with others in their group, develop a project on that topic.

One downside: Only one bus line stops nearby, so many families choose to drive, creating some congestion at drop-off and pickup. (Gail Robinson)

PS 221

57-40 Marathon Parkway
Queens, NY 11362
(718) 423-8825
www.ps221q.org

Who gets in: kids in zone
Grade levels: PK–5
Enrollment: 632
Low-income: 39%

Reading scores: *****
Math scores: *****
Ethnicity: 19%W 3%B 13%H 65%A 1%O

A charming, inviting school in a quiet residential neighborhood, PS 221 has strong leadership, consistently good teaching, and a nice balance between academics and the arts. It has a well-deserved reputation as one of the top schools in the city.

Reading, writing, math, and science are all strong. Classes are designed not only to build children's skills, but also to foster curiosity and a sense of wonder about the world. For example, in one 4th-grade science class, children posted their own questions, such as "How do snails breathe?" or "How does dust form?" or "What started the Black Death?" on a bulletin board. These questions form the basis of the children's explorations.

"It's so important to have joy in learning," said Principal Patricia Bullard. "There's a great big world out there, and we have the ability to inspire children or to turn them off. Instead of being passive recipients of knowledge, we want them to ask questions of each other and their teachers, to explore, learn, and laugh. They are not vessels to be filled."

In some ways, the school is traditional. Children recite the Pledge of Allegiance every morning. There's plenty of emphasis on grammar and spelling and on skills like memorizing multiplication facts. But there is also time for kindergartners to play dress-up or build with blocks. Teachers adapt their lessons to accommodate children's interests or special events. A 2nd-grade class took the occasion of my visit to interview me about what it's like to be a writer—and to write their own InsideSchools profile.

Class trips to the Bronx Zoo, Queens County Farm, and Alley Pond Environmental Center broaden children's horizons while building their knowledge of science. Children study ballroom dancing and learn to play the ukulele. (Clara Hemphill)

PS 94

41-77 Little Neck Parkway
Queens, NY 11363
(718) 423-8491
www.ps94.org

Who gets in: kids in zone
Grade levels: K–5   **Reading scores:** * * * * *
Enrollment: 366   **Math scores:** * * * * *
Low-income: 44%   **Ethnicity:** 25%W 6%B 22%H 45%A 2%O

In a neighborhood of one-family homes where most children walk to school, PS 94 hums with activity and purpose. No one-size-fits-all instruction here. Instead, teachers try different approaches with different children, targeting lessons to students at all levels.

Just a few blocks from the Long Island border, PS 94 could easily hold its own with neighboring Great Neck, considered one of the best school districts in the state.

Children have a choice of activities and tasks for reading and math, depending on their interests and level of skills: One child may work on a puzzle, another may write words with magnetic letters, while a third may read to himself. "Teachers understand we can't teach the same way to everyone," said Laura Avakians, principal since 2014.

Some classes are large—30 to 31. The day of our visit, one child had just arrived from El Salvador, another from Korea.

Science instruction is particularly strong, and the science room has more animals than we've seen just about anywhere, including a gecko, a hamster, a bearded dragon, a toad, and a rescued tortoise. In a lesson on composting, 5th-graders asked articulate questions, such as "What's the difference between decompose and disintegrate?" A LEGO club wins awards; some of the top-performing students join an early-morning STEM class where they may build a chair out of pasta and glue.

Lunchtime clubs include knitting, karaoke, and sports. Children may take part in a glee club or chorus, or take violin lessons. The school has a tiny playground, but children use the city playground on the corner or stay inside for clubs and games.

"We don't believe in showing videos during recess," said Avakians. "We want to improve social skills, and putting kids in front of television is not improving social skills." (Pamela Wheaton)

PS 188

218-12 Hartland Avenue
Queens, NY 11364

PK

(718) 464-5768
www.ps188q.org

Who gets in: kids in zone, plus kids who pass gifted exam
Grade levels: PK–5   **Reading scores:** * * * * *
Enrollment: 724   **Math scores:** * * * * *
Low-income: 24%   **Ethnicity:** 30%W 2%B 7%H 58%A 3%O

PS 188 sits in a quiet residential area in a part of Queens that most New Yorkers never see. But word of the school has spread as far as India and China. Principal Janet Caraisco says she occasionally receives calls from overseas families planning a move to New York who want to know how they can make sure their children can attend the well-regarded school.

By most measures, PS 188 is among the top New York City elementary schools. Attendance is high, and the school consistently receives top marks of "well developed" on the city's evaluation, called a Quality Review. Test scores are high.

The school sets rigorous standards, and students meet them. "We have high expectations for our students, and parents have high expectations. Put that together and we have a lot of success," said Caraisco, who has been principal since 2004.

Examples of student writing—starting in kindergarten—hang in classroom and hallway. Second-graders are expected to use correct, as opposed to "invented," spelling, at least in work selected for display. Compositions are striking for their neatness, the result of an effort to ensure that children write legibly and that older children can read and write in script.

PS 188 students read and write an increasing amount of nonfiction. Younger students hold forth on subjects they know about—scooters, say, or babies—while older children do research as well.

Along with its high-powered academics, PS 188 offers arts and athletics. Every grade produces an annual show attended by all. There is a full-time art teacher and a music teacher who provides guitar and recorder instruction.

Kindergarten and prekindergarten children attend classes in an annex. There are two classes per grade for students who test into the District 26 gifted and talented program. (Gail Robinson)

PS 46

64-45 218th Street
Queens, NY 11364
(718) 423-8395

PK

Who gets in: kids in zone
Grade levels: PK–5   **Reading scores:** * * * * *
Enrollment: 613   **Math scores:** * * * * *
Low-income: 48%   **Ethnicity:** 18%W 5%B 14%H 61%A 3%O

High test scores, a well-regarded special education program, and a commitment to inclusion are the hallmarks of PS 46. The school lets students make choices about what they read and write about and encourages them to have discussions. Teaching is lively and to the point.

The school is orderly, with seemingly nothing left to chance. Bulletin boards provide evidence of highly organized assignments, even for kindergartners. All grades make extensive use of Thinking Maps, which are intended to help students visualize problems.

Stamo Karalazarides, formerly the assistant principal, became principal in 2015. She replaced the scripted ReadyGen reading curriculum with the Teachers College Reading and Writing Project. The result, she says, is that the school challenges its students more and sets high expectations for them—and the children have responded. "Kids are much more excited about school," Karalazarides says.

The TC approach encourages children to read whole books—rather than short excerpts in anthologies or graded readers. In a 4th-grade class, students split into book clubs to read books of varying difficulty, but all set in a specific historical period—small-town America between 1849 and the mid-20th century.

A 2nd-grade class broke into small groups to debate issues that piqued student interest, such as whether children should have homework over school vacation.

Classes serve students in a range of academic levels and use the small groups to better tailor instruction. All children with low test scores or in self-contained classes for students with disabilities receive individualized extra help, particularly in phonics and math computation.

PS 46 offers hands-on work in science and technology, having students create something, such as a Play-Doh recipe or a design for a bridge. Fifth-graders take robotics, and the school offers some instruction in computer coding.

PS 46 has a visual arts teacher, and a variety of music offerings including a string ensemble (in most cases parents supply the instruments) and an after-school band. Evening programs celebrate student writers and feature math games. Students all take a 10-week musical theater program offered by a teaching artist, and 2nd-graders go swimming at a nearby park. "All year long, there's a lot happening here," Assistant Principal Stephanie Famoso says.

PS 46 has three Horizon Program classes for students with autism spectrum disorders and two Academic, Career, and Essential Skill (ACES) classes for students with intellectual disabilities or multiple disabilities. Karalazarides says students from these programs interact with other students as much as possible. The school also has ICT team-teaching classes combining students with disabilities and those in the general population at all grade levels, and some self-contained classes for students with disabilities. PS 46 moves students out of the self-contained classes into team teaching whenever possible.

Except for children in the ACES and Horizon programs, PS 46 admits only students from its zone. (Gail Robinson)

PS 173: Fresh Meadows School
174-10 67th Avenue
Queens, NY 11365
PK
(718) 358-2243
www.ps173q.org

Who gets in: kids in zone
Grade levels: PK–5   **Reading scores:** *****
Enrollment: 951   **Math scores:** *****
Low-income: 57%   **Ethnicity:** 27%W 1%B 12%H 58%A 3%O

PS 173 is a bustling, high-performing school with a sprawling building that feels like a suburban campus. The school has classes in technology, the arts, and instrumental music as well as a dual-language program designed to make children fluent in English and Mandarin.

"This school challenges every single child," says longtime principal Molly Wang. She says students are happy to come to school, even on Saturday (when there are classes for children learning English, those in the dual-language program, and those who need extra help). While that might raise eyebrows, the children of PS 173 seem exceptionally enthusiastic and are eager to discuss their school with a visitor.

Expectations are clear, and there are frequent assessments to make sure children are making progress. "They know what they're supposed to do and they know what they're supposed to do if they get stuck," a teacher explained.

Classes have as many as 32 children, but small-group instruction ensures they get the attention they need. While the teacher works with one group, other children may work on their own, with one another, or with another adult. Children help their classmates, which a 2nd-grade teacher said "makes them feel important."

Beginning in 1st grade, there is one dual-language class of 25 pupils in each grade. Parents apply at the end of kindergarten, and children are chosen by lottery; half are English speakers and half are Mandarin speakers. Children have instruction from two teachers, one who speaks English and one who speaks Mandarin. By the end of 1st grade, children are comfortable in both languages. "I'm amazed at how much they absorb and remember," Wang says. To help with the challenge, the dual-language students go to Saturday academy at PS 173, and every student receives a computer program to use at home.

In addition, some Chinese speakers are assigned to regular English-only classes in which they receive extra help from a teacher certified in English as a Second Language.

PS 173 stresses writing, and has long used the reading and writing program developed at Teachers College.

Two science teachers—one for kindergarten and 1st grade and one for the older children—use a well-equipped science room for hands-on activities. Science seems particularly popular with the students, who say the classes are fun but, one hastened to add, "not just fun. We also learn stuff." A technology teacher works with students at all grades, teaching computer coding to 3rd-, 4th-, and 5th-graders.

The school has a full-time music teacher and an orchestra and glee club. Children also take visual arts, culminating in a May exhibition of arts by children in all grades.

A very active PTA helps the school raise money for some of these activities and technology.

PS 173 has self-contained classes for students with disabilities as well as team-teaching classes with special education and general education in every grade. Staff are taking a close look at special education, partly because while the school as a whole scores above the city average on state standardized tests, its special education students score below the city average.

Application to the dual-language program is limited to children who attended kindergarten at the school. (Gail Robinson)

PS 205

75-25 Bell Boulevard
Queens, NY 11364
(718) 464-5773
www.ps205.org

PK

Who gets in: kids in zone
Grade levels: PK–5
Enrollment: 311
Low-income: 26%

Reading scores: *****
Math scores: *****
Ethnicity: 34%W 2%B 22%H 39%A 4%O

Small classes, supportive parents, and experienced teachers combine to make PS 205 a successful neighborhood school. Classrooms are cheerful and well equipped, and the school has a lively science program.

"It's a small school, and we reach all of our kids," said Karen Scott-Piazza, principal since 2008. "No one gets lost. I know every child. I know all their families." The school is small enough that everyone can eat lunch at once—rather than having staggered lunch periods, as is common at larger schools. Classes range in size from 24 to 27.

Scott, formerly assistant principal at MS 158, was a math major in college, and the school has a well-thought-out approach to math instruction. There is a good balance between lessons that focus on arithmetic drills and those that stress a conceptual understanding of math.

Reading and social studies are integrated as part of the Core Knowledge curriculum. Children may read books on topics such as *Aesop's Fables*, Greek mythology, Westward Expansion, or the human body.

A full-time science teacher offers classes once or twice a week to all grades. In a project called Tomatosphere, children grow tomato seeds that the Canadian Space Agency prepares in conditions designed to simulate those on a trip to Mars. PS 205 is one of several thousand schools that contribute data to the space agency's project studying the feasibility of growing edible plants on long journeys in space.

Twice a year, 5th-graders go to Alley Pond Environmental Center. They may bring back tadpoles and watch them grow into adult frogs, or look at water samples under a microscope to learn what makes a healthy pond. (Clara Hemphill)

PS 62

97-25 108th Street
Queens, NY 11419
(718) 286-4460
www.ps062.org

PK

Who gets in: kids in zone
Grade levels: PK–5   **Reading scores:** ***
Enrollment: 947   **Math scores:** ****
Low-income: NA   **Ethnicity:** 2%W 4%B 27%H 62%A 6%O

Kids at PS 62 come from 20 different countries; the most common native languages are Spanish and Punjabi. Longtime principal Angela O'Dowd, who grew up in Ireland, identifies with immigrant students and says that drives the school's culture.

During our visit we were impressed by the thoughtful ways in which teachers acknowledge their students' struggles. For instance, when a kindergarten student said the word "walk" started with a "v," the teacher smiled and responded, "I see why you thought that. Sometimes in Punjabi a 'w' makes a 'v' sound." In another class, the teacher immediately understood why a girl did not respond to a question. "Oh, did I not pronounce your name correctly?"

Through a grant from Studio in a School, art is woven into instruction for English language learners in grades K–2.

Children learn to work independently. On our visit, the teacher read with a few children in a 1st-grade class while others spread out across the room—at computers reading about elephants, writing at their desks, or playing word games on tablet computers.

Fifth-graders were chatty and enthusiastic as they worked in groups to complete table-size charts explaining their study of ecosystems in coral reefs, deserts, and the Arctic.

Parents are welcome: The longtime parent coordinator created a family room and leads workshops, book clubs, English classes, and other events for parents.

Visual arts, dance, and music are offered in all grades. Every year the entire 4th grade attends a performance of *The Nutcracker* ballet.

A downside: PS 62 does not offer after-school activities. (Laura Zingmond)

PS 254

84-40 101st Street
Queens, NY 11418
(718) 520-7878
www.ps254q.com

PK

Who gets in: kids in zone
Grade levels: PK–5   **Reading scores:** ****
Enrollment: 694   **Math scores:** *****
Low-income: 82%   **Ethnicity:** 6%W 5%B 75%H 12%A 2%O

Located in a gleaming new facility in a neighborhood of modest row houses, PS 254 has an intense focus on academics and conscientious teachers who work together as a team.

Their approach has brought PS 254 high test scores, glowing marks on school report cards, honors, and praise. PS 254 was one of six New York City schools that earned a U.S. Department of Education Blue Ribbon in 2014.

"We have great teachers who share their ideas and are willing to learn from one another," said assistant principal Heather Sosnovsky. Together, she said, they engage in "a never-ending discussion about education and how to help children." Everyone pitches in—even the gym teacher leads a reading group—and teachers spend lots of time planning lessons together.

Students get homework every day. Academics start early: Kindergarten classes don't have blocks or dress-up corners, and there is little time for play during class.

Children do go outside to play at recess, and there are trips every month to zoos, museums, a local environmental center, and community landmarks like the local firehouse. PS 254 has full-time music and art teachers, and all students have at least one of those subjects every week, with many having both.

Each grade has one class that is designated as a gifted class, called TAAP (Talented and Accelerated Academic Program).

The city's Quality Review praised PS 254's culture of high expectations. "Classes conduct research on colleges and organize a college fair. Students have opportunities to visit local colleges and learn about the expectations and post-secondary requirements," the review said. (Clara Hemphill)

PS 317: Waterside Children's Studio School

190 Beach 110th Street
Rockaway Park, NY 11694

PK

(718) 634-1344
www.watersidecss.org

Who gets in: kids in zone, kindergarten wait list
Grade levels: PK–5   **Reading scores:** ***
Enrollment: 489   **Math scores:** ***
Low-income: 79%   **Ethnicity:** 22%W 24%B 46%H 4%A 4%O

The Waterside Children's Studio School, also called PS 317, is an increasingly popular school with a strong arts curriculum, a well-regarded principal, and a welcoming, relaxed atmosphere. Just a block from the beach and surrounded by summer bungalows, single-family homes, and high-rise apartments, PS 317 serves a mix of different races, ethnicities, and income levels, including some children who speak Spanish, Bengali, Arabic, and Polish. Children seem comfortable with one another and with their teachers.

There are few textbooks; instead, children choose books based on their own interests, which they may read on their own or discuss with a partner. From kindergarten on, children do a lot of writing. They learn to give feedback and take suggestions from others on their work. In math, teachers try to spark discussions about how to solve problems.

"I don't necessarily like quiet classrooms," says Principal Dana Gerendasi, who founded the school in 2009. "I like to hear kids having conversations with each other."

Every student takes dance, drama, music, visual arts, and physical education. The school aggressively pursues grants to support its ambitious arts program. Students perform in the New York City Student Shakespeare Festival, and the Guggenheim Museum and the New York City Ballet offer residencies at the school.

Gerandasi get high marks from teachers on school surveys, and the children seem to like her too. "I'm a big fan of yours," a 2nd-grader told Gerendasi when she entered her classroom. Some children who find it difficult to deal with the hubbub of the cafeteria spend their lunch break in Gerendasi's office. The school seeks to ensure that every student has three or four adults they trust. Rather than meting out punishment, teachers seek to reward good behavior with various prizes. One eagerly sought by some students is being "principal for a day."

PS 317 shares a building with MS 318. Both schools replaced PS 225, which was closed due to poor performance. The school seems to be hitting its stride. Math scores, while still below the citywide average, have increased substantially. On our visit, children seemed happy and most were engaged.

The school population is shifting slightly as somewhat more affluent families move in, lured by the relatively low price of housing and the express buses to Manhattan. A ferry to lower Manhattan is a 5-minute walk from the school. Gerendasi said the school involves all parents, with a selection of workshops, student performances, exhibits, and student-led parent–teacher conferences, in addition to the traditional teacher-led meetings. The neighborhood is in the midst of change: A well-reviewed and cute frozen-yogurt shop is a block away. So is a residence for at-risk boys.

The school offers an array of after-school clubs and sports. A free after-school program also is available. There are three full-day Pre-K classes.

The school has two self-contained special education classes and team-teaching classes in every grade.

In spring 2016, the school had a wait list for kindergarten for the first time, although by summer all children who wanted to enroll were admitted. (Gail Robinson)

PS 196

PK

71-25 113th Street
Queens, NY 11375
(718) 263-9770
www.ps196q.edublogs.org

Who gets in: kids in zone, some wait lists
Grade levels: PK–5   **Reading scores:** *****
Enrollment: 901   **Math scores:** *****
Low-income: 21%   **Ethnicity:** 40%W 2%B 13%H 38%A 7%O

Long one of the top-performing schools in the city, PS 196 is a destination school. Parents move into the school zone just so they can send their children here—and are sorely disappointed if their child is placed on a wait list for kindergarten, as sometimes happens.

The school has very high test scores, especially for math, and many parents see it as a stepping-stone to the super-selective Hunter College High School in Manhattan, which begins in 7th grade.

It's not just the children in general education who do well on state tests; children receiving special education services score well above the city average for children with disabilities, and above average for general education pupils. Children do well because the teachers are effective, but motivated parents are also known to pay for private after-school tutoring.

Parents and teachers responding to the annual school surveys almost unanimously recommend the school; however, some parents say the quality of teachers varies—some are superstars, some are only so-so. Teachers and parents give high marks to principal Susan Migliano, who has been at the helm since 2009.

"The best thing about the school is the kids (well behaved, mature), some great teachers, a wonderful reading and writing curriculum, and a great math program," one mother told Inside-Schools. "The kids are well prepared for the state exams, but also develop a love for reading and writing."

Still, it doesn't work for all children. The same mother said her son, who had ADHD, was "treated so unkindly" that she withdrew him. His brother and sister, who were focused, strong students, loved PS 196 and did not want to leave.

"As long as your child is driven and smart, this is the school for her or him," she said. (Clara Hemphill)

PS 101

2 Russell Place
Queens, NY 11375
(718) 268-7231
www.ps101q.org

PK

Who get in: kids in zone
Grade levels: PK–6
Enrollment: 633
Low-income: 17%

Reading scores: * * * * *
Math scores: * * * * *
Ethnicity: 46%W 3%B 15%H 28%A 8%O

PS 101 is nestled is Forest Hills Gardens, a leafy community of Tudor-style houses and quiet streets. It has a stable staff, involved parents, and a principal well experienced in teaching children to write creatively and to think about books as literature.

Monique Lopez-Paniagua, who has led the school since 2012, gives her staff extensive training in the methods of the Teachers College Reading and Writing Workshop. In the classrooms we visited, children not only learned to sound out words, they also learned to analyze characters and plot development.

"It doesn't say he is sad," said a 1st-grade teacher, reading aloud from *Peter's Chair*, Ezra Jack Keats's story of a boy who is jealous of his newborn sister. "How do we know he is sad?"

Third-graders wrote essays with titles like "Why cops are wonderful" and "Stop hunting and poaching animals." In one class, kids flopped on a rug to read books they chose themselves.

The school has adopted GO Math!, a series designed to teach children the underlying concepts of arithmetic. "They really understand why we are re-grouping for subtraction," said a 2nd-grade teacher. "When I was in school, I just did it. I didn't know why I did it." Teachers have a chance to meet with one another to perfect their own understanding of the new methods, and the school offers parent workshops as well.

Over the years, some parents have complained that there is too much emphasis on academics and not enough time for play, particularly in kindergarten. Assistant Principal Irtiz Gonzalez, who gave us our tour, acknowledged that today's kindergarten classrooms look more like the 1st grade of a generation ago—with desks instead of blocks or dress-up corners. Gym is offered just once a week. But she said teachers encourage children to exercise in the classroom with activities like Zumba.

PS 101 has a 6th grade—unusual in the city. Many children leave after 5th grade, but for those who stay, PS 101 is a cozy alternative. (Clara Hemphill)

PS 144

93-02 69th Avenue
Queens, NY 11375
(718) 268-2775
www.pa144.com

Who gets in: kids in zone, plus kids who pass gifted exam
Grade levels: K–5   **Reading scores:** *****
Enrollment: 869   **Math scores:** *****
Low-income: 21%   **Ethnicity:** 35%W 3%B 18%H 36%A 8%O

PS 144 has a reputation as the most laid-back of the schools in Forest Hills. It's a place where kids can make puppets, learn ballroom dancing, and study acting, playwriting, and songwriting. The academics are solid—and the school's gifted and talented program attracts some of the top students in the district—but the arts are where the school really shines.

Principal Reva Gluck-Schneider told us that having a strong arts program is "non-negotiable." The school's administrators fervently pursue grants to fund the arts. Thanks to its partnerships with institutions such as the Queens Museum and the Guggenheim Museum's Learning through Art (LTA) program, PS 144 is able to bring in a number of teaching artists who work with students on a regular basis. Sculpture, book illustration, interior architecture, and bridges are just some of the topics kids have studied with the Queens Museum.

Every grade has an "artist in residence." Fourth-graders participate in the NYC Children's Theater (formerly Making Books Sing), which sends teaching artists to the school to help children create and perform a play based on a children's book. Second-graders work with artists from the Marquis Studios to design their own puppets and create a puppet show.

There are two science teachers. One 2nd-grade classroom planted seeds and used an in-class composting system. In a 5th-grade science class, students played a game called "Survival of the Sweetest," in which students learned about food chains by acting as wild animals competing over scarce resources, which were represented by candy. "We are simulating how animals would act in the wild," one student explained.

As part of Trout in the Classroom, students raise trout from eggs to fingerlings, monitor the tank's water quality, and eventually release them into the watershed. Students also receive weekly technology instruction in the computer lab.

During our visit, teachers had clear control of their classrooms. Whether students were taking turns counting by tens, measuring objects around the classroom, or listening to a story read aloud by the teacher, they were engaged and on task.

PS 144 is home to a districtwide gifted and talented program, and there is one G&T class in each grade K–5. The school also offers a push-in enrichment program for non-G&T classes so that all students can get the benefits of more challenging, project-based learning. "We recognize the gifts in all children," the enrichment program coordinator, Lois Olshan, told us. English language learners may receive extra support before school begins in the morning.

Parents say the school is welcoming to children with special needs. The mother of a boy with ADHD who was unhappy at nearby PS 196 said he thrived in the "more nurturing environment" at PS 144.

Gluck-Schneider is particularly proud of the school's partnership with the ArtAccess program at the Queens Museum, geared specifically toward providing tools and access to children with "great gifts and great needs," as she prefers to call children with disabilities.

Parents are devoted fundraisers and volunteers. Some help out during lunchtime, while others train to work one-on-one with students who need extra help. The Parents' Association organizes the school's fee-based after-school program. Students can choose from a variety of programs such as LEGO-building or gardening. A father runs an optional morning math club for 5th- and 6th-graders attended by some 60 children, filled with games and math challenges. "They run in here as though I'm giving them ice cream for breakfast," said Gluck-Schneider of this popular club.

The school has suffered from overcrowding in recent years, but an annex scheduled to open in 2019 will provide 330 new seats. (Lydie Raschka)

PS 161
101-33 124th Street
Queens, NY 11419
(718) 441-5493

Who gets in: kids in zone
Grade levels: K–5   **Reading scores:** ∗∗∗∗
Enrollment: 703   **Math scores:** ∗∗∗∗
Low-income: 89%   **Ethnicity:** 2%W 7%B 18%H 62%A 12%O

In this calm, well-rounded school that welcomes families from all over the globe, a rigorous curriculum, a rich arts program, and an emphasis on staff collaboration means that all students are prized and guided to achieve their best.

"Students here feel safe and they feel loved," said longtime principal Jill Hoder. On our visit, we saw students give her several impromptu hugs.

A grant from The Trust for Public Land in 2015 paved the way for a new playground, track, and set of tennis courts that 4th-graders helped design along with professional engineers. A joint program with PricewaterhouseCoopers lets 5th-graders work with accountants to analyze emerging job markets.

"It's important for our students to see the real-life applications of what they're learning," says Hoder. "When they learn something in math class, I want them to think, 'How am I going to use this?'"

Many children come to the school directly from countries like Guyana and Trinidad and have had their education interrupted. The school also has a high number of English language learners from South Asia. While Punjabi is the primary foreign language spoken here, Hindi, Spanish, Bengali, and Urdu are other popular languages. Five staffers speak Punjabi.

There is an emphasis on responsibility and self-assessment: children are encouraged to edit and grade much of their own work. Student safety monitors happily patrol the hallways to offer help to their peers, and good behavior is rewarded with "Arthur Ashe" dollars that can be used toward class prizes like ice cream or pizza parties.

We were impressed by the range and quality of special education services at PS 161, a barrier-free school. Assistive technology gives students with physical disabilities thoughtful access to physical education; several have participated in the Special Olympics. (Aimee Sabo)

PS 131

170-45 84th Avenue
Queens, NY 11432
(718) 480-2840
www.ps131.d29q.com

Who gets in: kids in zone, kindergarten wait list
Grade levels: K–5   **Reading scores:** * * * * *
Enrollment: 829   **Math scores:** * * * * *
Low-income: 82%   **Ethnicity:** 4%W 8%B 12%H 74%A 3%O

PS 131 is a beloved "melting pot" where new immigrants from China, Bangladesh, India, and Pakistan mingle with South Americans and a declining black and white population. The school does a good job teaching newcomers English.

This safe school is "well developed"—the highest rating a school can receive—according to the city's Quality Review. There are Smart Boards in classrooms, the science lab has been updated, and new English speakers may use the computer lab for extra practice with reading and writing.

Instruction tends to be on the traditional side, with teachers standing up front leading lessons, although that is beginning to change. For the first time in as long as anyone can remember, kindergarten teachers are trying out 40-minute "centers," during which kids learn through play. Dress-up corners, language games, and block-building have been helpful in sparking conversation among kids new to the English language, remarked one of the teachers.

Teachers receive ongoing help from trainers at Teachers College, a well-respected think tank for writing instruction.

Randolph Ford, a popular principal since 2003, retired in 2016. Veronica DePaolo, a capable assistant principal and former teacher at the school, took the helm.

There is no gymnasium. The creative physical education teacher makes do with exercises in a small foyer on bad-weather days, incorporating math and language lessons into jumping jacks and sit-ups.

The school usually has a wait-list for kindergartners who live in the zone. A handful are sent to another school for kindergarten but may return in 1st grade, and almost all do. (Lydie Raschka)

PS 176

120-45 235th Street
Queens, NY 11411
(718) 525-4057
www.schoolrack.com/PS176/

PK

Who gets in: kids in zone, plus kids who pass gifted exam
Grade levels: PK–5   **Reading scores:** * * * * *
Enrollment: 732   **Math scores:** * * * *
Low-income: 75%   **Ethnicity:** 0%W 81%B 3%H 5%A 11%O

PS 176 has deep roots in this middle-class, African American community of quiet streets and tidy single-family homes. Long-time principal Arlene Bartlett provides steady leadership for the benefit of all students—including those with special needs and those who come from across the district for the gifted and talented program.

Classrooms reflect an institutional culture that values hard work and order. The hallways are quiet, and, for the most part, students move through them in orderly lines. In most classes we saw on our visit, students worked on assignments at their desk or listened while a teacher taught from a Smart Board. Students were engaged, and classrooms were colorful, with much student work posted on the walls. Some of the classes in younger grades were more informal: In one kindergarten class, eager students sat on the rug for a presentation from a nature enrichment group, excitedly predicting the hidden animal with scaly skin that starts with "S." The students were thrilled that "snake" was correct, some cringing and some gleeful as the animal handler brought the snake to each in turn.

The school uses the GO Math! curriculum for all grades. For reading, K–2 classes rely on ReadyGen, supplemented by novels in 2nd grade. The older elementary students use Expeditionary Learning for reading and language arts, supplemented by novels. The school also has a Saturday Academy that provides extra help for 2nd- through 5th-graders in reading and math. For 2nd-graders, there's a Sunrise Academy, which provides extra reading instruction in the mornings before school.

The school has a partnership with the New-York Historical Society, through which 4th-graders will write a play that will be performed.

PS 176 has limited room for out-of-zone children. Students are placed in the gifted program based on their score on citywide assessments. (Elizabeth Daniel)

PS 251

144-51 Arthur Street
Queens, NY 11413
(718) 276-2745
www.ps251q.org

PK

Who gets in: District 29 lottery
Grade levels: PK–5
Enrollment: 325
Low-income: 73%

Reading scores: ****
Math scores: ***
Ethnicity: 1%W 92%B 3%H 2%A 2%O

Tucked behind two middle schools in a residential cul-de-sac, PS 251 has long been a stable school with solid academics. Established in 1972 as a magnet school for grades K–2, it has expanded to serve prekindergarten through 5th grade.

Pre-K classes feature blond wood lofts and are outfitted with puppets and other tools for learning to read, with objects and shapes for learning math and with dramatic play areas. All teachers incorporate STEAM (Science, Technology, Engineering, Art, and Math) activities into their instruction. During this time, kids may use blocks, science materials, LEGOs, and art supplies, among other hands-on activities.

The school has taken steps to maintain an orderly atmosphere by adopting a positive behavior management program; children receive small rewards or privileges for good behavior. The system was put in place when teachers indicated on school surveys that they did not have enough help with behavior management.

The instruction at PS 251 has an old-fashioned quality. Teachers are called by their surnames and pay attention to skills like spelling (the school holds a spelling bee), handwriting, and phonics. Young children chant the letter of the week in unison and trace the letter in the air in a practice called "skywriting."

Children play keyboard, and 2nd-graders swim at the nearby Roy Wilkins Recreation Center. Other activities include cooking and singing. On Saturdays about 70 children read with adult volunteers through a program called Reading Empowers.

Space is at a premium: A medium-sized room is used for assemblies and morning line-up. There is a tiny cafeteria; some children must eat lunch quite early. The school has a makeshift gymnasium, and gym also takes place outdoors during nice weather. (Lydie Raschka)

PS 122

21-21 Ditmars Boulevard
Queens, NY 11105
(718) 721-6410

www.mamiefayps122.wordpress.com

Who gets in: kids in zone, plus kids who pass gifted exam
Grade levels: PK–8   **Reading scores:** ✴✴✴✴✴
Enrollment: 1,385   **Math scores:** ✴✴✴✴✴
Low-income: 53%   **Ethnicity:** 39%W 6%B 21%H 30%A 4%O

Near the last stop on the N and Q trains in a quiet residential section of Astoria, PS 122 is a large neighborhood school with a sought-after gifted and talented program. The school has a sweet, welcoming tone, strong arts programs, and a focus on civic awareness.

Students have a chance to dig deeply into important topics such as the Civil War and Ancient Egypt, according to the city's Quality Review. They may make designs for a roller coaster in a math class, or research organic foods and study farms after reading *Charlotte's Web*.

Students take classes in music, dance, and visual arts; 5th-graders practice ballroom dancing to prepare for a citywide competition. Students in grades K–3 participate in the school's orchestra through a partnership with the Little Orchestra Society.

The quality of children's writing is good. Beginning in kindergarten, they write and revise multiple drafts of a variety of writing styles for different subjects. Thanks to a partnership with the Teachers and Writers Collaborative, students get to work with a poet each year to create their own anthology of poetry.

The school has two gyms, a library, an art room with a kiln, and a garden. It has a new schoolyard, a playground, track, and tennis courts. Unfortunately, the school lacks a full-service kitchen; school meals are prepared off-site and heated in warming ovens before being served in the cafeteria.

Children are admitted to the district G&T program based on their scores on the exam administered by the city. The school has long been home to The Academy, a selective middle school program open to graduates of gifted classes at other elementary schools in the district. (Clara Hemphill)

The 30th Avenue School
28-37 29th Street
Queens, NY 11102
(718) 726-0501
www.q300.org

Who gets in: kids who score in 97th percentile on gifted exam
Grade levels: K–8   **Reading scores:** * * * * *
Enrollment: 236   **Math scores:** * * * * *
Low-income: NA   **Ethnicity:** 31%W 6%B 9%H 45%A 10%O

The only citywide gifted program in Queens, the 30th Avenue School offers bright children the chance to explore their own interests and work with their classmates to solve problems. There is a focus on engineering and technology: Kindergartners study computer coding, 2nd-graders work in teams on engineering missions, and 6th-graders tackle LEGO robotics.

A whole room is devoted to wooden blocks, and, as the children build elaborate structures, they learn math concepts such as length, measurement, and balance as well as teamwork, collaboration, and cooperation.

Teachers foster curiosity, and activities often center around children's questions: "Teachers ask a lot of questions here, and now my child is starting to ask me a lot of questions," said a parent.

One year, kindergartners made their own musical instruments from paper towel rolls, round toothpicks, empty coffee cans or oatmeal containers, and rubber bands with the help of a father who volunteered.

Bill Biniaris, former algebra teacher at PS 122, became principal in 2016, replacing founding Principal Matt Willard. Biniaris led a schoolwide reform to better serve gifted students by incorporating standards of the National Association for Gifted Children.

Willard, formerly preschool science coordinator at the New York Hall of Science, wanted to give children in Queens the option of a progressive education, with time for exploration, projects, and play. "Experiential learning is motivating for kids," he said.

The school aims to build responsibility in kids and a cooperative culture. Younger children check in with one another during morning and closing meetings every day. The older ones meet four times a week in small advisory groups where they share goals and concerns. First-graders often work in groups of three; middle school students in teams of up to six. Parents said conflict resolution is actively and effectively pursued here.

The school uses a flexible approach to math, rather than one textbook. The rationale behind the choice of math programs, primarily Investigations and Contexts for Learning, is that they promote teamwork, projects, and exploration, according to the administration. These goals are also fostered through CMP3 (Connected Math Project 3) in the middle school.

Parents praised the school's balance of nurturing and academic challenge, and expressed relief at having found a school where their kids are "not criticized for being smart or nerdy." Yet they also seemed to be cautiously weighing the question of academic rigor and how it is best achieved. "Every G&T parent looks for a little bit of NEST and Anderson," said a 6th-grade parent, citing two schools known for fast-paced academics.

"If you are looking for a super-accelerated program, this is not the place to be," another parent said. "But if you are interested in a nurturing environment that promotes self-motivated learning, then it is a good fit."

Through 2nd grade, homework is limited to nightly reading and some optional assignments. Starting in 3rd grade, students receive homework in all core subjects.

The 30th Avenue School, also known as Q300, is housed at two locations. Grades K–4 share the PS 17 building; grades 5 to 8 share the IS 126 building at 31-51 21st Street.

All the elementary school students may participate in PS 17's fee-based after-school program. The elementary school is two blocks from N/R 30th Avenue subway station.

Families may apply to the elementary school (K–4) only after their children score high marks on the Department of Education's gifted and talented test. Bus service is available for some Queens students living within a five-mile bus route of the school. Others arrange their own transportation. Parents have organized a private bus service for a fee. See the school website for information about open houses. (Lydie Raschka)

PS 166

33-09 35th Avenue
Queens, NY 11106
(718) 786-6703
www.ps166q.com

PK

Who gets in: kids in zone, or who pass gifted exam; others in dual-language
Grade levels: PK–5   **Reading scores:** * * * * *
Enrollment: 1,180   **Math scores:** * * * *
Low-income: 71%   **Ethnicity:** 20%W 5%B 45%H 29%A 2%O

PS 166, a stable and thriving school on the border of Astoria and Long Island City, offers a highly regarded Spanish-English dual-language program and a districtwide gifted and talented program, as well as strong general education classes in each grade. Although the school is large and has several different programs in operation, there is a strong sense of community. Teachers cheerfully greet one another in the hall, and many know and connect with students beyond those in their classes. Each morning everyone in the school stops what they're doing for a lively, 2-minute dance or jumping-jack "fitness break."

A nice mix of Asian, Hispanic, white, and black students reflects the neighborhood's demographics. It is a rich soup where students and their families speak many different languages at home, and children whose parents are Bengali mix easily with children from Central and South America. Generally, the individual classes reflect the school's overall ethnic makeup, although the gifted classes, which admit students from throughout the district, have more white and Asian students and fewer Hispanics than the school as a whole.

The two full-time Pre-K classrooms are bright with play kitchens, reading nooks, blocks, and other stations. Students work together on art projects designed to encourage communication and collaboration. Although some Pre-K students continue into kindergarten at PS 166, the admission process is separate and they are not guaranteed a spot.

The school relies on scripted reading and math programs (ReadyGen and GO Math!, supplemented with manipulatives), but most classrooms we observed had a vibrant dynamic. For instance, kindergartners eagerly worked on poetry notebooks, sharing comments with one another. In an Integrated Co-Teaching class, 5th-graders working on math sheets appeared alert and interested as teachers moved among them, checking in and discussing concepts. In a lively dual-language class, a Spanish-speaking student led her classmates through an active lesson that included dancing. The students were delighted and attentive.

The school is large, and classes can be big. Hallways bustle as pupils move in loose lines from their classrooms to gym, music, or other specials. The atmosphere, though, feels active and friendly rather than crowded and hurried. For instance, a 2nd-grade teacher sang "Michael, Row Your Boat Ashore" brightly, keeping her students' focus as they walked back to the classroom; students from other classes streamed past happily. The full-size gym was busy but organized as two classes divided the space for different activities.

Jessica Geller has been principal since 2012 and was previously at the school for 9 years as an assistant principal and teacher. She is optimistic and upbeat about the school. There is little turnover in staff—and Geller is proud that the teachers who come to PS 166 tend to make a career there.

PS 166's dual-language program, one of the best-established in the city, is a point of pride for the administration. There are two dual-language classes in each grade, and the administration hopes to add a third kindergarten class. The students alternate classrooms, languages (Spanish/English), and teachers each day. Their lessons are consecutive but taught in Spanish one day, English the next. The program's supervisor said that most students who begin the program stick with it throughout their years in elementary school. Additionally, a nearby middle school has recently added a Spanish/English dual-language program, so PS 166's students will be able to continue their dual-language education.

The PTA is very active and pays for several enrichment programs, such as theater, 3rd-grade chess, and ballroom dancing. The PTA also sponsors an indoor recess program for cold or rainy days. There are two on-site after-school programs.

There are three small, self-contained classrooms for students with significant needs covering grades K–5. Some grades have an Integrated Co-Teaching (ICT) class with two teachers and a mix of special education and general education students.

Admission to the district G&T program is based on the city-wide assessment process. Call the school for information about admissions to the dual-language program. (Elizabeth Daniel)

PS 78

**48-09 Center Boulevard
Queens, NY 11109
(718) 392-5402**
www.ps78.com

PK

Who gets in: kids in zone
Grade levels: PK–8
Enrollment: 583
Low-income: 21%

Reading scores: *****
Math scores: ****
Ethnicity: 40%W 4%B 32%H 18%A 5%O

PS 78 takes good advantage of its location in a beautiful building on the rapidly developing Long Island City waterfront. Teachers use the nearby East River as an extension of the classroom, and students learn about the river through a variety of activities, such as maintaining their own oyster bed.

The school, housed in two buildings a 5-minute walk from each other, is popular—and overcrowded. There is no gymnasium or auditorium, and the school must use the lunchroom for large-group activities, art instruction, physical education, and meetings. For a number of years, it had wait lists for kindergarten; although there was no wait list in 2016, residents feared the reprieve was temporary.

Principal Louis Pavone says hands-on projects and fieldtrips, part of the school's Schoolwide Enrichment Model, get students excited about learning. Parents and others from the community come to the school to tell children about their careers—and to explain how math, reading, and writing skills will help them later in life.

The school has partnerships with the Metropolitan Museum of Art, Seaport Museum, the Department of Environmental Protection, NYS Parks and Recreation, Lincoln Center Education, Studio in a School, and St. John's University.

Students study topics ranging from simple machines to plant diversity and use the school's garden as well as the waterfront location for science lessons outside the classroom.

Students in kindergarten and 1st grade receive music instruction through the Music and the Brain program. Starting in 2nd grade, music classes use the Little Kids Rock curriculum, which teaches students to play guitar, keyboard, and drums with a method similar to the Suzuki method of violin instruction. Outside of music class, students may also choose to participate in the school chorus, the ukulele band, or musical drama after school. (Clara Hemphill)

Growing Up Green Charter School
39-37 28th Street
Long Island City, NY 11101

PK

(347) 642-4306
www.gugcs.org

Who gets in: lottery with District 30 preference
Grade levels: PK–8   **Reading scores:** ****
Enrollment: 707   **Math scores:** ****
Low-income: 52%   **Ethnicity:** 32%W 12%B 36%H 15%A 5%O

With a greenhouse, a chicken coop, plants in the classrooms, and an egg-laying duck named Walter, this charter school offers kids the chance to "grow up green," as its name suggests. Kids sail on a schooner at South Street Seaport to learn about the history of exploration, build shelters in Central Park to learn how Native Americans lived, or visit the Queens Botanical Garden to study "Trees and Me."

"We probably go on more fieldtrips than any other school in the city," said founding principal Matthew Greenberg, who blends the progressive practices honed at Manhattan School for Children and Bank Street School with lessons in building community he learned at a Roman Catholic school, where he also taught.

This charter school, opened in 2009, is meeting its mission so well that it's being cloned, with a new school of the same name opened in 2016 in Jamaica, Queens. Greenberg was tapped to be executive director of both.

Students here are assertive and eager to defend their positions. One class discussed writing a persuasive essay to the mayor and a judge urging them to reconsider the reversal of the ban on Styrofoam lunch trays. Citing research, one girl pointed out both sides of the issue.

The elementary school, housed in a former Catholic school building, has an old wing, complete with old-fashioned cloakrooms, and a brighter newer wing. Every inch of space is used. There is no library, so the corridors, some rather dimly lit, house the school's books, including those used for Read 180, a program for struggling readers. Twelve staff members share the main office, and special education guidance providers are in side-by-side small cubicles off the multipurpose gym. Fortunately, many staff members have been around since the school's inception and seem to get along well. Several bring their own children to the school, and staff children get priority in admissions, in the same way that siblings do.

Class size is about 28 per classroom in the elementary school, but with at least two teachers in each classroom it seems manageable. There are 24 students per class at the growing middle school. The middle school, located about a half-mile away at 36-49 11th Street, opened with a 6th grade in 2014. There is a small outdoor yard, with some picnic tables and basketball hoops. It is a long walk from the nearest subway train, and the city bus stop is four blocks away.

The green theme continues, encompassing not only recycling and the environment, but also community service. Every morning begins with an advisory, teaching organizational skills and addressing social–emotional issues.

Sixth-grade English students were doing a poetry slam about "where I come from"; 7th-graders were tackling Shakespeare and reading *Macbeth*, learning how Shakespeare's language differs from today's vernacular. Music students finishing a unit on Martin Luther King Jr. learned freedom and protest songs, and were asked to create a song or poem of their own.

About 75% of the elementary students stay for middle school; other popular choices are the Baccalaureate School for Global Education, Young Women's Leadership School, and Hunter's Point Community Middle School.

The school has a team-taught Integrated Co-Teaching (ICT) class in every grade, Special Education Teacher Support Services, and speech and occupational therapy.

Children are admitted by lottery, with priority to District 30, siblings, and children of staff members. In recent years there were 2,900 applicants for 125 spots schoolwide. Growing Up Green accepts students on every grade level, as spaces open up. (Pamela Wheaton)

PS 149
93-11 34th Avenue
Queens, NY 11372
(718) 898-3630

Who gets in: kids in zone
Grade levels: K–5   **Reading scores:** * * *
Enrollment: 1,177   **Math scores:** * * *
Low-income: NA   **Ethnicity:** 3%W 1%B 87%H 8%A 1%O

PS 149 is a happy, busy place that offers its many Spanish-speaking students lots of opportunities to perfect their native language even as they learn to speak, read, and write in English. At the same time, English-speaking children have the opportunity to learn Spanish.

Every grade in this gigantic Jackson Heights school has at least two dual-language classrooms in which a bilingual teacher teaches in English one day and in Spanish the next.

"The dual-language program is a fantastic opportunity," an English-speaking mother said. "My daughter reads, writes, and speaks, not to mention does math, in English as well as Spanish. Family and friends are amazed at this ability, something you would not get at most charter or private schools."

Children in the dual-language classrooms seem equally conversant in Spanish and English. Fifth-graders use sophisticated Spanish vocabulary words after reading and discussing Cesar Chavez and the farmworkers' strike.

"Dual-language outperforms the rest of the school," said Principal Esther Salorio. Students come from Mexico, the Dominican Republic, Colombia, and Ecuador, predominantly. The school's finely tuned dual-language program was started by Milady Baez, the current director of the Office of English Language Learners at the city's Department of Education.

In addition to dual-language classes, there are transitional bilingual classes, where the emphasis is on learning English rather than perfecting Spanish. There are also English-only classes, many of which are led by teachers certified in English as a Second Language.

Salorio, principal since 2009, is the daughter of Cuban immigrants and a "simpatica" leader, providing a warm and welcoming environment. She spends her days out and about in the classrooms, connecting with teachers and students as much as possible. "I try not to be stuck in my office," she said.

More than 85% of the students are of Hispanic heritage, and about 35% are not fluent in English. "Language acquisition is what we're focused on," said Salorio.

Teachers basically do double duty, she said, presenting their lessons in both languages. When the school adopted the city's recommended ReadyGen reading curriculum, there was no Spanish version, so the teachers created one. GO Math!, the city's recommended math curriculum, which the school also adopted, was in Spanish, and we saw students solving complicated word problems in Spanish.

"It's more work and it's a challenge," said one dual-language teacher. "But it's a good challenge."

PS 149 uses the Teachers College Reading and Writing Project curriculum, and students write essays, research papers, and "how-to" books in both languages.

Because of space constraints, there is no room for prekindergarten, but PS 149 hosts a weekly Mommy and Me program in the school library for 3- and 4-year-olds and their mothers.

Class size is high—up to 30 or 31 children—in the upper-grade dual-language classrooms, but teachers get help several periods a week from ESL teachers who come in to work with small groups of students. There are three dual-language classrooms in 3rd grade, when there's an influx of dual-language students from two nearby early childhood schools that end in 2nd grade, PS 228 and PS 222. That creates a crunch in the 4th and 5th grade. However, the principal has noticed increasing numbers of families leaving the school midyear, moving out of state where the cost of living is lower. Newcomers still arrive regularly from Latin America, she said.

Space is at a premium, but the principal is determined to hold onto the science lab, where there are three science teachers. There is also a dedicated art room and teacher. The principal would like to ramp up arts offerings, she said, and although there was some art on display, reading, writing, and math are clearly the focus.

PS 149's original building has worn wooden floors, old-fashioned closets, and charm; the newer wing is brighter, with colorful linoleum tiles. There is a huge schoolyard adjacent to a city park that is open only to PS 149 during school hours. Young children may play on climbing apparatus in an indoor courtyard.

Fourth- and 5th-graders lead an active student government, organizing an annual mitten drive for needy families, inviting the local police officers to talk about safety, lobbying for more recess and lunchtime clubs, and sharing breakfasts with the principal. (Pamela Wheaton)

Renaissance Charter School

35-59 81st Street
Queens, NY 11372
PK **(718) 803-0060**
www.renaissancecharter.org

Who gets in: lottery with District 30 preference
Grade levels: PK–12 **Reading scores:** * * *
Enrollment: 561 **Math scores:** * * * *
Low-income: 36% **Ethnicity:** 14%W 8%B 58%H 18%A 1%O

Imagine a large, nearly windowless cube filled with big and little kids playing games together, colorful student murals, and blue jean–clad students on a first-name basis with their teachers. This is Renaissance Charter, a small, superpopular Pre-K–12 school that prides itself on personalized, relevant, project-based learning for kids of all abilities.

Renaissance has a long history of integrating children with special needs in regular classes. Principal Stacey Gauthier is particularly sensitive to learning differences: Her own son, who has dyslexia, graduated from Renaissance and went on to graduate from law school. Renaissance shares the building with a small District 75 school for children with autism, who have been integrated into the general education classrooms, some going on to colleges such as Pace University.

Teachers stay and build their careers here, and one helped design the interior of the building, a former department store. There are interior windows so you can peer into classrooms, colorful couches, and centrally located tables on each floor, where teens like to gather to eat the excellent breakfast omelets, made by Chef Mo, the school's head cook.

Squarely in the progressive camp, the school has an active student body: Children take class trips, do hands-on projects, participate in an array of arts, and debate the issues of the day. A highlight is the school's weeklong celebration of learning called "Rensizzle" (named for Dr. Joseph Renzulli, the director of the National Research Center on the Gifted and Talented), which exemplifies the school's project-based teaching style. Some or all the traditional classes are canceled (depending on the grade), as students explore a topic such as robotics, journalism, or animal care, with trips to places like Howe Caverns, the *Huffington Post*, the Bronx Zoo, the Tenement Museum, or the Brooklyn Bridge.

Class trips and projects allow students to learn and to show their understanding in a variety of ways. For instance, students who have trouble reading a science textbook may study geology through a trip to the Sterling Hill Mining Museum. Global humanities classes rewrite history into plays about Apollo and Aphrodite or Hindu legends. Children in grades 4–6 take a 5-day trip to Lake George, where they learn about environmental science and reenact scenes from the Underground Railroad.

High school students must participate in a leadership, volunteer, or internship program each semester. We saw 9th-grade students leading games in a 2nd-grade class and a girls' leadership group called Sadie Nash. "I was shy at first," said a 9th-grade transfer student who found good friends in her leadership group. "Here we have space to talk about our issues as women." The Global Kids group picks social justice issues to explore such as poverty or health.

The school has no outdoor space, but it does have an indoor playground, and prekindergartners visit a playground down the block.

The school accommodates children with a wide range of disabilities, including autism, dyslexia, visual impairment, and emotional and physical handicaps. They participate in all elements of student life, from student government to the National Honor Society. Many of the school's teachers are dually certified in special education and another subject. We saw adults working one-on-one in the classroom and in small groups in separate rooms.

Renaissance accepts one incoming prekindergarten class of 18 students; about six spots open in kindergarten, and there is one class of new 5th-graders each year. There is one class per grade in Pre-K–4 and two per grade in 5–12. Priority is given first to siblings of enrolled students and then to residents of District 30. All available seats are awarded by lottery throughout all the grades as they come available. Applications for these grades are automatically wait-listed and will be considered if openings occur; however, there is a long wait list. (Lydie Raschka)

Staten Island
Schools

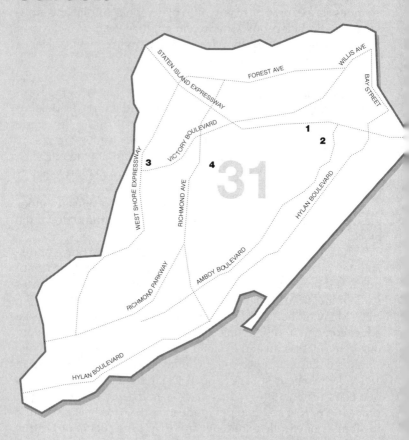

District 31
1 PS 80: Michael J. Petrides
2 PS 48
3 PS 26: The Carteret School
4 PS 69

STATEN ISLAND

Staten Island is a world apart from the rest of New York. Sleepy, suburban, even rural in parts, the island attracts people who are looking for quiet neighborhoods, nice backyards, and reasonably priced housing. Lots of Staten Islanders work on the island rather than face the long commute by ferry to Manhattan or the traffic jams on the Verrazano-Narrows Bridge to Brooklyn.

Politically conservative, Staten Island has long been a Republican stronghold in a predominantly Democratic city. For many years, Staten Island was home to mainly white, Italian and Irish American families with stay-at-home moms and dads who worked in construction or as firefighters or police officers. Those families still make up a large part of the island's population, but they have been joined by African Americans and immigrants from the Caribbean, Central America, India, and Korea—particularly in the northern, more urban parts of the island.

District 31, which includes all the schools on the island, has long been a stable, traditional district. For years the schools offered children a meat-and-potatoes kind of education: Most schools taught the basics adequately, but without a lot of innovation or imagination. In recent years that's been changing, and many schools have blossomed with the introduction of livelier teaching techniques. There is less reliance on textbooks and more on children's literature; children spend more time writing from their own experience and less time copying from the chalkboard. Teachers introduce math lessons that involve more conceptual understanding and less drill.

The North Shore schools are crowded, and housing development on the South Shore has led to overcrowding as well, but some Mid-Island schools occasionally have room for children from outside their immediate zone.

For prekindergarten, consider **PS 9, Naples Street School**, 1055 Targee Street, (718) 876-4610, open to children districtwide. Opened in 2013, the school offers dance, music, visual arts, and drama, integrating them into social studies, science, reading, and writing. Founder Deanna Marco, who lives on Staten Island, has 16 years of experience at Brooklyn's PS 295, The Studio School of Arts and Culture in Park Slope, where she was principal from 2006 to 2013. The school has a small ASD Nest program for children with autism.

The district office is at 715 Ocean Terrace, Staten Island, NY 10301, (718) 420-5667.

Michael J. Petrides School

715 Ocean Terrace
Staten Island, NY 10301
(718) 815-0186
www.petridesschool.com

PK

Who gets in: District 31 lottery
Grade levels: PK–12   **Reading scores:** ****
Enrollment: 1,330   **Math scores:** ***
Low-income: 47%   **Ethnicity:** 48%W 20%B 22%H 8%A 2%O

A highly sought-after school that draws children from across Staten Island, Michael J. Petrides offers a warm atmosphere, challenging academics, and the chance to stay at one school from pre-kindergarten through 12th grade.

Housed on the grassy campus of what was once the College of Staten Island, Petrides is surrounded by trees and nature trails. Classes are large—up to 32 in elementary and 34 in high school. But children rarely get lost in the shuffle because the total enrollment of the school is small. Teachers get to know children well because they stay at the school for so many years.

Children are admitted to the elementary and middle school grades via lottery, and there are far more applicants than seats available. The school has 75 children in kindergarten and about 125 students in 9th grade. Many students stay there for 13 years, but there are usually a few seats open in the upper grades and a larger number of seats in 9th grade.

One big advantage of the PK–12 model is that students can avoid the often-stressful middle and high school choice processes. "The next decision is college, and we're going to hold your hand for that," Principal Joanne Buckheit said.

The school provides extra help to students who need it and also offers opportunities for more proficient students. One year, a high school math teacher worked with advanced 4th- and 5th-graders.

Another advantage to the PK–12 structure: High school students may work with elementary school students. But being with younger children also is a responsibility, one senior who had been at the school since 2nd grade told us. "They look up to you. We know we have to do what's right," he said.

Yellow school bus service is provided for elementary school students. (Gail Robinson)

PS 48

1050 Targee Street
Staten Island, NY 10304
(718) 447-8323
www.nylearns.org/ps48pta

PK

Who gets in: kids in zone
Grade levels: PK–8
Enrollment: 948
Low-income: 42%

Reading scores: ★★★★★
Math scores: ★★★★★
Ethnicity: 60%W 4%B 18%H 17%A 2%O

PS 48 has an impressive new building with two science labs, a soundproof music room, an art room, a theater and dance studio, a physical therapy room, and a fourth-floor library with panoramic views of the treetops of Emerson Hill and the Manhattan skyline.

The school, in a neighborhood of single-family homes and small apartment buildings not far from the Staten Island Expressway, has old-fashioned values; children wear uniforms, host firefighters, and salute veterans at a special breakfast.

The arts make PS 48 shine. On our visit, students worked with instructors from the Guggenheim Museum to build kinetic models of simple machines. In a 5th-grade science classroom, students used a grid to create a three-dimensional model of the schoolyard while studying geographic land formations.

Students play recorder and violin. They create puppets and write puppet shows with teaching artists from Marquis Studios, and learn about the importance of setting in a story as they place puppets in their own handmade scenes.

Through a partnership with Cultural After School Adventures (CASA), students visit the Staten Island Zoo and study animal adaptations and the importance of animal skull shapes and teeth. PS 48 also has a basketball league for 5th-graders and fee-based after-school clubs such as fencing, robotics, dance, art, and martial arts.

Allison O'Donnell became principal in 2016, replacing longtime Principal Jacqueline Mammolito, a champion of the arts. O'Donnell was an assistant principal at the Michael J. Petrides School for 7 years and an assistant principal at PS 69 for 3 years.

The school promotes close ties between parents and staff. The parent coordinator plans birthday celebrations and monthly fun nights, and surveys families in the spring to plan the next year's workshops. (Lydie Raschka)

PS 26: The Carteret School
4108 Victory Boulevard
Staten Island, NY 10314
PK
(718) 698-1530

Who gets in: kids in zone
Grade level: PK–5   **Reading scores:** ***
Enrollment: 236   **Math scores:** ****
Low income: 51%   **Ethnicity:** 51%W 4%B 34%H 9%A 2%O

PS 26 combines small-town traditions with cutting-edge instruction. Kids take part in the community's Fourth of July parade, as they have for 100 years. They attend class in a building (a wing of which was constructed in the 19th century) that is probably the closest thing New York City has to a little red schoolhouse. "It feels like it's in a time warp," said Parent Coordinator Diane Heinz, whose family has sent six generations to the school.

But the school is up to date when it comes to teaching methods. Principal Laura Kump has a knack for helping ordinary teachers aim higher. She adopted the ambitious Math in Focus program, even though it was a challenge to retrain her staff, some of whom are admittedly math-phobic. ("We weren't brought up on this type of math," she said.)

Math in Focus requires a high level of student involvement and self-assessment during lessons. We saw 4th-graders use strips of paper to study angles, and 2nd-graders hold small wipe-off boards so they could break up numbers to solve subtraction problems. "Math is sometimes frustrating," said a 5th-grader, "but you have to work through it to understand it."

The school's special education population is ably served in two self-contained classes that mix ages. Some children leave class for extra help with a teacher. Children with serious special needs receive support from aides who work one-on-one with kids. "My child is mainstreamed beautifully here," said the mother of a child with autism.

PS 26's enrollment is growing after several years of decline. Parents like new features, like more teaching assistants for kids with special needs, a new after-school option, and an early-morning drop-off. (Some staff work extra hours for free to make the early-drop-off option happen.) (Lydie Raschka)

PS 69

144 Keating Place
Staten Island, NY 10314
(718) 698-6661
ps69.org

PK

Who gets in: kids in zone, kids who pass gifted exam
Grade level: PK–5   **Reading scores:** * * * *
Enrollment: 950   **Math scores:** * * * *
Low income: 52%   **Ethnicity:** 59%W 3%B 22%H 14%A 1%O

PS 69 families come together for old-fashioned fun such as a carnival with face-painting and ice cream cones. Parents attend awards ceremonies, pizza nights, and a father/guardian–daughter dance.

The school has a spacious playground with a running track and a baseball diamond, an inner courtyard with climbing equipment, and a cozy gazebo on school grounds. It boasts a gymnasium, science lab, media lab, and dance studio.

Children participate in creative lessons. One 2nd grade watched a movie about sheep-shearing, then glued sheets of cotton on cardboard boxes, "sheared" their own sheep, and dyed the "wool." Other children dressed as Betsy Ross, Johnny Appleseed, and other famous figures and posed in a "wax museum," coming to life to tell their stories. A firefighter visits the school to demonstrate "stop, drop, and roll" and lets kids try on a heavy firefighter's coat. Children take trips to Freshkills Park.

Principal since 2007, Doreen E. Murphy has spent her entire career at PS 69, starting out in 1995 as a classroom teacher and later serving as an assistant principal. Murphy gets high marks for her leadership, based on teacher and parent responses to the annual school surveys.

The school offers dance, band, violin, and community service opportunities. One group of students helped refurbish and restore a piano at an adult day program at the Sea View Hospital Rehabilitation Center.

There are after-school activities and a fee-based morning-care program that allows parents to drop off their children as early as 6:55 a.m.

PS 69 has gifted and talented classes as well as programs for students with Autism Spectrum Disorder (ASD) and others with special needs. The school offers multiple approaches for children with disabilities. An Intensive Kindergarten (IK) class serves ASD students with average or high aptitude. (Laura Zingmond)

WHAT TO LOOK FOR
ON A SCHOOL TOUR

Use this checklist from InsideSchools when you go on school tours. No school is perfect, so think about what you can fix, what you can live with, and what you simply can't live without. The overall tone of the school and the quality of leadership are critical. Extras like a great after-school program or foreign language classes are nice, but don't make or break a school.

First impressions
Trust your instincts. First impressions count.

Security guard and office staff

◁ □ □ □ □ □ ▷

Unfriendly.   Friendly.

Physical plant

◁ □ □ □ □ □ ▷

Dark, dirty,   Bright, clean,
messy.   orderly.

Student work on display

◁ □ □ □ □ □ ▷

Bare walls, cookie   Artwork, essays,
cutter-work, store-   science & social
bought decorations.   studies projects,
                          math problems.

Leadership
A principal can make or break a school.

Does the principal have a clear vision?

◁ □ □ □ □ □ ▷

No.   Not sure?   Yes!

Is there a clear plan to achieve that vision?

◁ □ □ □ □ □ ▷

No.   Not sure?   Yes!

Academics
Great schools explore all subjects.

Reading

◁ □ □ □ □ □ ▷

Book excerpts or   Kids enjoy picture
really simple   books, science
books, even in   books, historical
5th grade.   novels and complex
                          chapter books.

Writing

◁ □ □ □ □ □ ▷

Short essays with   Lots of high-
copied facts.   quality essays on
                          a range of topics.

Math

◁ □ □ □ □ □ ▷

Nothing but   Legos, blocks, dice,
worksheets or little   play money,
evidence of math.   different ways to
                          solve problems.

Social studies

◁ □ □ □ □ □ ▷

No evidence of   Maps, globes,
history or   timelines, thematic
geography.   studies on bridges
                          or subways.

Science

◁ □ □ □ □ □ ▷

No evidence of   Plants, animals,
science.   cooking supplies, eggs
                          hatching, experiments
                          in every class.

Teaching
A great teacher will make you envy your child.

Are students engaged?

Kids distracted, bored, aimless. → Kids so focused they don't notice visitors in the room.

Who does the talking?

Teachers do all the talking. → Teachers encourage kids to talk.

Do teachers challenge top students?

One-size-fits-all lessons. → Teachers encourage children to read harder books, write longer essays, do more complex math.

Do teachers support struggling kids?

One-size-fits-all lessons. → Teachers work with individual children or small groups.

Do teachers plan together?

Random units without a big-picture plan. → Projects in art/technology reflect lessons in history/math.

Culture & tone
You don't want anarchy... or a police state.

What's the noise level?

Can hear a pin drop. → A productive hum.

What do you hear?

Shouting and yelling. → Grown-ups and kids speak in respectful voices.

Are parents involved?

Parents shut out. → Parents & staff work as a team.

Gym, recess & play
Kids shouldn't sit still all day.

Work/play balance?

All work - no play or recess. → Purposeful play, guided by teachers.

Are students physically active?

No gym, dance or movement in class, watching movies at lunch. → Outdoors every day, jumping, dancing and skipping.

After-school

After-school programs?

Limited, expensive. → Free for all students, extensive opportunities.

Lunch

What's the lunchroom like?

Rowdy, messy, smelly. → Orderly and clean.

INDEX

Index

ABOUT THE AUTHORS

Clara Hemphill is the founding editor of InsideSchools, a website housed at The New School's Center for New York City Affairs, and the author of *New York City's Best Public Middle Schools* and *New York City's Best Public High Schools*. She leads the Center's policy work on economic segregation of the city's schools, examining why there are schools with high concentrations of poverty even in mixed-income neighborhoods. She was a reporter and editorial writer for *New York Newsday*, a foreign correspondent for the Associated Press, and a producer for CBS News based in Rome. Clara lives in Manhattan with her husband, Robert Snyder. Their two children, now grown, attended New York City public schools.

Lydie Raschka is a writer and teacher. A graduate of Bank Street College of Education, she taught grades 1 to 3 in the Yonkers, NY, public schools. She is a Montessori teacher trainer and writes reviews for InsideSchools. As a teacher, parent, writer, and consultant, she has been inside hundreds of New York City schools. Her son attended public elementary school in Manhattan.

Pamela Wheaton, one of the founding members of InsideSchools, edits the blog, reviews schools, and leads workshops about school choice in New York City public schools. She was a producer of PBS television programs and a reporter and editor at the *Buenos Aires Herald*. Her two daughters graduated from New York City public schools.

Laura Zingmond, who has visited hundreds of New York City schools for InsideSchools, advises parents on school choice. She has served as Manhattan Borough President Gale Brewer's appointee to the New York City Panel for Educational Policy. She has a law degree from Benjamin N. Cardozo School of Law and was a litigation attorney and administrative law judge. She is a lifelong New Yorker, and her two children are the fourth generation in her family to have attended the city's public schools.

Gail Robinson is a writer who specializes in education and other public policy issues. Based in New York City, she also is an adjunct professor at Baruch College/City University of New York. For more than 10 years, Robinson was editor-in-chief of *Gotham Gazette*, an award-winning publication on New York politics and policy. Her two children attended New York City public schools.

Aimee Sabo has visited elementary, middle, and high schools throughout the city and continues to be inspired by the dedication and creativity of the students, parents, and educators she meets. Before joining InsideSchools, she served on the Board of the Lungevity Foundation, raising much-needed funds for research in lung cancer. Her two children attend public school in Manhattan.

Mahalia Watson is the founder of Let's Talk Schools, which produces events and provides services that inform and educate parents and families so that they can make good-fit education choices from prekindergarten through high school. She has been a project manager and producer in print and broadcast production for more than 15 years. Her son attends a public school in Manhattan.

Elizabeth Daniel reviews schools for InsideSchools. She is a lawyer who has litigated voting rights cases, represented capital defendants, and represented plaintiffs in employment discrimination cases. She has an abiding interest in public education and is a New York City public school parent.